# COMMITMENT to EXCELLENCE

## Developing a Professional Nursing Staff

Excellence in Nursing

Professionalism of Staff

Edited by

**SueEllen Pinkerton, RN, PhD**
Vice President for Patient Services
St. Michael Hospital (A Member of the Wheaton Franciscan System)
Milwaukee, Wisconsin

**Patricia Schroeder, RN, MSN**
Quality Assurance Coordinator
St. Michael Hospital (A Member of the Wheaton Franciscan System)
Milwaukee, Wisconsin

AN ASPEN PUBLICATION
Aspen Publishers, Inc.
Rockville, Maryland
Royal Tunbridge Wells
1988

Library of Congress Cataloging-in-Publication Data

Commitment to excellence.

Contains detailed description of the growth of the
St. Michael Hospital Department of Nursing.
Includes bibliographies and index.
1. Nursing services—Personnel management.
2. St. Michael Hospital (Milwaukee, Wis.). Dept. of
Nursing—Personnel Management. I. Pinkerton, SueEllen.
II. Schroeder, Patricia S. [DNLM: 1. St. Michael Hospital
(Milwaukee, Wis.). Dept. of Nursing. 2. Nursing—
standards. 3. Nursing Staff—organization & administra-
tion. 4. Nursing, Supervisory—methods. 5. Quality
Assurance, Health Care. WY 105 C734]
RT89.3.C66   1987      362.1'73'0683      87-19531
ISBN: 0-87189-882-9

Editorial Services: Mary Beth Roesser

Library of Congress Catalog Card Number: 87-19531
ISBN: 0-87189-882-9

Printed in the United States of America

2   3   4   5

# Table of Contents

# Contributors

SUSAN MATYAS BLACK, R.N.
Staff Nurse
St. Michael Hospital

MIKE BLEICH, M.P.H., R.N.
Vice President–Patient Service
St. Mary's Medical Center
Racine, Wisconsin

MARY BRUSKEWITZ, M.S., R.N.
Diabetes Clinical Nurse Specialist
St. Michael Hospital

NORMA CARR, M.S., R.N.
Psychosocial Clinical Nurse
Specialist
St. Michael Hospital

TRACY DUSENSKE, B.S.N., R.N.
Staff Nurse
St. Michael Hospital

ALICE ECKES, B.S.N., R.N.
Staff Nurse
St. Michael Hospital

MARY GERSTNER, M.S., R.N.
Pain Center Clinical Nurse
Specialist
St. Michael Hospital

DOUG HALEY, B.S.N., R.N.
Staff Nurse
St. Michael Hospital

SUE KASPRZAK, R.N.
Staff Nurse
St. Michael Hospital

MARY BETH A. KENNEY, B.S.N.,
R.N.
Staff Nurse
St. Michael Hospital

ELEANORE KIRSCH, M.S., R.N.
Emergency/Outpatient Services
Director
St. Michael Hospital

CONNIE KRAUS, B.S., R.N.
Nurse Manager
St. Michael Hospital

JANET KREJCI, M.S., R.N.
Special Projects–Clinical Nurse
Specialist
St. Michael Hospital

REGINA MAIBUSCH, M.S., R.N.,
S.S.S.F.
Respiratory Clinical Nurse
Specialist
St. Michael Hospital

SHELLY MALIN, M.S., R.N.
Assistant Vice President–Nursing
St. Michael Hospital

MAUREEN MARCOUILLER, B.S.N.,
R.N.
Staff Nurse
St. Michael Hospital

JEFF MARTZ, B.S.N., R.N.
Staff Nurse
St. Michael Hospital

LILLIE MCALLISTER, B.S.N., R.N.
Staff Nurse
St. Michael Hospital

MARY BETH MCNICHOLS, B.S.N.,
R.N.
Staff Nurse
St. Michael Hospital

MARGARET MEYER, B.S.N., R.N.
Director of Nursing
St. Michael Hospital (formerly)

JEFFREY G. MILLER, B.S.N., R.N.
Staff Nurse
St. Michael Hospital

SUEELLEN PINKERTON, Ph.D.,
R.N.
Vice President–Patient Services
St. Michael Hospital

KAREN RAUEN, M.S.N., R.N.
Parent/Child Clinical Nurse
Specialist
St. Michael Hospital

DEBBIE REITMAN-JUDGE, M.S.N.,
R.N.
Psychiatric Clinical Nurse
Specialist
St. Michael Hospital (formerly)

ALVIN SCHACHTER, M.D.
Director–Pulmonary Medicine
St. Michael Hospital

KATHY SCHMIDT, R.N.
Staff Nurse
St. Michael Hospital (formerly)

PATRICIA SCHROEDER, M.S.N.,
R.N.
QA Coordinator/Research
Facilitator
St. Michael Hospital

MARY T. SINNEN, M.S.N., R.N.
Staff Nurse
St. Michael Hospital

MARGIE SMERLINSKI, M.S., R.N.
Gerontology Clinical Nurse
Specialist
St. Michael Hospital (formerly)

LILA SMICK
Office Coordinator–Nursing
Office
St. Michael Hospital (formerly)

GREGORY A. SMITH
Director of Marketing
Wheaton Franciscan System Inc.–
Milwaukee

CHRISTINE SPERRY, B.A.
Business Manager–Nursing
St. Michael Hospital

SUE STRAUB, B.S.N., R.N.
  Nurse Manager
  St. Michael Hospital

PEGGY L. WAGNER, M.S.N., R.N.
  Cardiovascular Clinical Nurse
    Specialist
  St. Michael Hospital (formerly)

NANCY WILDE, M.S., R.N.
  Alcohol and Drug Treatment/
    Mental Health Center Services
    Director
  St. Michael Hospital

ROSS J. WORKMAN, B.S.N., R.N.
  Nurse Manager
  St. Michael Hospital

# Foreword

Some tasks are more pleasant than others. Preparing this foreword has been a complete pleasure. My reasons are quite personal. I knew this book before it was written. I watched it happen. I can validate the contents. I can share in the pride of achievement it reflects. I can envision its importance and impact. Such moments have been far too rare in my career, so I take enormous pleasure in this one.

The book model depicts an incremental development of excellence in nursing and professionalism of staff. Quality assurance, clinical research, shared governance, and a climate of professionalism were the components enabling this growth. Accountability, autonomy, critical thinking, and political negotiation were the necessary tools. These terms are all engaging. They are the stuff of professional nursing's dreams. They activate our hope. And, too often, they elicit skepticism. So it is a pleasure to say in this foreword that you, the reader, should trust your impulse to hope. Somewhere, a group of dedicated, hard-working nurses made it all come together. I know, because I was there.

I am not an employee of St. Michael Hospital. I am, however, an active participant in the life of its nursing community. I have served as a consultant to the Nursing Department in several capacities, with diverse groups, all under a general rubric of professionalism and excellence. I have watched the tenuous beginnings, the nervous apprehensions in the struggle for change, the moments of fear and doubt, the days and weeks of disruption, the one step backward that seems inevitably to accompany three steps forward. I have actually been an active observer of the pain and struggle of growth more often than I have been a participant in the sweet celebrations of victory and achievement. In a very palpable way, I know the price the nurses at St. Michael Hospital paid to create the world they have described in this book. It was not an easy journey, but it was a courageous, sometimes exhilarating one. They have earned anew my admiration and respect in every step along the road. The story they tell you is true.

The story they tell is important, not only for them, but for all nurses who entered this profession with a spirit of idealism, a belief that enhancing the quality of life for persons who were ill and suffering was a good thing, of moral worth, that could bring significant personal satisfaction. Nurses are not dissatisfied with nursing; they are dissatisfied with the institutions where they do their nursing. We don't need to change nurses on nursing. We do need to change our institutional realities. The nurses at St. Michael Hospital have done that. We all need to know that it can be done. We need to know that a commitment to excellence and professionalism is a viable starting point.

John W. Gardner, in his seminal discussion of excellence, states that "Men and women of integrity, by their very existence, rekindle the belief that as a people we can live above the level of moral squalor. We need that belief; a cynical community is a corrupt community." (Gardner, 1984, pp. 159-160). I believe contemporary nursing runs the risk of such corruption. Nurses, frustrated by decades of paternalism and exploitation, often find cynicism becomes seductive; the moral squalor of manipulation, coercion, and adversarialness begins to seem reasonable. The men and women of integrity who elected to pursue excellence in nursing care and who share their experiences with you in this book demonstrate the possibility of "living above" and they have indeed, repeatedly, "rekindled" my beliefs. I hope they do so for you.

As all nurses know, the ultimate endorsement nurses make of their peers is stated when they seek health care for themselves and those they love. Because my daughters are at the athletic injury stage of development, I have become something of a regular at St. Michael Hospital Emergency Room. Once, while again sitting in one of the curtained cubicles, I observed the energetic activities swirling around me. They were busy, as they often are. In the cubicle next to me, an elderly woman was wheeled in on a cart from X-ray. The woman was clearly in severe pain, agitated, confused. From her garbled comments, I gathered that she lived in a nursing home, had fallen, and was here, I suspected, for X-rays for a potential fracture. She wandered mentally, crying out in pain, saying she was afraid she needed to go to the bathroom. A nurse came, gently comforted her, acknowledged her pain, helped her with the bedpan, and encouraged her to verbalize—a set of familiar commonplaces. The woman continued to mix and scramble thoughts, locations, and experiences while moaning and mumbling. Yet, in the middle of all these meanderings, for one brief bracketed moment, in a clear and direct voice, she said to the nurse assisting her, "You're a good nurse." It was so clear and direct, and so fleeting that it startled me. This book is about a lucid moment in the midst of the pain and confusion which too often shapes the institutional experiences of practicing nurses. It is about being a "good nurse."

The future, I believe, belongs to nurses like the authors of this book, people who asked the best and the most of themselves. I encourage you to read and study it with the same spirit and courage that created the story it tells. I have often told the nurses I've worked with at St. Michael Hospital that the future will not be shaped by academicians like me, but by practicing nurses like them. I believe that. It is my hope that nurses who read this book will come to share in the adventure described because, having read this book, nurses will begin to create this future in their nursing world. Hope always feels better than despair and, ultimately, courage is more fun.

*Phyllis Kritek, R.N., Ph.D., FAAN*
*Professor and Director, Doctoral Program*
*University of Wisconsin-Milwaukee School of Nursing*

---

**REFERENCE**

Gardner, J.W. (1984). *Excellence*. New York: W.W. Norton.

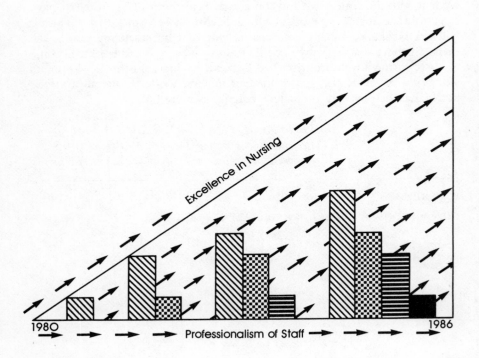

Excellence in Nursing

1980     Professionalism of Staff ⟶     1986

Unit Based Quality Assurance
Research Process
Shared Governance
Professional Growth

# Preface

In 1983, St. Michael Hospital was one of 41 in the country cited as a "magnet hospital" by the Task Force of Nursing Practice in Hospitals of the prestigious American Academy of Nurses (American Nurses' Association, 1983). A magnet hospital was defined as one especially successful in attracting and retaining nurses.

In 1976, St. Michael Hospital was one of the first in the country to implement primary nursing to optimize patient care. In 1978, it was one of the project sites in the National Study of Nursing Care Modalities (Van Servellen, 1980), which focused on primary nursing as a care delivery system.

St. Michael nurses have been published extensively in national nursing periodicals and have conducted workshops around the country in their specialties. Publication of the book *Nursing Quality Assurance: A Unit-Based Approach* (Schroeder & Maibusch, 1984), with chapters by 11 St. Michael Hospital nurses, meant national recognition of the professional level and achievements of the hospital's nursing department.

The hospital's vice president of patient services received an American Nurses' Foundation grant to study shared governance in a nursing department (Pinkerton, 1985).

St. Michael Hospital has a strong physician-nurse committee structure. It has seven different nurse-physician committees, each a specialty area, that practice under a problem-resolution model.

The Nursing Department at St. Michael Hospital was one of the first in the country to adopt formally the Social Policy Statement of the American Nurses' Association Congress for Nursing Practice (ANA, 1980). The Social

Policy Statement has been integrated into the philosophy, the purposes and objectives, the committee structure, and the job descriptions of the department.

Advanced degrees are the rule among nurse leaders at St. Michael Hospital. Nurses pursue professional development to maintain a high level of practice and to benefit their patients and families.

Given this variety of experiences, a book coauthored by the nurses who participate in the variety of activities seemed to be a worthwhile pursuit. Reflecting over the years, a growth in the professionalism of the staff was evident, as portrayed in the Book Model. This professionalism could be related directly to the activities in which the members of the nursing department engaged: unit-based quality assurance, the implementation of the research process, shared governance, professional growth of the staff, and the marketing of professional development activities to other nurses. These activities were introduced over a six-year period of time and, as each new activity was introduced, the already existing activities grew and became stronger. Concomitantly, excellence in the nursing department grew and became increasingly evident.

The following chapters describe the four activities of the nursing department from the viewpoint of the players. The concepts that linked the four activities together—accountability, autonomy, critical thinking, and negotiation of organizational politics—seemed to give the department direction while enhancing excellence and growth. Therefore, as the authors of the chapters describe the staff growth of excellence and professionalism through the activities of unit-based quality assurance, the research process, shared governance, and professional growth, the authors have also included the threads of accountability, autonomy, critical thinking, and negotiation of organizational politics.

As Kirsch explains in the introduction of Part V, the actual timing of the events in this book at times paralleled, preceded, or followed the progression of development in quality assurance, research utilization, and shared governance. They did not always proceed in an orderly step by step process as might be expected.

This book is intended for nurses who are interested in the strategies for action it contains, or in the detailed description of the growth of the St. Michael Department of Nursing, or in the perceptions of the many staff nurses who authored or coauthored chapters and clearly elucidated the significance of professional development for them.

This book is for nurse administrators interested in comparing approaches or trying new ones. It is for staff nurses interested in implementing new projects and programs.

It also is for faculty and students. Faculty members will gain insight into the practice setting to help to prepare new graduates; new graduates will have hope of a practice setting in which autonomous practice is a reality; graduate students will analyze the segments of the book that may become their own clinical or administrative projects.

This book is for the advancement of the nursing profession. It provides a futuristic and microcosmic view of the evolution of nursing. It is intended to stimulate the development of perceptions and insights in these individuals.

**REFERENCES**

American Nurses' Association. (1980). *Nursing: A Social Policy Statement* (ANA Publication Code: NP-63 35M 12/80). Kansas City, Mo.: Author.

American Nurses' Association. (1983). *Magnet hospitals: Attraction and retention of nurses* (Catalog No. G160 5M). Kansas City, Mo.: Author.

Pinkerton, S.E. (1985). *Evaluation of shared governance in a nursing department*. Milwaukee: St. Michael Hospital.

Schroeder, P.S., & Maibusch, R.M. (1984). *Nursing quality assurance: A unit-based approach*. Rockville, Md.: Aspen Publishers, Inc.

Van Servellen, G.M. (1980). *Final report: A comparison of the effectiveness of primary nursing units in hospitals serving as project sites* (National Study of Nursing Care Modalities). Los Angeles: University of California, Center for the Health Sciences, School of Nursing.

# Acknowledgments

To complete a book which reflects the work and progress toward professional practice of an entire hospital of nurses is a complex and at times overwhelming task. For the support and interest offered, John A. Comiskey, President, is thanked, along with the sponsors, The Wheaton Franciscan Sisters.

This book is organized by sections, and the section editors, Eleanore Kirsch, Janet Krejci, Shelly Malin, and Peg Wagner, are thanked for their hours of editing time, their great ideas, and their continued support.

Leann Hammann is most appreciated for her magic with the word processor and her continuation with the project. Germaine Wagner and Joan Wendelberger are thanked for their assistance in typing; Vicki Schluge and Madeleine Knasinski for their assistance with library services.

Most of all the nursing staff at St. Michael Hospital is thanked. They are the individuals who make nursing what it is and inspire us to support them as they pursue excellence.

*SueEllen Pinkerton*
*Patricia Schroeder*

# Part I

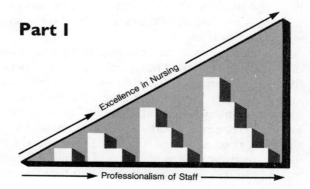

Excellence in Nursing

Professionalism of Staff

# The Professional Environment

*Patricia Schroeder*
Section Editor

A nurse's ability to practice well is dependent, in part, on the professional environment. An environment committed to excellence must possess a variety of characteristics, many of which are described in current popular literature on excellence in organizations. Managers who are enthusiastic, provide support, and trust the abilities of their staff members play a significant role in setting such a climate. The ability of members of an organization to change and adapt also is important.

Subsequent parts of this text describe growth of nursing excellence in one organization. This could not have occurred without continuing attention to the issue of professional climate or environment. Part I sets the stage for growth. Chapter 1 describes the quest for excellence and the value of striving for professional achievement. Chapter 2 provides perspectives on individual and group trust issues, both of which are essential to taking professional risks and being open to change. Chapter 3 addresses the change experience from the perspective of nurse managers. The initial decentralization of decision-making through implementation of unit-based nursing quality assurance is used as an example.

Placement of this information at the beginning of the book is not accidental. The importance of professional climate cannot be underestimated. It also cannot be addressed once, then considered finished. The climate in which nurses practice changes, based on many relatively uncontrollable variables such as societal attitudes, pressures from other disciplines, and effects of federal legislation. It is nursing's continuing challenge to mold the environment, to the extent possible, to be one that is professional, creative, and nurturing. This work must never stop.

## Chapter 1

# The Commitment to Developing Excellence

*SueEllen Pinkerton*

*Committing oneself to professional development goes beyond personal growth. Nursing leaders are obligated to create organizational climates in which staff members thrive and mature professionally. When the standards for organizational climate are being set, nothing less than excellence should be the goal.*

The concept of excellence implies superiority. However, this conflicts with the main tenet of nursing, which is equality of nurses regardless of education or experience. McClure (1978) states that excellence and equality are mutually exclusive. She reports that nurses tend to err on the side of overemphasizing equality and are reluctant to differentiate among practitioners on the basis of their ability or knowledge.

Evidence of this is found in the practice setting, where nursing assistants, practical nurses, and professional nurses alike are assigned to many of the same tasks and functions. This promotes the idea that little, if any, education is required in nursing. The result is a curbing of potential among the brightest and best nurses, which in turn leads to general mediocrity pervading nursing practice.

Excellence therefore seems to be diluted by the expectation of equality in nursing. For example:

1. All nurses take the same state board examination.
2. There is limited integration between education and service, resulting in little planning for the use of superior practitioners.

3. Nursing service often is asked to react to changes in education without adequate forethought, such as a shift from a medical model to an integrated curriculum in which all specialty areas are integrated, usually by age groups of clients, as opposed to keeping them separate (e.g., medical, surgical).
4. Students who are taught to be change agents by schools of nursing and thus pursue organizational excellence are not taught the details and practicalities of assessing the entity's climate before they go in and begin to try to make changes.

Based on these examples, excellence cannot be a unilateral professional pursuit. Collaboration is a key in reaching this goal. The literature is replete with information singling out the gap between education and service as the barrier to growth in such areas as research and the advancement of clinical practice. In this instance, the gap must be narrowed if nursing is to commit to excellence.

## WHOSE COMMITMENT?

When individuals commit themselves to excellence in an organization, they first must commit to the integration of education and service; the professionalization of nursing requires that education and service collaborate.

> Professionalization is the process through which an occupation gains a monopoly of specialized knowledge and high degree of competence in its utilization. In nursing, it requires . . . the maintenance of educational and professional standards through increased reading of professional literature, committee work, and participation in . . . professional associations . . . (Corwin & Taves, 1960, p. 223).

A professional nurse is one who is involved in work that is predominately intellectual, requires discretion and judgment, cannot be standardized in production time, requires advanced scientific knowledge, and is predominately original and artistically creative in character (McManus, cited in Bowden, 1967). It is imperative, therefore, that nursing support the concepts of autonomy, accountability, critical thinking, and political negotiation if nurses are to be conceptualized as professionals and a climate conducive to their growth is to be established.

The process model for examining professions involves several steps in a long-term negotiation for professional recognition, including:

- a sense of mission that relates to the contribution the specialty can make
- functions identified as core professional acts

- methodologies and techniques for accomplishing functions
- client relationships
- colleagueship within the profession
- professional interest and associations
- professional unity and relations with the public (Bucher & Strauss, 1961).

This process for professional recognition often occurs with segments of a profession such as in a particular specialty area. As that segment gains increased recognition and power, a total sense of the professional movement can develop.

In nursing, observations can be made of nurses negotiating for increased identity in clinical specialty areas and in independent practice. As these specialties achieve status and become influential, a sense of the entire profession's enhancement is discernible.

It is clear that there needs to be a commitment to individual groups in nursing in order to advance the entire profession. This involves endeavors such as political negotiation and lobbying as well as collaboration with other health professionals as to nursing's role definition to promote autonomy, accountability, and critical thinking.

Two key questions are: (1) How does this happen in a practice setting? (2) How can nurses commit themselves to excellence? To answer these questions, it is necessary to examine the components of an organization's climate, specifically: (1) interaction of group and individual behaviors, (2) leadership styles, and (3) decisionmaking (Gibson, Ivancevich, & Donnelly, 1982).

## CREATING AN ORGANIZATIONAL CLIMATE

### Behavioral Interaction

The first component of an organizational climate is the interaction of individual and group behaviors, which sometimes can lead to conflict. Bucher and Stelling (1969) report results of their interviews and observations in various hospital organizations spanning a ten-year period. They note the importance of bargaining by professionals for autonomy and role creation. They also describe segments of professional groups integrating through a political process involving meetings and committees.

The process also includes competition and conflict that may result in attempts to influence decisionmaking in favor of self-interest groups through the use of power. Bucher and Stelling conceptualize a professional organization as an establishment in which persons classified as professionals exert control and influence. This type of organization can be identified by the extent to which professionals control the policies and operations of their own sector and influence goals and policies for the entire entity.

Bates (1970) also describes instances in which negotiation takes place between nursing and other hospital subsystems, adding to the process of professionalism and to autonomy. These negotiations result in role clarity and expanded functions for clinical nurse specialists.

In hospitals, many groups interact. Ashley (1976) describes the subservience of nurses to doctors and hospital administrators. It is unclear how this history in nursing affected the development of nurse administrators and hospitals since there is such a strong focus in the literature on the effect of education on the advancement of nursing.

Another group interacting is staff nurses, who continue to represent nursing, medicine, hospital administration, and other departments in the facility in their daily exchanges on nursing units. In this instance, the youngest and least experienced professionals must face and interact with all other groups in the hospital organization. In other group interactions, nurse managers continually are found acting as buffers with other departments, yet this frequently is a role not explored with them when they assume such positions.

Although educators have attempted to teach assertiveness in nursing, they often have not included the process of negotiation and compromise. Nursing cannot ignore its history of subservience to the hospital system and must teach newcomers how to enter it appropriately. Credentials reflecting achievement and excellence are important both for practitioners and managers.

As progress is made creating superior organizational climates that promote positive resolution of individual and group conflicts, continuing analysis of interactions between the groups is essential. This can be very profitable for service and education groups in nursing, as well as for groups of nurses and other professionals who may be meeting in combined committees to resolve hospital issues.

Conflict in itself usually involves individual groups' striving to achieve autonomy and, in many instances, to acquire power. However, one group can increase its power without taking it away from another group, or what is described as power not being a zero-sum game. A gain for one person or group is not necessarily a loss for another person or group. For example, a head nurse who teaches staff nurses how to justify additional staff now has several people, rather than only one, who can perform the task, which leads to stronger justifications, better rationale, and an understanding of several people rather than just one. Most noteworthy is the fact that both education and service can move the profession by uniting it, which can stimulate progress.

## Leadership Styles

The second component of organizational climate involves leadership styles. Leaders often are described by the dimensions of both the task requiring leadership and of the individual. Individual traits and characteristics most often ascribed to leaders are that they are analytical, take initiative, are risk takers, have integrity, are experts in their field, are goal oriented, are able to delegate and coordinate, are empathic, and have verbal dominance or the ability to communicate.

These traits are characteristics of leaders that enable them to stimulate the integration of education and service and to commit to the growth of excellence in an organization.

## Decisionmaking

Decisionmaking is the third component of organizational climate. Decisionmaking that involves participation of all groups in an organization has been shown to increase productivity and decrease turnover. Some facts that should be considered when including groups in decisionmaking are:

- Some individuals do not want to become involved in decisionmaking, sometimes because they feel they do not have the expertise or feel incompetent in a particular area.
- Group members can be affected by differences in their individual status.
- Some feel that their input into decisionmaking is not being utilized.

The National Commission on Nursing study (1983) supports the creation of a climate for the promotion of excellence. It recommends that:

1. Trustees, administrators, physicians, and nurses should have an obligation to establish a suitable environment for the practice of nursing. Nursing should be involved in policy development and decisionmaking throughout the organization.
2. Nurses and physicians, who are essential to the care of patients, should know and recognize the particular contributions of those having the special knowledge and skills of both professions in assuring that decisions on care are of the highest possible quality.

The task force on implementing this study is continuing to address these areas, its report to be published beyond this book's deadline.

The first key to creating an organizational climate that promotes, encourages, and commits to excellence in nursing is to examine the environment that affects the institution, while considering the history of nursing and acknowledging that in some instances the profession is not ready to advance in new areas. The second key is the professional development of leaders and their use as mentors, along with analysis of potential new structures and the interrelationship of existing structures within organizations in which bureaucratic hierarchies are flattened and professionals within the bureaucracy are recognized for their abilities and are given corresponding accountability and autonomy.

## NURSES SUPPORTING NURSES

The last element in the striving for excellence is the commitment to individuals. It is important to develop leaders who invest in creating a growth-producing organizational climate. The leadership factor that promotes this growth is the willingness to invest in human potential. Investing is different from smothering and controlling. It is the willingness to let go when signs of readiness appear. It is the willingness to support, encourage, and be there. It involves wanting others to achieve, knowing that others want the same.

This element seems most difficult for nurses to understand and accept, perhaps primarily because of their socialization or the way in which they were introduced to nursing and their role as nurses. A climate without trust, however, will never be one that supports excellence.

## EXCELLENCE IN NURSING

The main tenet of this book is a commitment to excellence. The book's conceptual model shows the growth in excellence in nursing, but this can only occur concomitant with professionalization of the staff. Once the groundwork is in place for staff interaction and decisionmaking, a domino effect occurs stimulating professional growth.

In summary, it is imperative for leaders to make individual commitments to developing excellence in nursing. Nursing is composed of professionals who, once in an open, trusting climate, can progress rapidly into positions where they assume accountability, practice autonomously, and engage in critical thinking. But the first step is believing enough to make the investment in human potential; the obligation is nursing's.

---

**REFERENCES**

Ashley, J. (1976). *Hospitals, paternalism, and the role of the nurse.* New York: Columbia University, Teachers College Press.

Bates, B. (1970). Doctor and nurse: Changing roles and relations. *New England Journal of Medicine, 283,* 129-134.

Bowden, E.A.F. (1967). Nurses' attitudes toward hospital nursing service: Implications for job satisfaction and transfers between services. *Nursing Research, 16,* 246-251.

Bucher, R., & Stelling, J. (1969). Characteristics of professional organizations. *Journal of Health and Social Behavior, 10,* 3-15.

Bucher, R., & Strauss, A. (1961). Professions in process. *American Journal of Sociology, 66,* 325-334.

Corwin, R.G., & Taves, M.J. (1960). Some concomitants of bureaucratic and professional conceptions of the nurse role. *Nursing Research, 11,* 223-227.

Gibson, J.L., Ivancevich, J.M., & Donnelly, J.H., Jr. (1982). *Organizations: Behavior, structure, process* (4th ed.). Dallas: Business Publications.

McClure, M.L. (1978). The long road to accountability. *Nursing Outlook, 26,* 47-50.

National Commission on Nursing. (1983). *Summary report and recommendations* (Hospital Research and Educational Trust, Catalog No. 654200). Chicago: Author.

**Chapter 2**

---

# Trust Relationships

*Norma Carr*

*There are several factors that may influence trust in a nursing organ-
ization that is becoming self-governing. A closer examination of group
process can provide an understanding of the role of trust in the dynamics
of nursing groups.*

Soon after World War II, interest in the dynamics of group function became
the focus of several research investigations. Out of these grew an interest in
T-groups (training in human relations) and the subsequent formation of the
National Training Laboratory in group development. The information that
has come out of T-groups has formed the basis for most of the current theory
on task-oriented groups. Kurt Lewin's field theory, which emphasizes the
relationship of an individual's behavior to his or her environment, also has
had a major influence on the interpretation of behavior in groups.

## INTRAGROUP RELATIONSHIPS

For a group to work well, each member must develop an understanding
of how to contribute to its success. For many years most of the emphasis
has been on leadership. However, the effectiveness or success of a group
depends on how each member functions within its dynamics. According to
Bradford (1978), Bennis and Shepard (1978), and Gibb and Gibb (1977),
the establishment of trust among the group members as well as trust in the
leader is an essential part of the initial phase of group development.

10

Bradford (1978) identifies four phases that groups go through in a repetitious cycle: (1) initial group formation, (2) confronting a difficult problem or barrier, (3) overcoming the problem through cooperative problem solving, and (4) group reorganization.

## Initial Group Formation

A simple gathering of individuals does not comprise a group. A group forms when tasks have been identified, patterns of communication established, and a niche set for each person. For this phase to be dealt with adequately, trust needs to be established. A leader who fosters trust and shared leadership with the members is the ideal. If these tasks and concerns are not dealt with, the group will be unproductive.

## Confronting a Problem or Barrier

This phase may manifest itself as an insurmountable task. During the initial stage of group formation, the members will have developed a sense of cohesiveness and pride about their function and purpose. Such factors as reversal of a decision by a higher level, interpersonal difficulties, or conflict may cause members to feel pessimistic and disillusioned about the group's progress.

During this phase, participants may revert to arguing, subgrouping, and fragmented discussion. One earmark of this phase is that statements may be totally unrelated to ideas discussed previously. If the group is to move forward, some member must give the others a new perspective on the task, identify the group's strengths, and reduce the emotionalism generated by the problem.

## Cooperative Problem Solving

In this stage, members redefine the problem and identify what needs to be done to overcome the barriers to solving it. It may be necessary to redefine the participants' roles in order to complete the tasks. On the other hand, members may need to be more accepting of diversity and disagreement.

## Group Reorganization

The last phase develops when the group is able to identify the problem clearly and all members participate openly, without being judged, in an environment of trust. This is a new stage of formation of the group and is essentially a reorganization.

These stages are played out in different ways and on different levels repeatedly throughout the life of a group. It is to be hoped that the members will grow with the group to achieve higher and higher levels of success.

## COMMUNICATION AND TRUST

Bennis and Shepard (1978) identify overcoming of obstacles to valid communication as one of the most basic tasks in the development of any group. The members bring differing orientations toward authority and intimacy, which results in varied interpersonal behaviors. Behaviors such as withdrawal, aggressiveness, rebelliousness, and destructive competition can interfere with the free flow of ideas. The group members need to overcome such behaviors and develop a means to achieve consensus.

The ideal balance is achieved when a group is able to arrive at a consensus while allowing the members to retain their individuality. If nonconformity becomes a standard of rejection, individual members will tend to strive toward uniformity. The free flow of accurate information in a group may be affected adversely by conformity and an intolerance for individuality (O'Reilly, 1978). Moreover, the more varied and heterogenous the group, the greater the likelihood that it will succeed through a balance of interpersonal strengths and weaknesses.

Trust can affect the flow of information and decisionmaking in a group. O'Reilly (1978) conducted several laboratory and field studies to determine the causative factors and consequences of the intentional distortion of information by senders in organizations. One of the variables that affects information flow at the individual level is the sender's trust in the receiver— and vice versa. A high trust was demonstrated to have a favorable influence on the total amount of information and an unfavorable influence on the delivery of important information to supervisors. Under conditions of low trust, subordinates passed on more favorable important and unimportant information.

The impact of these distortions on the flow of information may impair decisionmaking at higher levels. Organizational conditions such as hierarchism, specialization, and centralization restrict the flow of information to appropriate decisionmakers. Accordingly, shared governance, which focuses on decentralization and autonomy, promotes trust in leadership and the free flow of information in the organization and thus increases the likelihood of sound decisionmaking.

Ashley (1976) describes the political forces in hospitals that have influenced nursing. Specifically, nurses' problems are an outgrowth of a profession dominated by women that has its roots in the paternalistic hospital setting. Several factors related to the socialization of women in society or the manner in which they were introduced to their role as women affect the way women relate to one another in the work setting. This, combined with nursing's historical background and place in the hospital bureaucracy, has contributed to the identification of trust relationships as an important theme in the professional status of nursing.

Openness, self-disclosure, and inner honesty are basic qualities in the development of trust in interpersonal relationships. Jean Baker Miller (1976) finds that subordination and authenticity of the individual are incompatible. Miller's basic tenet in this description of women in society is the recognition that they have been given unequal status. Miller, along with Bardwick (1979), suggests that such inequality promotes distrust. Distrust may be mixed with intimacy. Moreover, openness in interpersonal relationships can be frightening to women who decide to speak up. Women's tendency to use indirect communication patterns may contribute to the weakening of interpersonal trust. Bardwick says it is necessary to use direct, focused communication patterns in the work setting to develop trust.

## THE ROLE OF POWER

A common pattern in the hierarchy of nursing can be seen in the supervisor's unfeeling attitudes toward those who are subordinate. "Queen-beeism"— the tendency of those who achieve status to treat those in subordinate positions unfeelingly—still exists on the hierarchical ladder in hospitals. Miller (1976) attributes this and other destructive behaviors among women to the fact that subordinates treat other subordinates as destructively as superiors have treated them. Ashley (1976) reports that various attempts of nurse reformers were undermined by others in the profession who joined forces with hospital administrators.

This often has contributed to the breakdown of trust among nurses and thus to a weakening of their power base in nursing groups in the hospital organization. Women at work not only have to learn to express their opinions in an appropriately open, assertive way but have to feel better about themselves so that fear of rejection, especially over work disagreements, no longer dominates what they do. Both authors say women must use their adaptiveness and creativity to enhance their strengths.

The professional development of a nursing staff necessitates change on both the group and individual levels. With the restructuring of nursing's power base in shared governance there must be changes that promote autonomy of groups and individuals to replace the passivity of the bureaucratic model.

## IMPASSES AND DEFENSIVENESS

The assistance of a group process facilitator may be needed when the members reach an impasse. Similarly, groups that do not meet on a formal basis may need the help of a facilitator to expedite problem solving. The author, in the role of psychosocial clinical nurse specialist, has assisted nursing groups in problem solving. Group difficulties may be manifested in different ways, such as a conflict between shifts or an impasse in the peer review process. The approach taken to help a group with a problem will depend on the magnitude of the issue as well as the group's history.

Individual members of the group need to feel free to speak up about the issues and to understand that the disclosure of feelings and ideas (with their subsequent vulnerability) will not result in some sort of unfavorable inter-personal consequences. Work with group members frequently begins with focusing on reducing defensive behavior with the goal of improving com-munication. Defensive behavior, which is a coping mechanism used by in-dividuals to protect their image, is most likely to occur during times of conflict (Silber, 1984).

The most effective method of removing defensive barriers is to encourage group members to focus on the interests of others through empathizing, listening, and validating feelings. (Sometimes a great deal of talking takes place before an individual is ready for the real issue.) Group members need to know that if issues are not dealt with openly, they frequently are manifested in the form of hidden agendas or subgrouping.

When group members reach the point at which they want to reduce their defensiveness, a briefing on the rules of assertive communication may be of value. A role-playing exercise may accomplish this for some groups, while a simple review is all that is needed for others. Even though group members have had assertiveness training, their communication may have either an aggressive or an indirect approach. Assertive behaviors must be practiced until they become incorporated as part of the individuals' repertoire.

Learned helplessness is a common coping mechanism in centralized bu-reaucratic organizations that perpetuate powerlessness and passivity in their membership. Women and those working in social service agencies are two groups especially prone to this trait. Some of the manifestations—such as depression, stress, apathy, and resignation—can affect group process just as it affects the way individuals function in the work setting.

Learned helplessness perpetuates low productivity, poor self-esteem, and failure. The cycle tends to be self-perpetuating. Martinko and Gardner (1982) say that people may remain passive even after the organization changes significantly, eliminating the original cause for such self-defeating behavior.

## LEADERS AS CHANGE AGENTS

A large share of responsibility for change rests with nursing leaders who can identify problems such as learned helplessness and influence individuals who are in a position to effect change. For an organization to become increasingly self-governing, much effort needs to be directed toward the fostering of new behaviors and attitudes.

The initiation of staff participation through self-governance systems does not guarantee that staff initiative and autonomy will occur spontaneously, however. Through the process of working with various nursing groups, the psychosocial clinical nurse specialist can observe that the boundaries for participative decisionmaking need to be tested initially even though the process may seem cumbersome to the staff.

Nursing leadership needs to encourage staff nurses to participate in decisionmaking, to test new behaviors, and to take some risks in assuming responsibilities formerly thought of as off limits. Participative decisionmaking, like learned helplessness, can become self-perpetuating. When new behaviors are tested, decisions made, and their positive results felt, the process will serve as an impetus for future participative decisionmaking.

The development of trust is a necessary prerequisite for shared governance. Nurse leaders can serve as role models for effective, assertive communication. The fostering of mentor relationships can do much to encourage the self-confidence, skills, and networking necessary to prepare nurses for leadership positions.

The professional development of a nursing staff necessitates change on both the group and individual level. Nursing leaders can provide the objectivity needed to identify behaviors that need changing. With the restructuring of nursing's power base in shared governance, there need to be changes that promote autonomy of groups and individuals to replace the passivity of the bureaucratic model.

---

**REFERENCES**

Ashley, J. (1976). *Hospitals, paternalism, and the role of the nurse.* New York: Columbia University, Teachers College Press.

Bardwick, J.M. (1979). *In transition.* New York: Holt, Rinehart & Winston.

Bennis, W.G., & Shepard, H.A. (1978). A theory of group development. In L.P. Bradford (Ed.), *Group development* (2nd ed.). LaJolla, Calif.: University Associates.

Bradford, L.P. (1978). Group formation and development. In L.P. Bradford (Ed.), *Group development* (2nd ed.). LaJolla, Calif.: University Associates.

Gibb, J.R., & Gibb, L.M. (1978). The group as a growing organism. In L.P. Bradford (Ed.), *Group development* (2nd ed.). LaJolla, Calif.: University Associates.

Martinko, M.J., & Gardner, W.J. (1982). Learned helplessness: An alternative explanation for performance deficits. *Academy of Management Review, 7,* 195-204.

Miller, J.B. (1976). *Toward a new psychology of women.* Boston: Beacon Press.

O'Reilly, C.A., III. (1978). The intentional distortion of information in organizational communication: A laboratory and field investigation. *Human Relations, 31,* 173-193.

Silber, M. (1984). Managing confrontations: Once more into the breach. *Nursing Management, 15,* 54-58.

## BIBLIOGRAPHY

Vance, C.N. (1982a). The mentor connection. *The Journal of Nursing Administration, 12,* 7-13.

Vance, C.N. (1982b). Women leaders: Modern-day heroines or societal deviants? In E.C. Hein & M.J. Nicholson (Eds.), *Contemporary leadership behavior: Selected readings.* Boston: Little, Brown.

# Chapter 3

# The Change Experience

*Ross J. Workman and Mary Beth A. Kenney*

*Change is a process that occurs in increasing frequency in health care today. This chapter, written by nurse managers, describes the example of and reactions to the change of decentralizing decisionmaking on a nursing unit. Strategies have been described which influenced the success of the process.*

For growth to occur, there first must be change. Whether the growth is physical, intellectual, or social, some form of differentiation has to occur. Just as change is associated with growth in individuals, so can it also be seen in organizations. For example, the implementation of a unit-based quality assurance program can precipitate significant change, both for individuals and the organization. This, in turn, results in professional growth.

If growth is to be stimulated, there first must be a thorough understanding of change and its process. This chapter provides a theoretical review of these topics. It also analyzes the initial decentralization of decisionmaking at St. Michael Hospital to describe the realities of major organizational change.

## CHANGE THEORY

The concept of change is characterized in the literature as being inevitable, constant, universal, and powerful. If in fact it has such a pervasive and potent influence on individuals and groups, it is critical that it be defined clearly.

Change means to "make different." In human terms, it can be defined as "a process which leads to alterations in individual or institutional patterns of

17

behavior" (Brooten, Hayman, and Naylor, 1978, p. 79). Two important components of this definition are analyzed further: (1) how change affects human behavior and (2) how it should be viewed as a process.

## The Effect of Change on Behavior

Given the wide diversity of human attitudes and behaviors, change affects each person (and group) in a different manner. Some people thrive on it while others react negatively to even the slightest alterations in their routines. By nature, most people prefer what they have become comfortable with and accustomed to. Disruptions in the status quo (i.e., change) lead to psychological tension that prompts a response.

Asprec (1975) describes four main ways in which individuals and groups react to change. The first is through frustration and aggression (active resistance), which can develop when its consequences are perceived to be in conflict with personal needs or values. Manifestations of aggressive behaviors include deliberate sabotage (e.g., providing false data on a new system by committing intentional errors) and artificially slowing the work pace. These acts can be overt or covert and may become disruptive or destructive in a group setting.

The second is organized (passive) resistance, which occurs when individuals band together to resist change collectively. The basis for this resistance may include actual or merely perceived threats to self-interest, inaccurate perceptions of the intended action, objective disagreement with it, and low tolerance for it (New & Couillard, 1981). Examples are withholding vital information from management or covering up mistakes by group members to bias quality appraisals.

The third is indifference as characterized by two manifestations: (1) ignoring the situation, or (2) attempting to divert attention to other nonpertinent subjects. An example would be several group members who do not acknowledge any problems with their time management skills so they simply ignore the recommendations of a consultant.

The fourth is to meet change with acceptance. Although this is gratifying to the individual promoting the action, it may not always represent genuine support. The acceptance may be a conscious alternative to resistance, which can be energy-depleting and destabilizing (e.g., "the last guy that resisted that was fired").

## The Process of Change

Theoretical models have been developed that depict change as a systematic, and therefore predictable, process. This process is equivalent in many ways to the one undertaken when problem solving; therefore, it permits most changes to be planned and controlled.

Kurt Lewin's (1951) force field analysis has been used widely to describe the change process. Since individuals naturally strive for equilibrium, there generally is a balance of the driving (promoting change) and restraining (inhibiting change) forces impinging on any situation. By analyzing and altering the relative strengths of these forces, Lewin says the equilibrium can be broken and changes thus facilitated.

Lewin (1947) describes three distinct phases in the process: unfreezing, changing (moving), and refreezing. Unfreezing occurs when disequilibrium is introduced into the system and homeostatic forces acting on the individual or group begin to "melt down." As the status quo is disrupted by the introduction of the change, people become ready to explore alternatives and accept change. Changing (moving) allows an exploration of alternatives that will return the system to a new equilibrium. Once the best alternative is found, it is implemented. Refreezing occurs when the change becomes integrated as the new norm within the system. The new behaviors now are "frozen" until the next move comes along.

Most organizations face considerable internal and external pressures for change. Organizational viability and success depend in large part on how effectively the group and its leaders respond to these pressures. Successful organizations view change opportunistically, and actively plan for and adapt to it.

## Planned Change

"Planned change is a purposeful, designed effort to bring about improvement within a system, with the assistance of a change agent" (Spradley, 1980, p. 34). Instead of reacting haphazardly to each shift in the equilibrium, effective organizations respond to change (pressures) in a deliberate and systematic process. This process shares attributes with the decisionmaking and nursing process models, as outlined in Table 3-1.

It is important to remember that all change takes time. Major organizational moves require significant shifts in behaviors and attitudes and may take several years to accomplish fully.

For this process to be followed in a systematic manner, a facilitator or change agent is essential. Brooten, Hayman, and Naylor (1978) describe a change agent as a professional who relies on a knowledge of change to guide the process, who has good interpersonal skills, and who has been given (or has assumed) a mandate to help plan and implement a move or action. Managers in the institutions often serve as change agents but individual members or someone from outside the group (e.g., consultant) also can play this role.

**Table 3-1** Planned Change Model

| Nursing Process | Planned Change Process (Internal and/or External Stimulus) | Problem-Solving Method |
|---|---|---|
| Assessment | 1. Recognize need for change (unfreezing) | Problem identification |
| | | Problem definition |
| Planning | 2. Plan for change (moving) | Problem analysis |
| | • assess organizational climate for change | |
| | • identify various alternatives | |
| | • analyze pros and cons of each alternative (assess the driving and restraining forces) | Alternative solutions |
| | • select best alternative | Recommended action |
| Implementation | 3. Implement change (moving) | Implementation |
| Evaluation | 4. Evaluate effectiveness of change and either: | Evaluation |
| | • accept and stabilize change (refreeze), or | |
| Revision | • reject change and revise plans | |

Effective leadership is critical to the efficient and successful accomplishment of change in an organization. Managers must become skilled with each phase of the planned model and strive to develop a climate that supports it constructively. Successful managers can predict when and how best to introduce changes based on their knowledge of the underlying theory and their group's motivation and maturity. They seek to minimize resistance through various strategies, including group participation, education, and incentives. Finally, they view the process as a challenge instead of a burden, which helps foster a positive and progressive organizational spirit.

## Organizational Change in Nursing

The health care system continues to undergo dramatic changes in a response to economic, social, and political demands. To meet these challenges (actively and assertively), nurses should strengthen their knowledge base in areas such as health care economics, the change process, leadership theory, and politics.

Changes within nursing organizations, as with any group, must be planned carefully to enhance the likelihood of their success. One of the important roles that the nursing leader plays is that of the change agent. The leader should strive to create a "professional environment" (Porter-O'Grady, 1986, p. 81) in which the nursing staff learns to share the accountability and responsibility for change decisions.

The nursing profession has made tremendous strides over the last century, but the challenges and opportunities it faces are great. Nursing history and organizational theory have shown that although change is inevitable and constant, it must be addressed in a systematic process to promote a positive outcome. As nurses at all levels become more skilled at planning for new moves and situations, they will gain an increased sense of control over their practice and can search for innovative strategies to confront the future successfully.

## UNIT-BASED QUALITY ASSURANCE AS A MODEL

One strategy nursing departments can utilize in responding to challenges is to promote a decentralized approach to decisionmaking. Decentralization is defined as the dispersion or distribution of functions and powers from a central authority to regional or local authority. In the nursing department, this generally implies that the centralized authority figures (e.g., directors, head nurses) share their power and responsibility for decisionmaking with their staff nurses.

The first step toward decentralization of decisionmaking at St. Michael Hospital was the development and implementation of unit-based quality assurance (UBQA) (see Part II for a full discussion). While this participative approach has many advantages over a centralized or authoritarian style of leadership, it represents a major shift in philosophy and is not without its risks and costs. Some of these are highlighted in the following description. Lewin's model of the change process serves as the framework for discussion.

### Change Theory and Implementation of UBQA

The concept of UBQA and decentralized decisionmaking was introduced in the unfreezing phase by a small group of clinical nurse specialists. This core planning group saw great potential for expanding interest and accountability for quality assurance by involving staff nurses in the process at this unit level.

After initial planning, this core group's next critical task was to educate and involve the formal unit leaders so they could provide the support necessary for successful implementation of the project. As the designated unit leader, the head nurse plays an integral role not only by teaching the staff, but also by helping to create a supportive environment. After inservice training was held for the nurses, key staff members began to realize the potential benefits of a decentralized approach to unit problems and needs. These key nurses, in conjunction with the unit leadership, were ready to consider change.

The changing (moving) phase of the process is the time during which new ideas developed during unfreezing actually are tested and fine-tuned. With the implementation of UBQA, as with many innovative projects, a pilot model was established. This small-scale test allowed the leadership and staff time to experiment with alternative formats before hospitalwide implementation. The success of the pilot project proved to be a further positive stimulus for change and UBQA was initiated throughout the institution.

The structural shifts in quality assurance created expectations of significant attitudinal changes as decisionmaking was decentralized. For the managers, this meant sharing responsibility, authority, and control with the staff, and at least at the outset, slower decisionmaking and mistakes during the learning phase. For most of the staff members, the concept of participative management was relatively new and they did not resist the managers' continuing to control other decisionmaking.

For others, however, this was a period in which to test their new powers and determine the authenticity and sincerity of the decentralized organization (e.g., taking a stand in opposition to the head nurse, asking for more meeting time, or reordering priorities). After this growing together period, both the leadership and staff began to feel comfortable with the changes and experienced initial successes in the unit-based quality assurance program.

The refreezing phase is probably the longest of Lewin's three steps since it involves long-term behavioral and attitudinal changes. In the case of UBQA, refreezing did not begin until there was an atmosphere of mutual trust and collaboration between staff and leadership, evidenced by positive group process and constructive involvement of all members.

After that point, the quality assurance committees (QACs) became more independent and productive. Staff nurses now were initiating proposals for study (such as patient falls) and helping to set quality unit nursing standards (for example, acceptable numbers of primary/associate patients for daily assignments based on budget equivalent and acuity). The unit leadership continued the development of the staff in decisionmaking and research methods through inservice training, literature review, and experiential learning while attempting to reinforce professional growth.

As the staff members took greater responsibility for QA and began to accept accountability for their practice, the managers responded by promoting independent decisionmaking (e.g., allowing the nurses to set the agenda and priorities) and ultimately by encouraging them to lead QACs. This point was a long way from having one centralized quality assurance committee with only marginal staff representation and power.

## Barriers (Restraining Forces)

The major obstacle to implementing the change is breaking away from established norms. The unfreezing of the status quo requires the work of determined change agents willing to chip away at years of bureaucratic routines that prevent effective staff involvement.

Even after the leadership has decided to support this participative approach, staff members may resist this apparently desirable new phase for several reasons: lack of trust in managers, low self-confidence, and/or unwillingness to take on additional responsibilities. Passivity, ambivalence, and apathy all have inhibited major changes in nursing's past; they should have no place in the present or future.

Another potent barrier to decentralization is the cost in terms of time and money. In simple terms, participative decisionmaking takes more time than an autocratic approach. Orientation, planning, meetings, and inexperienced decisionmakers all consume time. In a fast-paced and cost-conscious age, these factors must be weighed carefully before implementing such a change.

This decentralization requires that staff members accept their new responsibilities for decisionmaking and power in a professional manner. An immature or novice staff may appear to be resistant. Although this may affect strategies for implementation (e.g., leader maintaining greater control at first, more gradual introduction of change), continued staff development eventually should promote a higher level of involvement. An analysis of organizational readiness for decentralization (La Monica, 1983, p. 71) is an important component of planning for this move and is addressed in Chapter 12.

## Advantages (Driving Forces)

The implementation and support of a participative program such as UBQA should provide a clear message to staff members that the leaders value their input and welcome their involvement in decisionmaking. The leaders' attitude of including nurses and supporting and following their recommendations helps foster a professional environment by promoting trust within the work unit and enhancing skills relating to group process, problem solving, and change. As individuals and groups evidence growth, their self-confidence builds and their willingness and readiness to accept responsibility is enhanced. These factors should contribute to job satisfaction and prove to be a motivating force toward improved staff performance.

Although there obviously are expenses associated with a program of decentralized decisionmaking, the long-term benefits may be worth the price. For example, a unit may develop and implement a new flow sheet or patient teaching record that not only will promote adherence to quality standards but also may save money through reducing staff time with more efficient documentation. Decisions may take longer; however, since they are the collaborative product of a group, there should be broader support and commitment from the members. Ultimately, the group's ability to plan for change will be strengthened.

## The Role of the Nurse Manager

As noted earlier, the nurse manager plays a critical role in the successful establishment of any unit-based program founded on the concept of shared decisionmaking. Before implementing a program such as UBQA, management groups should discuss their feelings openly about the changes in their roles. Managers must deal with the fact that they no longer will make all decisions for their units. An effective change agent will portray these shifts in terms not of managers' losing power or control but of their gaining the collaborative expertise of staff members, a situation that can only make the managers look better through improved decisionmaking.

Theoretical arguments alone may not be enough to dispel the skepticism of some nurse managers toward sharing the decisional process with their staffs. The core planning group can play an important role in demonstrating the wide array of positive outcomes to these managers through practical examples such as pilot study results. Peers are another excellent source of support during the transition period to help work through problems and uncertainties. The sharing of professional growth experiences in the staff (enhanced commitment of quality care, greater accountability for problem solving) and personal satisfactions (improved staff-management relations, more time as a result of delegation) should help convince even the most skeptical manager.

## The Value to Nursing

UBQA has proved to be a successful model for decentralization of decisionmaking. Increased involvement of staff nurses in the organization helps them become more committed to promoting positive change. Avenues for professional development have broadened as staff members now chair most unit QACs and participate in many other decisionmaking forums. By fostering a professional environment, nurse managers also will benefit as staff members become more able to share in the responsibility and accountability for providing quality care.

The change experience of decentralization at St. Michael Hospital has been a positive one as a result of systematic and thoughtful planning. Attention to historical lessons and theory has allowed nurses to confront the challenges before them assertively and to prepare for future moves.

## REFERENCES

Asprec, E.S. (1975). The process of change. *Supervisor Nurse, 6,* 15-24.

Brooten, D.A., Hayman, L., & Naylor, M. (1978). *Leadership for change: A guide for the frustrated nurse.* Philadelphia: J.B. Lippincott.

La Monica, E. (1983). *Nursing leadership and management: An experiential approach.* Monterey, Calif.: Wadsworth Health Sciences Division.

Lewin, K. (1947). Frontiers in group dynamics: Concept, method, and reality in social science; social equilibria and social change. *Human Relations, 1,* 5-41.

Lewin, K. (1951). *Field theory in social science.* New York: Harper & Row.

New, J.R., & Couillard, N.A. (1981). Guidelines for introducing change. *The Journal of Nursing Administration, 11,* 17-20.

Porter-O'Grady, T. (1986). *Creative nursing administration.* Rockville, Md.: Aspen Publishers, Inc.

Spradley, B.W. (1980). Managing change creatively. *The Journal of Nursing Administration, 10,* 32-37.

## BIBLIOGRAPHY

Crowder, E.L.M. (1985). Historical perspectives of nursing's professionalism. *Occupational Health Nursing, 33,* 184-190.

Griffin, G.J., & Griffin, J.K. (1973). *History and trends of professional nursing* (7th ed.). St. Louis: C.V. Mosby.

Huffman, M.L. (1983). The process of change. *Critical Care Nurse, 3,* 44-46.

Kemp, V.H. (1984). An overview of change and leadership. *Topics in Clinical Nursing, 6,* 1-9.

Shoemaker, H., & El-Ahraf, A. (1983). Decentralization of nursing service management and its impact on job satisfaction. *Nursing Administration Quarterly, 7,* 69-76.

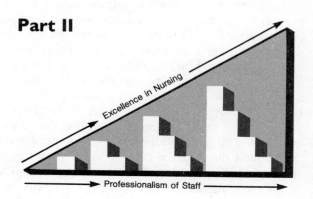

# Unit-Based Quality Assurance

*Patricia Schroeder*
Section Editor

In 1984, 11 nurses who practiced at St. Michael Hospital in Milwaukee coauthored *Nursing Quality Assurance: A Unit-Based Approach* (Schroeder & Maibusch, 1984). The book, born of a nursing department dedicated to the achievement of excellence in nursing practice, focused on the development of a decentralized approach to nursing quality assurance activities. The program grew to become the foundation of subsequent professional development (see book model). Professional activities such as research and shared governance built upon the knowledge and skills developed through unit-based quality assurance (UBQA), and as a result all three programs were enhanced.

Part II of this book begins another look at the nursing department of St. Michael Hospital, this time seven years after the 1979 implementation of UBQA. Although a tradition of excellence had been established long before, the passage of time has demonstrated that the program served as a catalyst for elevating the role of the professional staff nurse at this community hospital.

Chapter 4 discusses the effects of quality assurance on professional development and Chapter 5 describes the UBQA program as it has evolved. Given the expectations that UBQA activities would develop the accountability of professional staff nurses, the roles involved in facilitation of such a program must be planned carefully. Chapter 6 explains needs for and strategies to facilitate QA in a decentralized program.

Together, these three chapters describe a dynamic, valuable professional program that was enhanced further by the development of activities described in each subsequent Part—the research process, shared governance, and professional growth.

Chapter 4

# UBQA: A Catalyst for Professional Development

*Patricia Schroeder*

*The unit-based quality assurance (UBQA) program in nursing was developed to affect the quality of care. It also has become the foundation of and catalyst for professional development of nurses at St. Michael Hospital.*

The process of assuring the quality of nursing care is complex. Nurses have worked for many years to develop mechanisms that can be used to assess quality and then fit them into a process to assure that result. One process or program for quality assurance (QA) in nursing is unit-based quality assurance (UBQA). It is a program involving a QA committee on each nursing unit and requires the involvement and commitment of staff nurses in achieving its goals.

## THE LITERATURE

Several works describe the potential benefits to the organization involved in implementing such a program (Schroeder, Maibusch, Anderson, & Formella, 1982, Schroeder & Maibusch, 1984). Little is written, however, about the professional development of the individual staff nurses involved.

Smeltzer, Hinshaw, and Feltman (1987) studied nurses to determine whether those who participated in QA programs had professional characteristics different from those who did not. They discovered that the two groups did differ in a variety of ways. Nurses involved in QA in that setting (1) had a

29

higher level of education, (2) were more involved in continuing professional educational activities, (3) held higher management positions in that hospital, and (4) generally had worked longer than the randomly selected noninvolved nurses.

The study also investigated whether QA participants perceived the care they delivered to be more positive than nurses who did not participate. Overall, those in the involved group felt that they had performed five out of seven care activities more frequently than the uninvolved group and believed the QA program had positive impact on services they delivered.

There is little other research to describe the impact of QA participation on practicing nurses elsewhere; however, what can be described here is the knowledge, skills, and ability to conceptualize what is necessary to carry out a UBQA program successfully.

## PROFESSIONAL EXPECTATIONS OF STAFF

The components of a comprehensive QA program include at least the development of standards, monitoring of practice, evaluation and resolution of problems, and reporting of activities and accomplishments. Each of these components is described next, in terms of knowledge and skills necessary to implement them successfully.

### Development of Standards

The ability to develop standards involves a blending of knowledge and skills in a variety of areas. The individuals involved must have a sound understanding of the nature of nursing in the particular practice area, its science and technology, and that of overlapping disciplines. Continuing use of literature is necessary to remain current.

This information then must be balanced with the specific practice environment, including the population served, resources available (peers, other services, tangible resources, available time with clients, etc.), and professional values held. All these issues must be integrated in order to develop appropriate standards for nursing practice in a given setting.

### Monitoring of Nursing Practice

Monitoring of a UBQA program begins with an understanding of standards of practice and adds the elements of observation, selection of critical elements for review, organization and perseverance in carrying out a plan over time, and critical assessment of data. It is necessary to have the capacity to view practice from a perspective larger than the day's caseload. Trends or patterns in care must be considered in determining what is controllable and should be maintained or changed and what is uncontrollable and must be incorporated into standards.

For example, shorter lengths of stay are not totally within the control of nursing, yet they have a great impact on nurses' capacity to deliver care. Trends in length of stay and clients' abilities to achieve certain outcomes must be tracked and reviewed routinely in order to know that standards for practice are valid. The ability to conceptualize, and then extrapolate from this information, is a high-level skill.

## Evaluation and Resolution of Problems

The knowledge and skills necessary to evaluate and resolve problems build on the previous components. An ability to use the literature is essential in gaining access to what already is known and/or what may help deal with the situation. Use of the research process in varying degrees of rigor is necessary in studying an issue. Resulting data must be analyzed and interpreted in relation to the clinical setting, the population served, and the practitioners involved.

Problem resolution then depends on an accurate interpretation of the information as well as effective use of a sound political process, that is, approaching the issue with full knowledge of the parameters, using good interpersonal skills, and attempting to achieve win-win solutions. Leadership skills and change agent characteristics are necessary for successful problem solving, as is creativity in developing ways to resolve practice problems.

## Reporting Activities and Accomplishments

Members of a QA committee must be able to demonstrate their accountability. In almost any organization, this involves documentation. The ability to organize and communicate one's work in writing is yet another skill. It paves the way for evaluating work and projecting the activity beyond the immediate unit setting.

When the knowledge, skills, and abilities necessary for contributing members of UBQA are reviewed, the picture that emerges is of nurses who are excellent practitioners, scientific thinkers, and change agents. Although it would be wonderful to assume that all nurses do this all the time, that is not realistic. The UBQA program is a viable avenue for promoting the use of these skills if present and developing or refining them if necessary. It also provides structure and support, which are necessary given the decisionmaking and interpersonal effects of their use, as well as the potential conflicts that otherwise would result with traditional management.

Once established, these skills and expectations go beyond a UBQA program and affect how a nurse views nursing practice and the organization. The program greatly affected the professional environment at St. Michael Hospital and set the stage for subsequent staff development in the research process, shared governance, and the growth of excellence in general.

## REFERENCES

Schroeder, P., & Maibusch, R. (Eds.). (1984). *Nursing quality assurance: A unit-based approach*. Rockville, Md.: Aspen Publishers, Inc.

Schroeder, P., Maibusch, R., Anderson, C., & Formella, N. (1982). A unit-based approach to nursing quality assurance. *Quality Review Bulletin, 8,* 10-12.

Smeltzer, C., Hinshaw, A., & Feltman, B. (1987). The benefits of staff nurse involvement in monitoring the quality of patient care. *Journal of Nursing Quality Assurance. 1,* 1-7.

# Chapter 5

# UBQA: The System Revisited

*Patricia Schroeder*

*Professional nurses are the key to the delivery of quality care. Nurses at the bedside must be the ones to define standards of practice, monitor achievement of standards, and evaluate and resolve practice problems.*

Unit-based quality assurance (UBQA) is a title originating with Schroeder, Maibusch, Anderson, and Formella (1982) and describing a decentralized nursing quality assurance (QA) program in a hospital. This program, which was initiated in 1979 at St. Michael Hospital, Milwaukee, has since become a common model for quality assurance implementation in hospitals across the country.

A major reason for its appeal has been its underlying tenet: that professional staff nurses are accountable for practice. This chapter discusses factors that have supported the growth of decentralized quality assurance programs, reviews the structure and function of UBQA at one hospital, and describes common evolutionary changes in the program.

## FACTORS SUPPORTING UBQA GROWTH

Many organizations across the country have joined the trend toward participative management. Not exclusive to health care, this trend is built on the use of input from staff members in managing and charting direction for the organization. The increased "valuing" of such input by administrators and managers has supported the idea that staff nurses should be accountable for practice.

The ever-growing move toward professionalism in nursing also has supported the development of UBQA programs. The American Nurses' Association's *Social Policy Statement* (ANA, 1980, pp. 7, 8) describes nursing's contractual agreement with society. Society grants the profession the ability to carry out its work in exchange for nursing's being responsible and accountable for its actions. This can be accomplished only if professionals agree to define the care they will deliver, monitor its performance under those standards, and resolve problems in practice.

Bergman (1981, p. 55) identifies accountability as having three preconditions. To be "accountable," one must:

1. have the knowledge, skills, and values to be able to make judgments and carry out actions
2. be given responsibility to carry out actions
3. have the authority or right to carry out the charge.

Accountability for nurses would be based upon their having knowledge and skills about professional practice as well as the QA process. Implementation of the UBQA program gives staff members the responsibility and authority to be truly accountable for the care they deliver.

## THE UBQA PROGRAM

The UBQA program is developed around the concept that most quality assurance activities are planned and carried out by staff members on individual nursing units. Unit quality assurance committees (QACs) generally are composed of four to eight staff nurses, with a staff nurse as chairperson and a clinical nurse specialist as facilitator. The head nurse also is a member. Exhibits 5-1 and 5-2 describe the responsibilities of QAC members and chairpersons. (Responsibilities of nurses in other roles are described further in Chapter 6.) This group is responsible for defining standards of practice, monitoring them, and evaluating and resolving problems at the unit level.

Standards of practice are developed for populations of patients and must be congruent with the organizational mission and philosophy, institutional standards for nursing practice, standards from nursing specialty organizations, and current scientific knowledge. These standards then are promoted housewide, if not developed in collaboration between units that have similar populations.

Each unit is responsible for establishing ongoing monitors of practice, determined by considering major areas of clinical practice, significant practice concerns, and available data. To support this process, common QA data such as information on patient falls, medication errors, cardiac arrest staff per-

**Exhibit 5-1** Responsibilities of QAC Members

1. Assist in development of standards of practice.
2. Be accountable for monitoring nursing practice by identifying and prioritizing critical practice issues.
3. Conduct evaluation studies; assist in the development of study criteria, data collection, data analysis, and recommendations for corrective action based on the findings.
4. Follow up to see that corrective actions are completed and documented and that problems are resolved.
5. Promote resolution of multidisciplinary problems.
6. Participate in housewide studies.
7. Monitor progress and assist in the completion of unit QA projects.
8. Establish annual quality assurance goals based on priorities and reevaluate as necessary.
9. Provide input for the annual review and evaluation of quality assurance activities.

formance reports, etc., are routed automatically to QAC chairpersons. This allows those involved with unit-level monitoring to use their limited time either collecting other more specific data or analyzing what they have already.

When a practice problem is suspected or known, it is the responsibility of the QAC members to take one of three courses of action:

1. They can study the problem, in an attempt to identify its nature, extent, and the direction for its resolution.
2. They can develop standards, if the problem is based on lack of consistency.

**Exhibit 5-2** Responsibilities of QAC Chairpersons

1. Set agenda, keep minutes, call and conduct meetings, and monitor attendance of committee.
2. Update QAC members on information provided on Quality Assurance Coordinating Committee (QACC) meetings and other hospitalwide issues.
3. Facilitate the QAC's work in the quality assurance process.
4. Complete a quarterly report on unit QA activities and submit to QACC chairperson.
5. Complete annual evaluation report form and submit to QACC chairperson.
6. Participate actively in completion of QACC's yearly and standing objectives.
7. Assist in the development of standards of care.
8. Facilitate the monitoring and documentation of standards of care on a continuing basis.
9. Provide education on quality assurance:
10. Assist in the development of projects, forms, and methodologies.
11. Facilitate the completion of evaluation study reports.

3. They can implement corrective action, if the problem is understood enough to determine the appropriate course of action.

It is the members of the QAC themselves who determine which of these actions to take; however, ultimately they must resolve the problem.

Departmentwide coordination of the program is accomplished by the Quality Assurance Coordinating Committee (QACC). This is composed of the chairpersons of QACs, the clinical nurse specialist facilitators, the assistant vice president for nursing, and the vice president for patient services. Its main functions are to review trends in practice across the nursing department and to support chairpersons in solving problems that arise in QACs. Information shared in this group demonstrates that QA work is progressing, and sufficient rigor in QA activities can be maintained. The QACC also is the mechanism for pursuing interdepartmental concerns and for communicating nursing QA activities to the hospital quality assurance committee.

At St. Michael Hospital, all decisions made at the QACC are forwarded to the Nursing Practice Council (NPC), which is the practice decisionmaking body. Composed predominantly of staff nurses, with one representative each of the assistant head nurses/clinical coordinators, head nurses, and clinical nurse specialists, this group is structured according to the shared governance model. The NPC is responsible for coordinating all practice-related activities, committees, and projects in the department of nursing.

## EVOLUTIONARY CHANGES IN UBQA SYSTEM

The UBQA program at St. Michael Hospital has changed over time. Such evolution is typical of what is seen across the country in decentralized QA programs. The development and implementation of a major program requires so much effort and energy that it would be helpful if, once in place, it would remain stable. However, development of a progressive professional nursing staff requires that the UBQA program grow. Evaluation of the program commonly involves examining the leadership, process, and functioning of QA committees; the focus of QA work; the rigor involved in the evaluation process; and integration with other disciplines and departments.

### Leadership of Committees

Effective and timely implementation of UBQA requires the skills of a qualified leader. When the program is new to a nursing department, the most common choices for QAC leaders are nurse managers. Nurses in institutions that place nurse managers in the role of committee chair report both positive and negative responses. It often makes the initial development of the groups go more smoothly. The manager is aware of unit practice issues and is comfortable acting in a leadership role. The staff nurse members know the manager and are familiar with the individual's leadership style.

However, the structure does not support the concept of increasing staff accountability for practice. One nurse called it a process of "having six nurses sit and watch the head nurse make a decision." Some have suggested they were reluctant to identify practice concerns because they might be interpreted as saying the head nurse did not do the job well enough. At the very least, if the head nurse is responsible for staff performance evaluations, the group may remain on guard.

The trend across the country is to have professional staff nurses lead unit QA committees. This can be done either when a program is implemented or at a defined point thereafter. The benefits to staff members in assuming this role are significant. Nurses practicing on a unit acquire "ownership" of the committee much more quickly. They are able to test its wings in dealing with issues of real concern. The QA process also is labeled clearly as the staff's domain.

There may be some difficulties in identifying staff nurses as committee chairpersons. Many have had limited experience leading groups. They may have to learn such skills as developing agendas, preparing for and following up on committee business, and dealing with group process. Furthermore, some settings may not allow time for the nurse to carry out these activities. There is no question that skills can be learned and time set aside, but there must be a conscious plan to do so to provide the greatest likelihood of success.

## Structure and Function of QA Committees

The unit-based QA system is a major move toward decentralization. Many hospitals adopt this system from a much more centralized program that has the benefits of structure and well-developed communication. In an attempt to maintain these benefits, the initial development of a decentralized program often appears very structured. This is not to say that this is bad, because the program must have a framework. The components can include the chair, a specified number of group members, when and how long the group is to meet, the type and amount of work to be completed, and sometimes even the degree of impact to be seen on the unit.

As the program becomes involved with other unit activities and issues, it needs to change. One unit may need the head nurse to chair it while another should have a staff nurse leader. One unit may choose to meet formally every other month on second shift while others may not find this effective or feasible. Some units need to spend more time developing standards while others may devote their energies to evaluating practice problems. All must maintain certain monitoring functions, given the standards of the Joint Commission on Accreditation of Hospitals (JCAH, 1986, p. 206).

The shift from standardized structure and functioning of QA committees is healthy. It unquestionably requires greater efforts in coordinating or tracking activities on a housewide basis, but the time is well spent. It demonstrates that the QAC is an integral part of practice.

## Focus of QA Work

It is an accepted premise that individuals and groups must begin with the simple before moving to the complex. Even though this is acknowledged in many other situations, it often is bypassed in professional groups. There is a sense that QA groups should make a significant impact on practice very early in their existence or they may not be worth continuing. This is unfair.

By focusing on specific practice issues, even selecting those that are resolved easily, the group can test the system, learn the process, and get immediate positive feedback. As the group progresses in its development, the focus of work becomes more complex. Issues with many variables should be and routinely are discussed, pursued, and resolved. The move from simple to complex, or task oriented to more conceptual, is a step that cannot be skipped or rushed. It must be nurtured so it can develop with time and experience.

This is not to suggest that groups do not need to be accountable. Some feedback mechanism should (indeed, must) be established to assure that their work is progressing and that the degree of impact on practice is worth their time, effort, and expense.

## Rigor Involved in the QA Process

Quality assurance presents an interesting dilemma. It must use scholarly research methods to validate the results of studies on which decisions can be based. However, the research cannot be so complex and rigorous as to make the process too difficult for the staff to carry it out. Increasing rigor also requires the expenditure of time, money, and resources.

Increasing the number of professionals involved in QA activities expands the ranks of those dealing with this situation. Although it generally is accepted that QA is a scholarly method of evaluation that is not intended to demonstrate results that can be generalized outside of the immediate setting, greater direction may be necessary.

A typical strategy in the early stages of decentralization is to educate members regarding the research process. At St. Michael Hospital, greater structure for the study process was desired both to develop the staff and to improve studies. The research review process was added, supplemented by the development of selected nurses in various aspects of research methods.

When members of a UBQA committee develop a study idea, they write a brief proposal to identify the topic, objectives, time period, population, the conceptual framework, and the method of study. The proposal is submitted to the chair of the QACC. If the chair finds that the study is sound, it is approved and returned to the QAC within 72 hours. If the study involves the development or use of a new instrument, it is reviewed by one or two nurses who have expertise and interest in its development, with suggestions returned to the QAC promptly. Human subjects protection may compound the review process (see Chapter 10).

The evolutionary step of increased rigor in QA work is common in hospitals using a decentralized program. As the staff becomes more familiar with the research process, more questions arise as to the validity of study results. Implementation of a structured method of reviewing studies can assist committees that may need help, simplify studies from committees that are sophisticated, and overall provide a rough estimate of the potential cost/benefit ratio of studies before carrying them out.

## Integration with Others

As members of UBQA committees become more comfortable with their roles and activities, it is easier for them to carry out functions outside the nursing department. Opportunities to work on multidisciplinary issues do not cause resistance to dealing with foreign factors. Improved definitions of standards as well as the availability of monitoring data demonstrate the need to work with other disciplines and departments to close gaps in practice. This combination of greater skill and increased opportunity thrusts many professional nurses into the multidisciplinary QA arena.

Some suggest that QA operations are 10 percent activities and 90 percent politics. This is more likely to be true if the QA activities are multidisciplinary. The development of political skills and effective interdisciplinary relationships is a major step in working with other disciplines and departments.

## COSTS OF UBQA

A program such as UBQA cannot be discussed without at least acknowledging its costs. Indirect staff time is the most significant expense in the program. Methods have been established at St. Michael Hospital to track the amount of time spent on QA activities, both in and outside of committee work. Although the time varies significantly between units, overall it is considerably less than might be assumed. Time spent on specific activities also varies considerably. Malin and Buss (1986) describe the process of tracking cost and benefit on one QA activity carried out on an obstetric unit.

The cost of such a program cannot be addressed without reviewing the benefits. UBQA is based on nurses' accountability and responsibility for practice. Its decisionmaking requires staff members to invest in the pursuit of higher levels of professional practice. Their "ownership" of clinical issues makes change less difficult to implement. As a result, less time is expended by leaders trying to force change.

A number of QA activities also have demonstrated significant cost savings for nursing. Evaluation of aspects of practice that are time consuming and potentially unnecessary has resulted in the revision of standards and procedures, producing cost savings of thousands of dollars. The activities also have improved the quality of care while simultaneously decreasing the amount of time necessary to carry them out (Taylor, Wagner, & Kraus, 1987).

Unit-based quality assurance is a program that has broad applicability. It has been used successfully in a variety of settings with different populations of both patients and staffs. It has been implemented in large and small, urban and rural, resource-laden and resource-limited settings with the same conclusion.

If this program is supported by administrators and nursing leaders, if it is valued and nurtured, and if the results of its work are used and acknowledged, it can flourish. The benefit of quality of care is one that cannot be underestimated, but it is the professional development of participants that opens the door to tremendous potential.

## REFERENCES

American Nurses' Association. (1980). *Nursing: A Social Policy Statement* (ANA Publication Code: NP-63 35M 12/80). Kansas City, Mo.: Author.

Bergman, R. (1981). Accountability: Definition and dimensions. *International Nursing Review, 28,* 53-59.

Joint Commission on Accreditation of Hospitals. (1986). *Accreditation manual for hospitals.* Chicago: Author.

Malin, S., & Buss, J. (1986). Fetal heart monitor strip documentation: Examining cost and benefit. *Journal of Nursing Quality Assurance, 1*(2), 66-70.

Schroeder, P.S., Maibusch, R.M., Anderson, C.A., & Formella, N.M. (1982). A unit-based approach to nursing quality assurance. *Quality Review Bulletin, 8,* 10-12.

Taylor, B.N., Wagner, P.L., & Kraus, C.L. (1987). Development of a standard for time-effective patient assessment during blood transfusion. *Journal of Nursing Quality Assurance, 1,* 66-71.

## BIBLIOGRAPHY

Gortner, S.R. (1974). Scientific accountability in nursing. *Nursing Outlook, 22,* 764-768.

Hull, R. (1981). Responsibility and accountability analyzed. *Nursing Outlook, 19,* 705-712.

McClure, M.L. (1978). The long road to accountability. *Nursing Outlook, 26,* 47-50.

Singleton, E.K., & Nail, F.C. (1984). Autonomy in nursing. *Nursing Forum, 21*(3), 123-130.

## Chapter 6

# Facilitators of Quality Assurance

*Patricia Schroeder*

*Staff nurses are the key to a unit-based quality assurance program. The success of such a program is also dependent on strong support and assistance by other roles within a nursing department.*

The unit-based quality assurance (UBQA) program in nursing at St. Michael Hospital is a staff nurse approach. It is rooted in the foundation that quality assurance (QA) is a staff nurse accountability and must remain so in order to be integrated with practice and make a difference in patient care.

This does not mean, however, that nurses in other roles do not play a part in making the program successful. This chapter describes the needs for and roles of nonstaff nurses in the UBQA program, including managers, clinical nurse specialists/nursing educators, and a departmentwide QA coordinator.

## NURSE MANAGERS

Historically, as nurses rose up the bureaucratic ladder in an organization, their responsibilities for QA increased. Some institutions based much of a manager's performance evaluation or even pay raises on quality-of-care indicators of staff performance on the unit.

The UBQA program functions very differently, holding the professional staff rather than the managers accountable for quality of care. Nurse managers are expected to play a role in QA on the unit, but that can vary depending on the activities of individual units. Exhibit 6-1 describes the role of nurse managers in the UBQA program.

Broadly stated, nurse managers support UBQA in four ways: (1) facilitating QA work, (2) providing access to needed information to staff nurses, (3) expecting staff accountability, and (4) incorporating practice decisions into management expectations.

## Facilitating QA Work

The support of nurse managers as resource leaders for the unit can be significant in allocating time for meetings and assistance in patient coverage. This may span the gamut from adapting staffing patterns, to providing time for QA work, all the way to the manager's taking over a patient assignment during QA meeting time. The degree of the manager's support and expectation says much regarding serious commitment to QA in general.

## Providing Access to Needed Information

Accountability for practice cannot be possible until staff nurses have sufficient information to understand the issues. Such information may not be available to the staff generally but is known routinely by nurses in management positions. It is imperative that nurse managers assure appropriate access to information that provides perspective on patient care on the unit. Incident

**Exhibit 6-1** Role of the Nurse Manager in UBQA

---

1. May attend unit quality assurance committees as a member and/or as unit leadership liaison and/or as ex officio member (attendance is optional based on unit needs).
2. Facilitates meeting attendance of committee members (promotes attendance, helps to complete patient care activities, etc.).
3. Reviews with the quality assurance chairperson information on member attendance and activities.
4. Routes unit practice issues/information to QAC.
5. Identifies/validates problems for study or discussion.
6. Facilitates timely completion of quality assurance projects.
7. Collaborates with clinical nurse specialist (C.N.S.) facilitator and committee members to determine fiscal feasibility of quality assurance activities.
8. Incorporates QAC practice decisions into management expectations. (That is, as a manager, holds other staff members accountable to abide by the practice decisions of the QAC.)

reports and nonconfidential information on other departments are but a few of the items that must be shared. The manager also must display or present the information in a way that it can be understood and interpreted. A history of the issue and tips on interpersonal savvy can make a difference in a QAC's successful dealings.

### Expecting Staff Accountability

If staff nurses are given the challenge and resources to carry out a QA program, they also need the expectation that they will succeed. It is important that managers expect success from QACs in assuring quality of care. This would include timely completion of projects, successful resolution of practice problems, and continuing maintenance of quality assessment work. QACs may find it helpful to establish a time line for activities that would provide the manager with a realistic gauge for measuring progress.

### Using QAC Decisions

Managers must support QA work by using the resulting practice decisions whenever possible. Obviously, the QAC cannot make some unit decisions. Care must be taken to keep the focus of QA work on practice rather than on management issues. Nothing diffuses commitment and energy quite so much as having decisions undermined or ignored. A QAC will be more likely to produce and persevere if its work makes a difference and its authority is recognized.

## CLINICAL NURSE SPECIALIST FACILITATORS

Clinical nurse specialists (C.N.S.s) have long been involved with the UBQA program at St. Michael Hospital. Originally functioning as chairpersons of QA committees, they have shifted into a facilitator role to support the emergence of the leadership of staff nurses. Functions of the C.N.S. facilitator are described in Exhibit 6-2. Institutions that do not have C.N.S.s might consider the use of nurse educators or nurses with significant QA expertise in such a role.

Beyond the eight functions described in Exhibit 6-2, the C.N.S. facilitator role can be summarized by three unique contributions. First, being somewhat separate from day-to-day practice on the unit can provide the C.N.S.s with objectivity and perspective in addressing clinical issues. The distance can allow them to separate some of the clinical practice needs from the interpersonal issues between staff members that influence care. Although both issues require

**Exhibit 6-2** Clinical Nurse Specialist Facilitators

1. Attend all quality assurance committee meetings.
2. Review all study proposals.
3. Facilitate study review process as necessary.
4. Monitor and evaluate progress of unit quality assurance committee.
5. Assist in the development of standards of care.
6. Provide education on quality assurance.
7. Attend meetings of the Quality Assurance Coordinating Committee (QACC).
8. Participate actively in completion of the QACC's yearly and standing objectives.

attention, the focus and process for resolving them may be considerably different, based on the actual cause. Greater objectivity can help identify and define the parameters of clinical practice issues.

Second, the C.N.S.s, by virtue of their expertise and education, can help the group strive toward higher level functioning through use of the research process. Although the methodological rigor of QA activities always must be balanced with time and available resources, scholarly input can promote the use of a more scientific process. Greater use of the literature, consideration of validity and reliability issues, and the use of frameworks or models can strengthen the process and result in data that are more valuable.

Third, the C.N.S. facilitators can help nurses in the QAC learn to use the system. Practicing on one nursing unit may not give staff members a big-

**Exhibit 6-3** Responsibilities of the QACC Chairperson

1. Sets agenda, keeps minutes, calls and conducts all QACC meetings, monitors attendance.
2. Facilitates the flow of information on QACC activities to and from Nursing Practice Council.
3. Receives, reviews, and, as appropriate, routes all formal QA evaluation study proposals as outlined in the guidelines for such reviews.
4. Acts as ex officio member of the Research Development Committee (if not a permanent member).
5. Acts as contact person on Nursing Department QA activities.
6. Solicits quarterly reports from unit QAC chairpersons.
7. Prepares quarterly reports for hospital QAC and QACC members.
8. Solicits annual QAC reports and prepares final annual evaluation report.
9. Facilitates annual evaluation of QACC yearly objectives and files written report.
10. Facilitates completion of QACC's yearly/standing objectives.
11. Facilitates completion of QACC task force activities.
12. Acts as resource/consultant to assist unit committee chairpersons and/or facilitators.

picture perspective as to how to promote change and work through the organization. It is indeed helpful if such perspective can be provided. This can result in greater continuity across the nursing department as well as larger potential for success on the unit.

As staff nurses accept greater accountability for identifying and resolving practice problems, they take risks in dealing with the system or organization. The very nature of risk taking indicates that individuals can succeed or fail. The price of failure for a staff nurse inexperienced in organizational politics can be high. Even relatively low-risk activities such as scheduling inservice

**Exhibit 6-4** QA Coordinator/Research Facilitator Job Description

1. Coordinates nursing quality assurance program. Serves as a focal point for the gathering of information required by the program and documents all program activities.
2. Chairs the Quality Assurance Coordinating Committee and the Nursing Research Development Committee.
3. Collaborates with the chairperson of the Protection of Human Subjects Committee, Nursing Information System Coordinator, members of the Research Development Committee, and the Quality Assurance Coordinating Committee in carrying out the work of the program.
4. Reviews all nursing evaluation and research studies for content, appropriateness, and feasibility. Routes to others as described in research review process.
5. Participates in activities of Safety Committee and Pharmacy and Therapeutics Committee.
6. Acts as a liaison between the quality assurance programs of other hospital departments and the Nursing Department.
7. Is an ex officio member of the Protection of Human Subjects Committee and the Medical Staff Research Committee.
8. Plans and participates in continuing education related to quality assurance and research.
9. Promotes the use of the research process in evaluating nursing care.
10. Informs nurse researchers of potential external funding available for approved nursing department programs/projects.
11. Informs nursing staff of opportunities for professional presentations/publications of Nursing Department activities.
12. Promotes the awareness and utilization of research through a variety of mechanisms (nursing newsletter, bulletin boards, posters, memos, classes, special presentations).
13. Acts as a link with outside nurse researchers who propose to conduct research at St. Michael Hospital.
14. Maintains continuing communication with vice president of patient services.
15. Collaborates with the coordinator of the University of Wisconsin-Milwaukee Center for Nursing Research and Evaluation in supporting and facilitating utilization of resources. Documents utilization in collaboration with the Nursing Department business manager.

*Source:* Courtesy of St. Michael Hospital, Milwaukee, Wisconsin.

training, focusing attention on a different practice issue, or soliciting new members for group work can cause political fallout if not considered in the context of unit norms or managers' expectations. The C.N.S. facilitators can help the group use a process that can stack the deck in favor of success.

## QUALITY ASSURANCE COORDINATORS

The role of quality assurance coordinator is relatively new at St. Michael Hospital. It evolved from the role of quality assurance coordinating committee (QACC) chairperson (see Exhibit 6-3) and later was integrated with research facilitation (see Exhibit 6-4 on the facilitator's job description). Such evolution supports the development of the QA and research functions in the nursing department and meets the needs and expectations of nurses participating in the program. Just as the model for this book shows research building on the foundation of the QA program, so has the role of research facilitation built upon and enhanced the role of QA coordinator.

The contributions by the QA coordinator/research facilitator focus on overseeing nursing departmentwide QA/research functions, on integrating information from units to better identify and take action on clinical issues, and on providing direction for movement in development of the programs and those involved.

## CONCLUSION

The key to success of the UBQA program has been the development and commitment of professional staff nurses. However, the importance of the other players in this scenario cannot be underestimated. Only through nursing departmentwide support can such a broad program survive and thrive. The involvement of other nurses, such as managers, C.N.S.s, educators, and co-ordinators has been critical to staff nurse development. Facilitators must prepare the environment, set the stage for action, and support and praise the success of the efforts.

# Part III

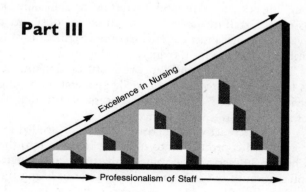

Excellence in Nursing

Professionalism of Staff

---

# Quality Assurance as a Base for Research Development

*Janet Wessel Krejci*
Section Editor

Actualizing the theory-research-practice cycle in the delivery of nursing care has been a high priority for the profession in the 1980s. The increase in rigor and relevance of quality assurance studies is the beginning of achieving this important goal. Quality assurance is the most logical vehicle for building research skills and interest at the staff nurse level. Through quality assurance, staff members have taken on responsibility and accountability for evaluating their practice. This section describes how quality assurance can be utilized as a base for moving toward a research-based practice.

The development and support of critical thinking is imperative if the staff is to contribute to valid knowledge generation by engaging in research activities. Chapter 7 discusses the concept of critical thinking as the foundation of the theory-research-practice cycle.

As research activities increase, support is needed in terms of research expertise and coordination to integrate research into the staff's daily practice. Chapter 8 describes the value of the research facilitator in coordinating the integration of research and practice without losing sight of staff needs.

Communication and collaboration among nurses in service settings and academic environments prevents isolation and can be helpful in generating valid, relevant knowledge. Nurses from each setting have invaluable contributions to offer each other and the profession as a whole. Chapter 9 analyzes how research can link the world of academia to the reality of daily practice.

As general research quality assurance studies focus more on systematic approaches to and evaluation of patient care, nurses must attend closely to issues of human subject protection. Chapter 10 discusses this topic and offers practical suggestions for developing a nursing human subject committee.

## Chapter 7

# Critical Thinking: Integration of a Concept

*SueEllen Pinkerton*

*The department of nursing, usually the largest in the hospital, is a complex structure. Its many responsibilities focus on patient care, professional trends, and professional practice. Creating a climate for sustaining this structure is complicated by the need for underlying support and the development of critical thinking—the substance of professional practice.*

This chapter begins with a review of some of the history of nursing service and the profession. It introduces critical thinking as the substance of professional practice and outlines its relationship to quality assurance, the theory-research-practice cycle, and professional development.

Schools of nursing were opening at a rapid rate in the late 1800s to provide staffs for hospitals caring for the increasing urban population. The population surge resulted from the Industrial Revolution, massive immigration, and a high birth rate. The economy was changing from agricultural to industrial, with population centering in large cities. Many hospitals opened to accommodate this urban shift and found that inexpensive service could be provided by student nurses. Schools of nursing thus increased from 323 to more than 11,000 between 1880 and 1890 (Sellew & Nuesse, 1946, p. 287).

These nursing schools followed England's traditional Nightingale model, which was based on the system utilized by religious orders and military units. But Florence Nightingale also recommended that nursing schools and hospitals be under separate administrations to prevent the hospitals from dominating the schools and the schools from having only minimal influence on the hospitals (Strauss, 1966, p. 66).

This recommendation was not followed and schools were organized under a single nursing administrator who was both the superintendent of the training school and the administrator of nursing service. The functions of supervisor of nursing care and teacher thus were combined in one role with responsibility to the hospital, patients, and students. As a result, hospitals were prevented from focusing on the continued development of staff and improvements in patient care.

It was not until after World War II that nurse administrators were recognized in their roles. Supportive mechanisms were developed through the National Committee for the Improvement of Nursing Services, a three-year program sponsored by a grant from the W. K. Kellogg Foundation (Sheahan, 1950). The program developed and implemented an action plan to improve nursing service, nursing education, and relationships with interprofessional groups, governmental agencies, and the public.

Miss Nightingale also developed a research approach to nursing problems, basing her reforms on meticulous investigations. She was known as a passionate statistician, having been a Fellow of the Royal Statistical Society and an Honorary member of the American Statistical Association. No earlier use is known of the observed and expected frequencies that Nightingale used to show actual and expected number of military deaths. As a result of her work in statistics, she attempted to establish an Oxford Professorship in Applied Statistics. The area was not covered by the examinations at Oxford, however, and the sum of money was inadequate, so the project was abandoned (Grier & Grier, 1978). She was also widely recognized as a scientist, and had requests from the British government to consult in India and the United States. Her research approach was not passed along as part of the Nightingale tradition, however. It was not until the recent past that there emerged a strong focus on nursing research as part of the development of a knowledge base. Linking this to practice has taken longer but it is meeting with success, as described in Chapters 8 and 9.

## CRITICAL THINKING

The process of critical thinking is applicable in any situation. It is a process of defining and analyzing problems, with the emphasis on questioning information rather than merely accepting it. In a complex nursing department this skill is important for staff nurses in reviewing physicians' orders, incorporating standard policies and procedures in practice, reviewing accepted nursing interventions and interpreting patient data. Nurses in their organizational role must analyze and problem solve with members of other hospital department committees (quality assurance, policy, procedure) and persons visiting the institution or their department.

Critical thinking is a skill that requires support and development. It is to be hoped that it begins early in life (Marbach, 1986), is fostered in schools of nursing, and is accepted as a vital part of practice. Obviously, acceptance of someone who constantly questions and challenges may be a problem if the climate is not one to nurture and support this skill. The questioner could develop into a pest or even a common scold.

## CRITICAL THINKING AND QA

The experience of unit-based quality assurance (as described in Part II) provides groundwork for critical thinking. Under UBQA, staff nurses can question practice and approaches to it. To conduct quality assurance activities on their own nursing units, they must be familiar with practice and all the influences on it, such as the usual medical and nursing diagnoses, physician practitioners, and organization of the unit. With the appropriate chairperson/ facilitator, an environment of questioning and challenging can exist. Nurses may question standing policies—for example, when the frequency of taking vital signs was changed during the administration of a transfusion (Taylor, Wagner, & Kraus, 1987).

Nurses may be motivated to research a topic further, and may need guidance with various steps of the process, i.e., review of the literature, the value of conceptual frameworks, methodology, and instrumentation. It is through integrating the steps of the research process into quality assurance studies that values and attitudes toward the importance of systematic study begin to emerge. This entire process can be enriched by the support of critical thinking.

Porter-O'Grady (1986) identifies as one responsibility of the collective nursing organization the developing of a conceptual framework—a quality assurance issue. Avant and Walker (1984) state that a conceptual framework provides a practical means of justifying nursing care decisions. Capers (1986) supports use of a nursing model to guide nurses' practice, believing that it will not interfere with their autonomy by directing their practice, even though the nurses may wish to have an eclectic approach to choosing their own theory or model to guide them.

However, Hardy (1986) says that using one model to direct practice closes nurses' minds to all but that one view. In an age when the need is for professionals who think and question, nurses instead are being taught to memorize a particular model or approach to care. Hardy suggests multiple models to stimulate creativity and exploration from different views, which is further validation of the role of critical thinking.

## RESEARCH, THEORY, CRITICAL THINKING

As nurses become more familiar with the research process, they develop a larger knowledge base and gain more experience so they have more information to apply to situations in which they engage in critical thinking. This helps them move into investigation of research findings and apply their findings to practice. This in turn leads to a natural link to theory-research-practice. Although conceptual models (just discussed) are not seen as theory, they are forerunners to theory development and are most likely to exist in health care institutions.

Kim (1983), discussing theory-research-practice in the nursing knowledge system, feels gaps exist because of the lack of dialogue among the practitioners from the three sectors and because of their segregation into different organizations. Kim suggests a new spirit of scientific investigation to incorporate the three functional areas of teaching, research, and practice into one role, such as is done in the Rush model. The Rush model, at Rush-Presbyterian-St. Luke's Medical Center in Chicago, is organized so that all nurses teach, participate in research, and practice in one role. The school of nursing faculty also have positions as staff nurses and managers in the hospital rather than separate teaching roles exclusive to the school of nursing. Kim summarizes: "It is through a close scrutiny of theory in practice and research that nursing can evolve into a viable science, and it is by grounding theoretical formulations in practice and aligning practice problems for research that nursing can expand its scientific richness" (p. 181).

As Kim demonstrates, practice is linked to theory and research. Dickoff, James, and Wiedenbach (1968) say that "theory is born in practice, is refined in research, and must and can return to practice" (p. 415). Walker and Avant (1983) propose using theory to challenge conventional views of clients, health/illness, and interventions—more support for critical thinking. If theorists and researchers are to work with practitioners in building nursing knowledge, nurses who think, question, and challenge are needed. The nursing documentation in the patient record of such practitioners will be replete with data and will complete the link to theory and research.

There is no better articulation of the need to pursue knowledge building than that of Styles (1982) in describing nursing's descent from Florence Nightingale, a model researcher:

> From these roots, how did we grow to believe that instinct, ritual, feeling, and obedience to others could combine to make a *total, trustworthy* response to the complex human health condition? How have we come to accept not knowing, to the extent that knowing is possible, the probabilities that one of our "merciful" acts will

benefit the patient more than another, or even that it will do him no harm? (p. 184).

## PROFESSIONAL DEVELOPMENT

Quality assurance has been a starting point for promoting and encouraging critical thinking. Expansion of the QA process to include the research process further propelled nursing staff members into an environment in which they may rightfully participate in the theory-research-practice cycle. This in itself would seem rewarding enough, but it provides direction for still further professional development.

Murphy (1985) describes external contexts that promote creative scientific work, such as:

- mentorship and sponsorship
- the institutional setting
- scientific collegiality
- freedom of ideas
- freedom from undue restraint as demonstrated through shared governance
- availability of financial and human resources
- ability to avoid becoming overloaded with extraneous responsibilities.

Nurses by virtue of engaging in critical thinking may be afforded the opportunity to extend their practice into creative, scientific work.

The implications for critical thinking and participation in the theory-research-practice cycle are obvious. There are still other supports, within a shared governance system, that promote development of the staff nurse as a contributor to nursing as a creative scientific work, one that requires critical thinking. Shared governance, by virtue of being a system in which staff nurses make practice decisions, supports critical thinking. By having staff nurses responsible for policies, procedures, and quality assurance (see Part IV), they learn to challenge, question, and gain confidence in their decisions.

This open climate for questioning is carried to the staff nurse role on physician/nurse committees (Chapter 19) and peer review (Chapter 24). Eventually, critical thinking goes beyond artificial boundaries imposed by organizational structures to permeate all aspects of professional growth in creative scientific work.

As Murphy (1985) points out, the next level of integration of creative scientific work is integration with nurses' life style for a total commitment to their pursuit and a total absorption in their work. Perhaps one of the first steps in this integration is becoming a contributing author to a professional publication.

## REFERENCES

Avant, K.C., & Walker, L.D. (1984). The practicing nurse and conceptual frameworks. *Maternal Child Nursing, 9,* 87-90.

Capers, C.F. (1986). Using nursing models to guide nursing practice: Key questions. *The Journal of Nursing Administration, 16,* 40-43.

Dickoff, J., James, P., & Wiedenbach, E. (1968). Theory in a practice discipline, Part 1. *Nursing Research, 17,* 415.

Grier, B., & Grier, M. (1978). Contributions of the passionate statistician. *Research in Nursing and Health, 1,* 103-109.

Hardy, L.K. (1986). Identifying the place of theoretical frameworks in an evolving discipline. *Journal of Advanced Nursing, 11,* 103-107.

Kim, H.S. (1983). *The nature of theoretical thinking in nursing.* Norwalk, Conn.: Appleton-Century-Crofts.

Marbach, W.D. (1986, January 27). Why Johnny can't reason. *Newsweek,* p. 59.

Murphy, S.D. (1985). Contexts for scientific creativity: Applications to nursing. *The Journal of Nursing Scholarship, 17,* 103-107.

Porter-O'Grady, T. (1986). *Creative nursing administration: Participative management into the 21st century.* Rockville, Md.: Aspen Publishers, Inc.

Sellew, G., & Nuesse, C.J. (1946). *A history of nursing.* St. Louis: C.V. Mosby.

Sheahan, M.W. (1950). A program for the improvement of nursing services. *American Journal of Nursing, 50,* 794-795.

Strauss, A. (1966). The structure and ideology of American nursing: An interpretation. In F. David (Ed.), *The nursing profession: Five sociological essays* (pp. 60-108). New York: John Wiley.

Styles, M.M. (1982). *On nursing: Toward a new endowment.* St. Louis: C.V. Mosby.

Taylor, B.N., Wagner, P.L., & Kraus, C.L. (1987). Development of a standard for time-effective patient assessment during blood transfusion. *Journal of Nursing Quality Assurance, 1,* 66-71.

Walker, L.D., & Avant, K.C. (1983). *Strategies for theory construction in nursing.* Norwalk, Conn.: Appleton-Century-Crofts.

## BIBLIOGRAPHY

Carnevali, D.L., Mitchell, P.H., Woods, N.F., & Tanner, C.A. (1984). *Diagnostic reasoning in nursing.* Philadelphia: J.B. Lippincott.

Drucker, P.F. (1985). The discipline of innovation. *Harvard Business Review, 63,* 67-72.

Poulin, M.A. (1979). Education for nurse administrators: An epilogue. *Nursing Administration Quarterly, 3,* 45-51.

Silva, M.C. (1986). Research-testing nursing theory: State of the art. *Advances in Nursing Science, 8,* 1-11.

Simms, L.M., Price, S.A., & Ervin, N.E. (1985). *The professional practice of nursing administration.* New York: John Wiley.

Smith, J.P. (1983). Concept of nursing literacy: An energizing force in health care. *Journal of Advanced Nursing, 8,* 69-75.

Stevens, B.J. (1979). *Nursing theory: Analysis, application, evaluation.* Boston: Little, Brown.

**Chapter 8**

# Research
# Facilitator Role

*Janet Wessel Krejci, Sue Straub, and*
*Margie Smerlinski*

*The role of the research facilitator can be invaluable to any nursing department that is committed to implementing research in nursing practice. The research facilitator can support the development of a research program utilizing quality assurance as a foundation for growth. This chapter discusses research roles in a hospital setting. It covers historical precedents, function of different roles, cost and benefits of the role, options for implementation, relationship to quality assurance, and differentiating titles such as research facilitator, nurse researcher, and research director. It also provides guidance for nurse administrators in planning for optimal and realistic use of resources to work toward identified research goals.*

## HISTORICAL PRECEDENTS

There have been many changes since the early 1970s that have influenced nurses' perceptions of research and its value to patient care. National health care policy and the American Nurses' Association (ANA) stance on increasing professionalism in nursing have encouraged increased quality and quantity in research, in academia as well as in clinical entities.

Many events have contributed to the increased value and quantity of nursing research. The ANA generic standards (1985) have incorporated nursing's responsibility for research. Schools of nursing have implemented research courses in undergraduate as well as graduate programs (McClure, 1981). Most master's programs in nursing now require a master's thesis rather than a nonresearch paper. Specialty organizations are writing research goals and standards for the members to follow.

A National Center for Nursing Research was formed in 1986. The number of M.S., D.N.S., and Ph.D. programs in nursing has increased. The ANA Social Policy Statement (1980) strongly supported the needs for further research. The inclusion of research activities in job descriptions and competency-based evaluations has expanded. Finally, the advent of diagnostic related groups (DRGs) and other cost constraints in health care challenge nurses to measure their impact on outcomes.

The consequences of these changes are many. More master's students, as well as faculty members, are seeking clinical agencies in which to conduct their research. Closer scrutiny of quality of care and the increased need to measure the impact of nursing have resulted in greater rigor in quality assurance studies. As nurses develop critical thinking and seek higher education, they more actively question the status quo and are more likely to request research resources to solve practice problems. Nurses utilize quality assurance as a vehicle for conducting systematic research to find answers for complex patient care problems. The result, for service settings, is increased demand from several directions despite resources that are limited by health care cost constraints.

In the past, research responsibilities of the nursing department were handled easily by the chief nurse administrator. Activities usually were limited to enlisting staff support for medical research and reviewing thesis proposals for the infrequent nursing graduate student. Quality assurance studies were limited to routine audits. There was no need for a nursing human subject protection committee, little emphasis on education for nursing research, or much interest in looking at theory- or research-based practice.

The chief nurse administrator still may be the one most responsible for influencing the research climate (Hunt, Stalk, & Fisher, 1983; Krueger, 1978; Sylvester, 1980). However, given the increasing demands on nurse executives to respond to changing external and internal forces, it is unrealistic for them to perform all the functions of the nursing research roles. It may be more realistic—and more beneficial for the nursing department in general—for them to facilitate research indirectly by creating and developing new research positions. This is accomplished more easily if a quality assurance program is in a place that has encouraged responsibility and accountability of staff nurses for monitoring their own practice.

## RESEARCH NEEDS AND RESOURCES

If the chief nurse executive is committed to creating or developing new research roles, specific needs must be assessed. Nursing must look first at its own philosophy and its department's purpose and objectives. Its leaders must decide its goals for implementing research. External influences must be identified in their relation to research. Leaders and staff members must identify what specific role research will play. Relevance to staff nurses and to quality of care should be key factors if research is to be integrated successfully with departmental practice.

These issues provide a baseline of information for assessment. The next step can be a review of research activities that have been identified as integral to research-based practice such as: assessing, creating and nurturing a research climate; developing staff; conducting studies for specific problems; maintaining liaison with the school of nursing; tracking trends in the profession; consulting on methodology and data management; developing data collection methods and procedures; facilitating outside research requests; chairing and leading the research committee, and many others.

The activities that support staff members in research fall into two general categories—coordination and consultation. As research activities increase, it may be necessary to assign one person to take sole responsibility for the tremendous amount of negotiation necessary for coordinating research activities. If this is not done, the result may be a chaotic and often destructive approach to research:

- chaotic because, without coordination, it can lead to a flurry of activities, none of them with meaningful direction
- destructive because there often is mistrust of research at the staff level and, if handled poorly, this will validate staff perceptions that research is time consuming and costly without benefits to patient care.

Consequently, without staff support, it will be impossible for a research-based practice to succeed.

Nursing departments also must have access to research expertise. Again, increased quantity of research without improved quality can be destructive to a research-based practice. Nursing departments can ill afford to conduct poorly designed studies that yield questionable results. The model for providing both coordination and expertise already has been implemented in the unit quality assurance structure. There often is a staff nurse familiar with the unit to coordinate the committee as well as a clinical nurse specialist to offer expertise.

Many titles have been used for nurses working with research in a clinical agency. Although this at times is a matter of semantics, it is important to assess the difference in functions behind the titles.

The literature most often refers to a "nurse researcher" in a clinical agency, although in larger systems an entire department may be devoted to research, with its head having the title "research director" or "research coordinator"

(Chance & Hinshaw, 1980; Marchette, 1985). The term research facilitator is fairly new in academic as well as service settings (Lieske, 1986; Timmons, 1986). For simplicity, the title "research facilitator" is used here for the role responsible for coordinating activities and "nurse researcher" for an individual who conducts research and/or consults on methodology.

To identify what type of position is needed, it is necessary to look first at the differences in function, expertise, and qualifications. The literature provides little insight. In a study that ran from 1973 to 1976, Krueger (1978) reports that 8 percent of a sample of 219 hospitals employed a full-time nurse researcher and 67 percent a part-time researcher. However, the study does not give the background of the positions involved or explain specific functions.

A more recent study by Hagle, Kirchoff, Knafl and Bevis (1986) surveyed 34 clinical agencies employing a nurse in some type of a research role. It identified 17 different titles, with varying responsibilities. Of the respondents, 59 percent identified as their main responsibility the facilitation of research and 47 percent the conduct of research. More detailed descriptions of functions were not included.

Most authors do support a doctorally prepared nurse researcher to fill the role, whether full time or part time (Chance and Hinshaw, 1980; Cronenwett, 1985; Kirchoff, 1983; McClure, 1981; Zalar, Welches, & Walker, 1985). However, several disadvantages were identified in employing a doctorally prepared nurse as a nurse researcher in a clinical (hospital, home care, or long-term care) agency. McClure (1981) makes the point that such nurses are in short supply and questions whether clinical agencies should even be competing for this supply when academia needs them more. This may be a questionable rationale, at least from the perspective of the clinical agency.

McClure also points out that it may be extremely difficult for a nurse researcher to exist in isolation from other scholars—that is, away from the academic scene. She believes that for a healthy exchange of ideas to occur there needs to be a critical mass of peers available, and she does not believe this exists in most clinical agencies. Her point may be one reason why clinical agencies look to joint appointments with academic entities for nurse researchers.

When the decision is made to hire a researcher on a joint appointment, the nurse brings research expertise from a faculty perspective but may be at a disadvantage when it comes to effecting change in a practice setting. The lack of in-depth knowledge of the hospital's political system may hamper the individual from enhancing the research climate. This may evidence itself by refusal of staff members to participate in research activities or the refusal of physicans to permit their patients to be subjects in the research until they get to know the researchers and accept them. Faculty members hired to be nurse researchers often have become disillusioned when they were unable to devote as much time to actual research as they had envisioned. They have found that they must attend to many organizational and facilitative functions that were obstacles to conducting research.

Essentially, then, the differences between the two roles are that a research facilitator coordinates and facilitates needs, goals, and resources and a nurse researcher conducts research and consults on methodological and data management issues (see Table 8-1).

The skills and educational requirements for each role overlap in some areas but are not the same (Table 8-2). The research facilitator at a minimum should have a master's degree, while the nurse researcher should hold a Ph.D. in nursing.

The research facilitators' expertise is based on a knowledge of the system as an organization and how different persons relate both between and in departments. It is ideal if facilitators are not too far removed from practice so they may be able to relate to staff needs and capabilities as well as identify motivating factors for nurses. In essence, the research facilitator provides another way to close the gap between research and practice.

Cronenwett (1985) suggests that the nurse researcher have solid knowledge based on such elements as patient classification systems, reliability and validity concerns, data collection methods and procedures, and administrative research methodology. The individual's research should be congruent with and supportive of the particular entity's philosophy. The nurse researcher also must be able to communicate effectively with persons in nursing conducting their own research or quality assurance studies and offer realistic consultation.

Once differences in functions, skills, and requirements are identified, nursing leaders in a department may be able to select the role best suited for their needs. If a specific project is a priority, a nurse researcher should be employed or contracted; if research already is being carried out or the development of the research environment is a priority, a facilitator should be hired.

## IMPLEMENTATION OF A RESEARCH PROGRAM

The model described here was used in St. Michael Hospital, a community hospital that attracts and retains master's-prepared nurses. It involved a nurse facilitator with access to a nurse researcher. Given the hospital's resources, quality assurance studies and other basic research could be conducted independently, along with more complex studies in consultation with the nurse researcher. Since the literature contains much material on the nurse researcher role, this discussion focuses on the implementation and functions of the research facilitator.

**Table 8-1** Functions of Facilitator and Researcher Compared

| Subject | Facilitator | Researcher |
| --- | --- | --- |
| Assessment of Climate | 1. Proposes and obtains approval to conduct study<br>2. Facilitates communication and logistics of study, engages management support<br>3. Disseminates results through appropriate channels, collaborates with Research Development Committee (*RDC*) and other roles (C.N.S., R.N.)<br>4. Coordinates recommendations | 1. Consults on design<br>2. Interprets results<br>3. Recommends approach |
| Research Development Committee | 1. Chairs committee | 1. Consults with committee |
| Education and Staff Development | 1. Helps set priorities with RD and QA committees along with other roles<br>2. Proposes and obtains administration approval<br>3. Coordinates offerings | 1. Consults for RDC and QAC<br>2. Provides selected educational programs |
| Outside Research Requests | 1. Acts as liaison with institutional review board (IRB)<br>2. Serves as researcher advocate<br>3. Communicates with appropriate staff members<br>4. Coordinates/facilitates process<br>5. Addresses feasibility with administration | 1. Conducts methods critique<br>2. Analyzes relevance to practice |
| School of Nursing | 1. Coordinates contract (if one exists)<br>2. Acts as liaison between needs and resources | 1. Employed by School of Nursing<br>2. Identifies appropriate resource for specific problem |
| Research Utilization | 1. Identifies feasibility<br>2. Communicates with staff and leadership | 1. Serves as methods expert<br>2. Consults with staff members for relevance to practice and process of utilization<br>3. Analyzes and synthesizes |
| Quality Assurance | 1. Acts as liaison between RDC and QAC<br>2. Coordinates support services<br>3. Coordinates activities and disseminates information | 1. Assesses methodology<br>2. Consults on statistics<br>3. Consults on form and method development |

**Table 8-2** Educational and Professional Requirements

| Subject | Facilitator | Researcher |
|---|---|---|
| Education | 1. Minimally M.S.<br>2. Major in nursing | 1. Ph.D. in nursing |
| Employer | 1. Clinical agency | 1. School of Nursing or joint appointment |
| Experience | 1. Solid clinical background<br>2. QA—in research studies | 1. Variety of research experiences<br>2. Evaluation methodology |
| Expertise/Knowledge | 1. Knowledge of organization/political system<br>2. Knowledge of community resources<br>3. Continual monitoring of practice concerns | 1. Patient classification<br>2. Reliability/validity<br>3. Instrument development<br>4. Data management<br>5. Trends in nursing profession/nursing research<br>6. Knowledge of statistical analysis |

## Research Climate

The research facilitator rarely works in isolation, given the nature of the position. One of the first tasks is to assess the research climate (this is a continuing concern). Published materials are available for measuring the research climate (Egan, McElmurry, & Jameson, 1981). Although these can provide valuable information, other qualitative information also is essential to evaluate nurses' readiness to engage in research.

Before addressing readiness, nurses must define specifically the goal of integrating the research into their operation. The study by Egan, McElmurry, & Jameson (1981) defines research climate in terms of eight conditions that affect the ability to conduct systematic studies—subject participation, professional participation, market factors, organizational systems, economic factors, legal/statutory, facilities and resources, and contributions to the research endeavors of educational institutions. This assumes that integrating research into practice means exclusively or primarily "conducting systematic studies." This may be a grave and frequent error. The facilitator needs to elicit staff and administrative support to identify clearly the meaning and goal of integrating research into the setting. Goals of research implementation may include conducting studies, utilizing research, and/or educating staff. These can be accomplished more easily if the facilitator builds on the skills already developed with those involved in QA.

It is essential to examine the range of research activities that may be used. Although conducting systematic studies obviously is one aspect of research, it may not be the most appropriate initial goal. If the goal is to obtain specific data on a problem, a systematic study may indeed be in order, and the integration of research for practice becomes a secondary objective.

However, if integration of research is the real primary goal, then different approaches may be necessary to meet the needs of nurses with varied levels of preparation. Many authors believe that utilization should be the first application of research activity in service settings (Horsley, Crane, & Bingle, 1978; Loomis, 1985; Stetler, 1985). But Kirchoff (1983) contends that even research utilization may be too complex for the staff members to implement as a first step. Variables such as awareness of research methods, exposure to research, varying levels of education, and access to research findings were cited by Kirchoff as reasons why it may be unrealistic for staff to utilize research.

To identify realistic research activities for staff nurses, a continuum of research activities has been developed in a matrix model (Figure 8-1). One of the first steps, cognitive application, is derived from Stetler and Marram's (1976) work on research utilization. They broadened the term to include the application of research review by staff nurses to aid them in their practice.

For example, nurses may read an article on pain research that is based on the assumption that giving patients more control over rating their pain will increase their comfort. Other examples may analyze risk factors of the elderly

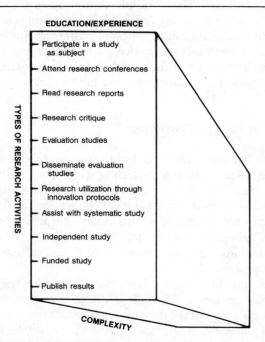

**Figure 8-1** Matrix of Research Activities in a Service Setting

in falls or high incidences of women entering the emergency department with premenstrual syndrome (PMS).

These examples influence the nurse's approach to assessment and intervention, thus improving quality of care. Although staff members are not engaged in a systematic study or adopting an innovative protocol, they definitely are utilizing research and should be rewarded and encouraged. Other types of activities are included in Figure 8-1.

It may be noted that research studies are not segregated from quality assurance studies because the distinction is not that helpful. Many studies carried out in a systematic and valid manner for quality assurance also can be classified as research.

The nursing profession has spent little time identifying the day-to-day research needs of practicing nurses. Because of their almost obsessive need to be classified as "a profession," nurses have attempted blindly to imitate other disciplines in their approaches to research. The result is an almost exclusive focus on conducting larger scale quantitative studies and, in the process, often losing the support and interest of staff nurses. The research facilitator is the crucial link in steering the nursing department toward a research-based practice while maintaining awareness of benefits to staff.

Given this perspective on research, the facilitator may want to assure access to appropriate resources. These include clinical nursing journals, librarian support, unit support for sharing articles, head nurse support for trying new approaches, and quality assurance interest in addressing cognitive application as a method of problem solving (as defined by Stetler and Marram, 1976). Once goals are developed and the climate has been assessed, the data from the assessment guide the facilitator toward further functions.

## Development of Research Activities

Development becomes one of the key functions of the research facilitator in realizing identified goals. If a research development committee (RDC) is not already in place, one should be created. It is crucial that nursing have a committee separate from the medical research committee. This is not to say that multidisciplinary research is not important, but it is more important to establish first a strong base for nursing research. It may be helpful to begin the research committee as a subcommittee of quality assurance until its development has progressed.

Membership and function are fundamental considerations when developing a research committee. The individuals chosen as members should be responsible for carrying out the nursing department's purpose and objectives. Therefore, it is imperative to include the target population—the staff nurses. A committee that includes informal as well as formal leaders of the staff nurse group will ensure that identified goals will be realistic for those nurses.

Representation from management also is imperative if support through all job classes is sought. The quality assurance director (if not already identified in the research facilitator role) should be included. This ensures a good working relationship between the RDC and quality assurance. As clinical nurse specialists (C.N.S.s) often are charged with bridging the gap between practice and the more esoteric goals set by the profession, they also must be included. The committee then could consist of seven to ten members. If the chief nursing executive is not a member, copies of the agenda and minutes should be forwarded to that executive to keep communication lines open.

The functions of the committee should be decided upon by the members. Issues to consider include: protocol review, length of membership, reporting structure, educational offerings, and budget concerns.

## Education

Given the external and internal constraints, the budget for education, and the difficulty of arranging time away from patients, staff education has to be accomplished in creative ways. Two factors to consider when dealing with education in research are content and the vehicle for its delivery.

Erroneous assumptions sometimes are made about the most appropriate content to offer to help staff nurses understand research. Although starting out with components of the research process may seem logical, it may be the beginning of the end of the nurses' interest. They may have difficulty retaining any information at all in trying to relate to the steps of the research process after they have delegated to other nurses the responsibility for six patients and know two more admissions are coming onto the unit. Inservice classes for 45 minutes at the end of the day may increase the nurses' anxiety over formalizing the research content and decrease their learning potential.

Creative elements for education include the use of different media. Videotapes could be made that are available to staff nurses at their convenience. Traveling inservice aids including posters and brief written materials could be used. Clinical nurse specialists can make informal rounds for short one-on-one discussions with nurses.

Taking into consideration both the content and the vehicle, several approaches were attempted at St. Michael Hospital. The first was a 20-minute dialogue with nurses over lunch breaks called brown-bag lunches. One presenter (at the outset, a clinical nurse specialist) would choose a research study that had clear clinical relevance to the staff. An abstract of the study would be presented and discussed for clinical applications. The study would be critiqued so the staff could begin to be exposed to the research process through that approach.

Also presented were quality assurance studies that the staff believed were related directly to practice—teaching needs of various populations, job satisfaction of R.N.s, and transfusion procedures. In this way nurses became exposed to research in a way they perceived as beneficial, rather than burdensome, to their daily practice.

Research education also can be offered in workshops away from the hospital. The Research Development Committee organized a workshop held in a conference center accessible to most employees. Members of the quality assurance committee were especially encouraged to attend. The workshop covered the research process and critiquing research, and small-group sessions discussed articles that had clear clinical relevance. A wine and cheese reception was included so participants could network with each other as well as the presenters. A small fee was charged to cover costs of food and materials. Differing environments often provide the opportunity to look at old problems in new ways.

The research facilitator can present brief inservice segments at quality assurance meetings, have research development committee members give brief informational presentations at unit meetings, or bring up research concerns at patient care conferences. The nursing newsletter can carry abstracted research articles with brief critiques and suggestions for clinical application. Again, applications can fall anywhere along the research activity continuum from cognitive application to conducting a research study.

The facilitator should become familiar with a computer software statistical package to help cope with the increasing focus on evaluation studies in quality assurance and research. Computer programs are both time saving and cost efficient if used correctly. It is beyond the scope of this chapter to identify specific software. However, the facilitator must become aware of resources that may support the research program. With virtually all hospitals now computer literate, it is logical to use their programs for statistical analysis.

Evaluation of educational offerings is crucial. The use of evaluation forms at the end of presentations can be helpful but other informal methods may provide more critical information. For example, staff members who are members of a research development committee should be open to input from their peers as to what the nurses really think. The facilitator may make informal phone calls to nurse managers to ask if they support the offerings enough to send staff members and to seek more detailed critiques of educational offerings. Assessing the climate definitely is a continuing process.

## COORDINATION ACTIVITIES

Another main function of the research facilitator at St. Michael Hospital is to coordinate research studies conducted in the nursing department. These include studies proposed from the outside (such as master's theses, doctoral dissertations, and faculty research) as well as larger studies done by the hospital staff. Despite the complexity of this system and the interactions necessary with other committees (i.e., those on human subjects protection, medical staff research, and quality assurance), a research review model (Figure 8-2) was developed by the Research Development Committee in coordination with the Quality Assurance Committee.

This model facilitates the flow of research through the system. When any research request comes in, the research facilitator meets with the researcher for an exchange of information and discussion of general feasibility. Depending on the extent of the proposal, the facilitator may have to limit the amount of research in which certain populations are asked to participate (e.g., staff and general medical-surgical patients). The vice president of patient services and the chair of the Human Subjects Protection Committee then review the study for methodology, administrative review, and human subject concern.

A problem that may face the facilitator is possible weakness in the proposed research methods. Although the hospital may want to support research, if the methodology is questionable it may be unethical to subject staff or patients to a poorly constructed study. A doctorally prepared nurse researcher is invaluable at this juncture to help identify such problems.

To assist students requesting to do research, a research review handbook was developed. It identifies expectations, the purpose and objectives of hospital committees involved in the research process, a step-by-step procedure for submitting research proposals, and a sample consent form. The handbook has decreased the number of poorly prepared researchers who approached St. Michael.

Along with coordination of the outside researcher, the research facilitator is responsible for informing management, clinical nurse specialists, and staff as to upcoming studies. This can be cumbersome when larger studies are involved because changes often are made along the way. This problem has been eased by requiring all researchers to summarize any and all proposed changes in writing as addenda to the original request. Each addendum is sent to appropriate hospital personnel to keep them up to date.

Once the study has been completed, the researcher writes a periodic progress report (in duplicate) for the research facilitator and the administrator of that specific area. The report gives progress on data analysis and conclusions of the study. This aids communication and ensures feedback for staff members participating directly or indirectly in the study, as they are often anxious to learn of study results which involved them. Researchers often are invited to present their findings at a brown-bag lunch so staff members may hear the results. Final copies of full research reports, as well as abstracts, then are filed with the facilitator.

The coordination element of the research facilitator function can be extremely time consuming if systems are not set up efficiently. It is important

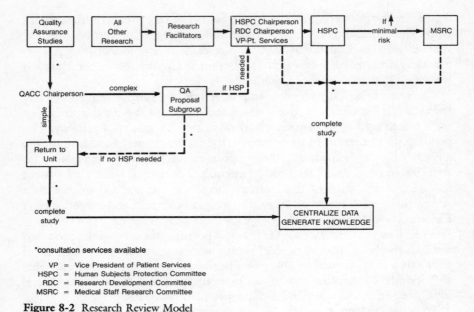

*consultation services available

VP   = Vice President of Patient Services
HSPC = Human Subjects Protection Committee
RDC  = Research Development Committee
MSRC = Medical Staff Research Committee

**Figure 8-2**  Research Review Model

that the facilitator clearly communicate expectations to outside researchers either in writing or orally; this will limit time-consuming meetings that may benefit neither the researcher nor the department.

## DISSEMINATION/COMMUNICATION

The research facilitator also acts as a liaison among staff members, departments, and the community at large, including schools of nursing, other hospitals, and the nursing profession. Many reports in the literature strongly support linking practice and academia to meet research goals (Chance & Hinshaw, 1980; McClure, 1981). A contract was signed annually from 1982 to 1985 between the University of Wisconsin-Milwaukee School of Nursing as coordinated by Dr. Phyllis Kritek, director of the Center for Nursing Research and Evaluation, and St. Michael Hospital for use of the university's resources. The research facilitator's role under this contract was to act as a liaison between the university and the agency in matching resources at the university with the hospital's clinical projects.

Other liaison responsibilities include informing staff nurses of upcoming conferences, calls for papers, workshops, and opportunities in the community. The research facilitator obviously must remain in close touch with the needs of the staff in order to disseminate appropriate information. The facilitator also may need to encourage staff members to submit their quality assurance projects, innovations, or proposed presentations.

As publishing and/or presenting is not always a regular task in hospitals, nurses may be reluctant in pursuing such endeavors. Support for increasing their skills in this area should be organized through the research facilitator. Workshops can be held on how to make a presentation, how to write a query letter, and how to write for publication.

## THE SUPPORTING ROLES OF OTHERS

Research facilitation is supported by others. Although the facilitator is primarily responsible for coordinating activities to meet the nursing department goals, other individuals are crucial for the success of any research program. The chief nurse executive's unfailing support is the catalyst in research projects. This executive must have the vision and the political savvy to present positions convincingly to other hospital administrators as well as the department of nursing at strategic times. The chief nurse executive also must be willing to give members of the leadership the confidence and support they need to implement a research-based practice.

Directors of nursing must work closely with the chief nurse executive to incorporate nursing research into everyday staff practice. This entails including research into job descriptions and competency-based evaluations and developing norms for nursing research in the department.

Head nurses are in a pivotal position to help bring a research-based practice to reality. They must actively support a climate of inquiry in which nurses feel the freedom to question practice and the status quo. They also can be helpful by finding creative ways to release nurses from patient care time so they can pursue research. Head nurses set the tone for the unit with subtle behaviors that often can have stronger influence than the spoken word.

Since head nurses have the major responsibility for budgets, it is not surprising that they may be ambivalent about supporting research activities that call for time away from patient care. It would be a strategic plus if head nurses could be members of the research development committee for input on budgets, time constraints, etc., and could foster positive attitudes in their peer group in supporting research.

Head nurses who are members of quality assurance committees can be instrumental in success because they understand that the application of research findings can improve quality of care and increase the efficiency of its delivery. They often are in the most difficult position in bridging adminis⁾ tration and staff. They need support, development, and encouragement to succeed.

Clinical nurse specialists perform key functions through their ability to translate research findings into realistic practice issues. If the head nurse is the link between administration and staff, the clinical nurse specialist is the link between the idealization and the reality of practice.

Clinical specialists can be responsible for educational offerings, consultation, or practice problems on their units. They can help staff members translate nursing problems into research and can identify studies and theoretical articles that may be relevant to their practice.They can recommend potential ways to apply research findings. Clinical nurse specialists are in a unique position as they have master's degrees, and have both the research skills to identify clinical problems and the clinical expertise to affect practice.

As noted repeatedly in this chapter, the staff nurses are the keys. Research must be relevant to them if the department is to move toward a research-based practice. The research facilitator must build in ways to keep in touch with the staff nurses' world to assure successful integration. The nurses should be rewarded for their efforts in research activities and listened to on their concerns for research.

There are many ways to approach the integration of research in a service setting. This chapter describes a variety of options and discusses one specific model. The underlying goal of this approach is to bridge the gap between research and practice while remaining accountable to the needs and reality of the staff nurse. Quality assurance was identified as the most logical building block for this endeavor.

## REFERENCES

American Nurses' Association. (1985). *Standards of nursing practice*. Monograph Pub. no. NP-68G. Kansas City, Mo.: Author.

American Nurses' Association. (1980). *Nursing: A Social Policy Statement* (ANA Publication Code: NP-63 35M 12/80). Kansas City, Mo.: Author.

Chance, H.C., & Hinshaw, A.S. (1980). Strategies for initiating a research program. *The Journal of Nursing Administration, 10*, 32-39.

Cronenwett, L. (1985). Hiring a nurse researcher. *The Journal of Nursing Administration, 15*, 5-7.

Egan, E., McElmurry, B., & Jameson, H. (1981). Practice-based research: Assessing your department's readiness. *The Journal of Nursing Administration, 11*, 23-62.

Hagle, M.E., Kirchoff, K.T., Knafl, K.A., & Bevis, M.E. (1986). The clinical nurse researcher: New perspectives. *Journal of Professional Nursing 2*, (5), 282-288.

Horsley, J.A., Crane, J., & Bingle, K. (1978). Research utilization: An organizational process. *The Journal of Nursing Administration, 8*, 4-7.

Hunt, V., Stalk, J.L., & Fisher, F. (1983). Networking: A managerial strategy for research development in a service setting. *The Journal of Nursing Administration, 13*, 27-32.

Kirchoff, K.T. (1983). Using research in practice: Should staff nurses be expected to use research? *Western Journal of Nursing Research, 5*, 245-247.

Krueger, J.C. (1978). Utilization of nursing research: The planning process. *The Journal of Nursing Administration, 8*, 6-9.

Lieske, A.M. (1986). *Clinical nursing research.* Rockville, Md.: Aspen Publishers, Inc.

Loomis, E. (1985). Knowledge utilization and research utilization in nursing. *Image: The Journal of Nursing Scholarship, 17*, 35-39.

Marchette, L. (1985). Developing a productive nursing research program in a clinical institution. *The Journal of Nursing Administration, 15*, 25-29.

McClure, M. (1981). Promoting practice-based research: A critical need. *The Journal of Nursing Administration, 11*, 66-74.

Stetler, M. (1985). Research utilization: Defining the concept image. *Journal of Nursing Scholarship, 17*, 42-44.

Stetler, M., & Marram, G. (1976). Evaluating research findings for applicability in practice. *Nursing Outlook, 24*, 559-563.

Sylvester, D.C. (1980). Nursing administrators responsible for research. *AORN Journal, 31*, 850-855.

Timmons, S. (1986). *A comparison of the research role of nursing executives in theory and in practice in acute care facilities.* Unpublished master's thesis. Milwaukee: Marquette University.

Zalar, M., Welches, L.J., & Walker, D. (1985). Nursing consortium approach to increase research in service settings. *The Journal of Nursing Administration, 15*, 36-41.

---

## BIBLIOGRAPHY

Chinn, P.L. (1985). Debunking myths in nursing theory and research image. *Image: Journal of Nursing Scholarship, 17*, 45-49.

Fawcett, J. (1985). A typology of research activities according to educational preparation. *Journal of Professional Nursing, 1*, 75-79.

Jacox, A. (1974). Nursing research and the clinician. *Nursing Outlook, 22*, 382-385.

Larsen, E. (1983). Combining nursing quality assurance in research programs. *The Journal of Nursing Administration, 13*, 32-38.

Lindeman, A.C., & Krueger, J.C. (1977). Increasing the quality, quantity, and use of nursing research. *Nursing Outlook, 25*, 450-451.

Werley, H.H., & Westlake, S.K. (1985). Impact of nursing research on public policy. *Journal of Professional Nursing, 1*, 148-156.

**Chapter 9**

# Practice and Education Collaboration: Toward Research-Based Practice

*Shelly Malin, Janet Wessel Krejci, and*
*Mary Bruskewitz*

*As research successfully builds on the quality assurance program, other resources from the larger nursing community can be utilized for continued growth and support of the theory-research-practice cycle. This chapter explores the many-faceted topic of collaboration between practice and education, primarily as it relates to research. A brief historical perspective provides a framework for understanding the efforts to move the profession toward the goal of a nursing practice based on a thoroughly researched foundation of knowledge. Models for research collaboration are critiqued, including issues from both the practice and the education perspectives. Advantages and disadvantages of joint research appointments are reviewed. Considerations for future work in the area of practice/education collaboration are suggested.*

The history of nursing education and research provides important background for a close examination of where the profession stands in the waning years of the 1980s. The history of health care and nursing has several versions, depending on which sources are used. In this synopsis, the work by Ashley (1976) and Dolan (1983) provides the framework. In the late 1800s and early 1900s, hospitals flourished in this country. They became a business venture for administrators (often physicians), with nurses as major financial revenue-producers and job beneficiaries as the hospitals kept the profits produced by private duty nurses and also provided the work force.

Initially, Florence Nightingale's ideas influenced hospital schools of nursing. She opposed the practice of using untrained servants to provide service so she introduced apprenticeship training to improve patient care. Her plan provided instruction in scientific principles and practical experience leading to mastery of skills. The training schools were organized and financed independently of the hospitals. Contracts were used to ensure access to hospitals.

## THE EARLY TRAVAILS

One important difference in the first hospital nursing schools in the United States was that they were not endowed financially, as were those in England. The schools faced financial problems from the start, which led to nurses' exchanging their work for hospital support to the school. Nursing schools became the most popular and least expensive way of providing care. While medical schools grew and prospered at the turn of the century, nursing schools did not.

Nursing schools grew in numbers, but education was not an important goal. They had no university connections and training was informal. As late as the 1930s, few training schools had paid instructors. From the administrators' viewpoint, the main goal was inexpensive labor. Ashley (1976) speaks of the family as the institutional model for hospital operations at that time. The role of the nurse (female) was that of caring for the "hospital family"; physicians (male) were the masters to be served.

From the 1900s on, training schools that had tried to exist outside the hospital were absorbed by or established for the institution. This prevented their independent development as educational institutions. Money went to the hospital to make it a better place, not to improve education. Because schools were run by hospital management, nursing leaders at that time had little control over standards. Several schools, such as Waltham Training School in Massachusetts and Johns Hopkins, attempted to change this by adding formal course work, but little was done on an organized basis. The tradition of uneducated teachers continued for years. In the mid 1930s, just under 30 percent of the salaried teaching staff in training schools had less than a high school diploma.

Student nurses worked long hours until a labor bill was passed in California in 1911 to protect them. Leaders were outraged by the fact that nurses were considered common laborers, although some conceded that they had done an inadequate job in informing the public about nurses. If they had, nurses would not even have been considered in this bill.

Hospitals had little need to hire graduate nurses because the training schools provided the most inexpensive source of labor. Graduate nurses often wandered from state to state looking for jobs, which they usually found in the private duty sector. Higher education first appeared in the 1920s. It was not until 1948 that the National League for Nursing (established in the 1920s) began assessing nursing education programs.

Financial support for nursing education fluctuated with war and peace until after World War II, when aid varied according to federal priorities. World War II saw the largest grant of money ever set aside for nursing education. During this time, the quality of education was monitored and curriculum changes were made. Funds for postgraduate education of faculty also were made available (Miller, 1985).

In the 1940s, conflicts between the goals of hospitals and nurse educators became apparent, with the institutions focusing on the provision of care, and the educators on nursing education. In many cases, the response of educators was to move completely out of the hospitals and into the academic mainstream. This brought a whole new set of problems. Tremendous time and energy were devoted to curriculum design and the academic credentialling of nursing faculties. This was deemed necessary to move the profession from training to education.

The response of nursing professionals in the practice setting was to begin viewing the nursing faculty as inexperienced and living in an ivory tower, detached from the real world of patient care. As faculty members were becoming credentialled academically, they began doing research, but it rarely was related directly to patient care because they often did not have direct access to patients in that setting. This widened the gap between education and practice. Practicing nurses had little regard for the research generated by faculty. More recently, nursing leaders have been working to bridge the gap between education and practice.

## MODELS OF COLLABORATION

Grace (1981) explores both early and current models of collaboration between practice and education. The early ones in the United States were called unification models, with practice and education totally merged under the governance of the hospital. Most models in the 1980s are contractual, with responsibility for education and practice handled by separate institutions.

The effort to bridge the gap between education and practice has been approached in a variety of ways. Grace describes one unification model as exemplified by Rush University, Rochester Medical Center, and Case Western

Reserve in which the same nurse acts as both faculty and practitioner. Although they differ somewhat, each provides a close working relationship between education and practice. The danger in such models is that they may run into the same difficulties as did the early unification ones, with service needs subsuming the needs of education.

Grace also discusses other models, including the collaborative, the affiliative, and the contractual. In the collaborative model key positions often are shared; for example, one person may serve as the assistant dean of nursing for both the hospital and the school of nursing. There may be a council to coordinate services and decisionmaking between education and practice.

Affiliative and contractual models are similar but have some important differences. Both attempt to create a relationship that benefits both education and practice. The difference is that in affiliative models a much closer connection is developed with implications of a set of rights and responsibilities for the partners. In a contractual arrangement, the contracted employees are guests in the contractor institutions; the contract is the only link.

Grace suggests that in any model of collaboration, the quality of both education and practice must be preserved and that this is best accomplished by establishing a working relationship (perhaps by contract) but keeping them as separate entities.

Aydelotte (1985) presents other approaches to bridging the gap, including:

- appointment of adjunct clinical faculty members on a part-time basis
- shared or joint appointments
- establishment of an advisory council to schools of nursing with members from practice settings
- periodic symposiums between nursing educators and nursing practitioners
- appointment of individuals in practice settings to university committees, and vice versa
- joint planning of continuing education offerings.

The options for collaboration are many and choices should fit the needs of all involved. An example of advantages and disadvantages of a particular link: One of the authors of this chapter, a clinical nurse specialist, works in a joint research/practice position at a university. In evaluating the position, she finds advantages and disadvantages:

- Advantages include acquisition of new skills, involvement in research that is readily applicable to clinical practice, the benefits of having practice input, informal liaison between settings, and fine tuning of personal writing and organizational skills.

- Disadvantages include time constraints, with both settings wanting more time; potential communication gaps; divided loyalties; and difficulty in peer support.

The author believes the outcomes have been valuable for both settings and the patient population is being served. A key to success in such a position is organization and a sense of self, permitting a workable division of time between the two institutions.

## EDUCATION/PRACTICE GAP

It is interesting to note that in a review of the nursing literature emphasizing the need to bridge the education/practice gap, research is mentioned only secondarily. The literature seems to assume that collaboration between the two will change research outcomes.

Reasons for the research/practice gap have been explored in the literature. McClure (1981) believes that faculty members lack both interest and ability in studying practice-related problems. She links this to the fact that most nurses with advanced degrees who work in academia "systematically disengaged from practice due to other faculty activities and obligations . . . [the] faculty withdrawal syndrome" (p. 66). McClure cites the consequence of this withdrawal as an estrangement between practice and education. Other consequences include:

- devaluation of academic preparation for nurses by nurses
- devaluation of academic preparation for nurses by others both in and outside of health care
- lack of patient-focused research
- lack of interdisciplinary research with other health care professionals
- isolation of nursing faculty.

She sees this as an all-encompassing problem that is reinforced by organizational and political systems that do not recognize practice-related activities.

Although the profession is experiencing an increase in academically generated research, three major obstacles remain in attempting to apply this research to the clinical setting:

1. lack of replicated studies (Brown, Tanner, & Padrick, 1984; Fawcett, 1980; Reynolds & Haller, 1986; Werley & Westlake, 1984)
2. lack of valid and reliable research models (Strickland, Waltz, & Lenz, 1986)

3. the predominance of quantitative research in a profession whose members work with primarily qualitative factors (e.g., human responses) (Chinn, 1986).

The lack of replicated studies makes it difficult and sometimes inappropriate to utilize research findings that may not be generalizable. The deficit of validated instruments was a major theme of the University of Maryland Measurement Outcome Project (1983-85). Strickland, Waltz, & Lenz (1986), in a review of research studies published in the 1980s, report few that reported on the reliability and validity of the materials or models used. They caution practitioners against applying findings without first testing the materials for reliability and validity with specific patient populations.

The most dangerous obstacle from one perspective is the continued proliferation of quantitative research. Several nursing leaders are beginning to speak to the need for a "new paradigm" in research. This includes utilizing appropriate qualitative methods to develop a sound nursing base of knowledge (Chinn, 1986; Kritek, 1986; Munhill, 1986).

These are but a few of the blocks that must be addressed in the academic setting; obstacles in the service setting also need to be dealt with. In the service setting, terms such as nursing research, practice-based research, and research-based practice have become the buzzwords of the 1980s. Although there are well-intended reasons for implementing research, the reality is that much of the current focus results from response to external influences. Institutions now compare notes on what each is doing in the area of professionalism and research, much as they compared themselves on efficiency in the late 1940s. Hospitals perceive themselves as lagging in progressiveness if they lack research.

## APPROACHES TO KNOWLEDGE

Before beginning the process of negotiating a relationship with an educational institution, it is crucial to conduct a critical analysis of the meaning of research to practicing nurses. As discussed in Chapter 5, this can be done most productively by building on previous experience with quality assurance. Research as an activity may be foreign to practicing nurses, but when linked with accountability for evaluating practice, it becomes more relevant.

One important area in assessing the meaning of research to staff nurses is the ways they approach knowledge. Belenky, Clinchy, Goldbager, and Tanile (1986) identify different ways of knowing by women based on five years of extensive and repeated interviews with women. In analyzing the data, they develop five categories of knowing: silence, received knowledge, subjective, procedural, and constructed. Because most nurses are women, this research is helpful in understanding their differences. Although it is beyond the scope of this chapter to provide an in-depth analysis of this work, the categories provide a framework for a beginning analysis of different ways of knowing in nurses.

Nurses come with a wide range of maturity, education, and experience. All of these factors influence their approach to knowledge. Based on Belenky et al.'s categories, here are several examples of differences in individual nurses:

- There are those who practice "by the book"—that is, they follow authority to the letter without questioning. They are likely to respond, "this is the way we've always done it," when a particular practice is questioned (received knowledge).
- There are those who are comfortable with their practice and, when asked how they know what they know, might respond, "I just know in my gut, my way is right" (subjective knowledge).
- Still other nurses follow logical reasoning as a way of knowing (procedural knowledge).
- There are those who rely exclusively on rational, "proved" knowledge as their approach to care.
- There are those who may be open to learning from experience, theory, and research (constructed knowledge). They are characterized by their openness and continual search for and integration of new knowledge. But often, these are the nurses who have gone on for higher education and/or have taken a promotion that removes them from day-to-day clinical experience. Silence is the one area that does not seem to be represented in nursing, as the interactional nature of nursing would not support nurses who were "silent."

Although these examples are brief, this organization of ways of knowing is useful in beginning to assess nurses. Understanding different ways of knowing is important in moving the profession toward research-based practice.

One of the more difficult areas in the service setting is educational preparation of the nurses. Most authors believe that all nurses can engage in some type of research activities (Fawcett, 1985). Many contend, however, that lack of baccalaureate or higher education may impede them in critiquing and applying findings (Kirchoff, 1983). McClure (1981) sees a direct relationship between level of education and positive research outcomes.

Fawcett (1985) delineates a typology of research activities according to education preparation. She describes three major research activities: (1) generation of knowledge, (2) dissemination of knowledge, and (3) utilization of knowledge. Fawcett believes that all levels are responsible for utilization.

Baccalaureate or higher levels are responsible for dissemination and master's or doctoral levels for generation of knowledge. She acknowledges that she may be criticized for writing that generation of knowledge is an activity exclusive to master's or doctorally prepared nurses. However, given the complexity of most research, it may take a M.S. or Ph.D. to identify whether it is even appropriate for application.

Most acute care settings have a predominance of diploma or associate degree nurses, fewer with baccalaureates, and even fewer with master's and doctorates. If Fawcett's model is to be followed, it is evident that health care institutions will need to place a higher priority on hiring nurses with advanced degrees to integrate research and patient care.

Another critical factor in making a success of a research department in a clinical setting, as noted earlier, is the strong support of the nurse executive. Unless that individual is willing to support research activities financially (budget) and professionally, it is not likely that there will be much collaboration between researcher and practitioner. Many authors (Hunt, Stark, & Fisher, 1983; Jacox, 1974; Marchette, 1985; McClure, 1981) also have cited the nurse executive's support as the one ingredient that is imperative in the development of research.

There are other obstacles to conducting and utilizing research in the clinical setting that are related to the staff nurse. Jacox (1974) points out the role conflict between nurses as caretakers and as researchers; the terminology and language of the researcher also contributes to staff nurses' feeling alienated in that world. All of these factors lead to a lack of understanding by staff nurses of the researcher role, which in turn discourages them from becoming involved in a research project.

Given the acknowledged gap between university-generated research and the application of clinical research, the profession is looking for ways to close the gap. Models of collaboration on research utilization are described in the literature. Several projects, both large and individual, are discussed next.

## RESEARCH UTILIZATION MODELS

The Western Interstate Commission for Higher Education (WICHE) regional program for nursing research development was a six-year project funded by the Division of Nursing of the Department of Health, Education, and Welfare. Three theoretical approaches were used to develop major project activities: (1) collaborative nontargeted research; (2) collaborative targeted research; and (3) research utilization.

Major outcomes included funded research projects, generation of materials and models tested for reliability, and new programs in participating hospitals. The program's coordinators concluded "that no further large-scale utilization projects should be attempted until the products of research have been indexed and made available" (Krueger, 1978, p. 29). Lindeman and Krueger (1977) also report that working in groups is time consuming and that attrition of group members influenced the outcome of many projects. It is hard to measure the direct impact of this model or project in relation to a research-based practice.

The Conduct and Utilization of Research in Nursing (CURN) project was a five-year (1975–1980) development project awarded to the Michigan Nurses Association by the Division of Nursing of DHEW. Its major objective was to increase utilization of research through dissemination and encouragement of collaborative research studies. Collaborative research was defined as involving projects in which university-based researchers and hospital-based clinicians had equal roles (Loomis & Krone, 1980). Innovation teams from 17 hospitals participated in a series of workshops. The organizational impact of the project was measured through a survey of utilization in control hospitals.

The CURN project resulted in clinical protocols as well as two findings that relate to research utilization:

1. Clinicians were reluctant to take time away from their other obligations, even when nurse administrators were supportive of time allowance, and thus became overwhelmed and frustrated with their inability to complete the projects.
2. Clinicians found that the project's function in linking them with a researcher was extremely important because mechanisms do not exist that allow this to happen without a third party.

The project recommended development of models to assure linkage so the goal of research-based practice could be realized (Loomis & Krone, 1980).

The consortium model (Zalar, Welches, & Walker, 1985) is exemplified by Stanford University Hospital. In this model, nursing service and education agencies are brought together to share knowledge and resources to encourage research endeavors. This project, funded by a Division of Nursing of DHEW grant, promoted the creation of a cost-effective approach that supported the conduct of nursing research and implementation of its findings.

The project staff included three full-time master's-prepared nurse researchers, a project evaluator, a statistician, and an editor. Educational workshops were provided for two levels—beginning and advanced—with both conducting research studies. Workshops on the change process and scientific writing were included.

The project staff was available to all members of the consortium, which provides greater access to study populations and the opportunity for cross-site studies. Replication is facilitated, which, as mentioned, is an important aspect of clarifying research findings. The consortium completed a large study at several sites investigating wound healing of decubitus ulcers.

## ST. MICHAEL/U.W.-MILWAUKEE

This chapter would be incomplete without discussing the Center for Nursing Research at the University of Wisconsin-Milwaukee. This center exemplifies the entire university's commitment to serving the community.

The center has made itself available to community agencies in a variety of ways. Several hospitals may buy out a percentage of an experienced researcher's position and the expert then will utilize services at the Center for Nursing Research and Evaluation to provide data analysis and computer and research assistant services to the hospital requesting support.

Experienced doctorally prepared researchers might be instrumental in developing a research committee at the hospital or serving as consultants. If a research committee already exists, the researcher might provide consultation on studies, on education for various levels of nurses, and on developing the nursing department's plan for research in the hospital.

St. Michael Hospital has the benefit of a contract arrangement that allows its nursing department to pick and choose services to be used by the staff. The model was developed by SueEllen Pinkerton, R.N., Ph.D., and Phyllis Kritek, R.N., Ph.D., in 1984. For several years, a nurse from the hospital has filled the facilitator role. She works directly with a facilitator from the Center for Nursing Research and Evaluation. St. Michael Hospital staff has the freedom of using any of the center's staff or university faculty as consultants on projects; the center data analyst is used frequently as a consultant.

Inservice training was offered on developing code books to code data. Informal lunches were held at the university and at the hospital. Project assistants provided valuable resources for specific research efforts. They also are available to work on literature searches, data collection, data coding for input into the computer, and a myriad of other services. Media services are available and used for developing research posters for presentation at research meetings. Through project collaboration, one St. Michael Hospital clinical nurse specialist worked half time on a federally funded project. The center's library also is readily available.

The benefit of this collaborative effort is clear when outcomes and benefits are examined. Many of the quality assurance projects in the hospital were improved by increasing their rigor. Data analysis was available on a more sophisticated level through the university.

A study examining the needs of families in the intensive care setting provides a prototype for how the hospital benefits from services. With the experience from this study, the clinical nurse specialist involved with critical care helped the staff interface with the university. Staff nurses were comfortable enough to go to the Center for Nursing Research, communicate with researchers and statisticians, and complete a complex study. The study was written up by the staff in conjunction with the clinical specialist and published in *Quality Review Bulletin* (Spatt, Gonas, Hying, Kirsch and Koch, 1986). Many other quality assurance studies have resulted in publications as well. The experience of being able to exchange ideas through informal brown-bag lunches and more formal education series provides networking opportunities that enhance the growth of professional nurses.

## OTHER APPROACHES

Many different approaches to linking education and practice for research are described in the literature. It is important when deciding which might best meet the needs of a particular practice or education setting to review potential advantages and disadvantages. One approach is to have the school of nursing faculty provide education on research in the practice setting. Hospital staff members may choose to attend formal classes in research at the educational site. This approach alone, or in conjunction with others, is advantageous when a university is in close proximity. Success depends on the nurses' ability to bridge the gap and translate formal education into practice. The entity that houses the practice setting might provide more specifically focused education by hiring faculty to offer education for the staff. This is likely to be more expensive in the short term but is cost effective in the long run if a large number of staff members could thus be educationally prepared to participate in the research planning but are presently unable to due to lack of the necessary education.

Courtesy appointments to committees can be accomplished with practicing staff as members of education committees, or vice versa. These appointments promote sharing of knowledge. Responsibilities need to be delineated clearly and committee members must have voting privileges.

## THE FUTURE

Despite progress, nursing has more obstacles to overcome in its movement toward research-based practice. Academicians still tend to view themselves as a step above the practitioners. Practitioners tend to devalue what educators and researchers have to offer. Grass-roots activity and dialogue are needed in education and practice settings to make possible the development of trust and working relationships between both to successfully bridge the gap. Clinical nurse specialists and research specialists can lead the way in establishing collaborative research efforts.

Nursing's position in the service setting is changing as nurse leaders assume control of finances for the department. This puts the department in a better position to provide time and money for research. It behooves nurses to increase their skill in writing grants to compete for research funds. With involvement in carrying out research or product testing for health care manufacturing companies, funds might be set aside for research and continuing education. It is important for nurse educators and researchers to learn more about nurses' ways of knowing (Belenky et al., 1986) and to make needed changes in their education.

Nurse researchers must look beyond the dominant example—i.e., logical positivist approaches for knowledge—and develop methods that will answer the questions that exist in the profession. The dominant paradigm approach, although scientific, does not address the complexities of human responses, which are the core of nursing; rather, it is a method developed for the natural sciences, not the human sciences.

In reviewing nursing's history and current models, it is clear that progress has been made. Progress continues slowly and education provides only a partial answer. All nurses in practice are encouraged to establish links and to address the research issues relevant to their particular work. With the increasing governmental involvement in health care, nursing's opportunity to demonstrate its impact is at hand.

Nurses need to continue that forward movement toward the goal of research-based practice. As both academic and service settings are focusing more on research, each should look to the other for growth. Research then can indeed be the vital link for closing the gap between education and practice.

## REFERENCES

Ashley, J. (1976). *Hospitals, paternalism, and the role of the nurse.* New York: Columbia University, Teachers College Press.

Aydelotte, M. (1985). Approaches to conjoining nursing education and practice. In J. McCloskey and H. Grace (Eds.), pp. 288-316. *Current issues in nursing.* Boston: Blackwell Scientific Publications.

Belenky, M., Clinchy, B., Goldbager, N., & Tanile, J. (1986). *Women's ways of knowing: The developing of self, voice, and mind.* New York: Basic Books.

Brown, S., Tanner, C., & Padrick, K. (1984). Nursing's search for scientific knowledge. *Nursing Research, 33,* 26-32.

Chinn, P. (1986). *New methodologies in nursing research.* Rockville, Md.: Aspen Publishers, Inc.

Dolan, J. (1983). *Nursing in society: A historical perspective.* Philadelphia: W.B. Saunders.

Fawcett, J. (1980). A declaration of nursing independence: The relation of theory and research to nursing practice. *The Journal of Nursing Administration, 10,* 36-39.

Fawcett, J. (1985). A typology of nursing research activities according to educational preparation. *Journal of Professional Nursing, 1,* 75-78.

Grace, H. (1981). Unification, reunification; reconciliation or collaboration: Bridging the education/service gap. In J. McCloskey & H. Grace (Eds.), *Current issues in nursing.* Boston: Blackwell Scientific Publications.

Hunt, V., Stark, J., & Fisher, F. (1983). Networking: A managerial strategy for research development in a service setting. *The Journal of Nursing Administration, 12,* 27-32.

Jacox, A. (1974). Nursing research and the clinician. *Nursing Outlook, 22,* 382-385.

Kirchoff, K. (1983). Using research in practice: Should staff nurses be expected to use research? *Western Journal of Nursing Research, 5,* 245-247.

Kritek, P. (November 9, 1986). Class discussion. University of Wisconsin-Milwaukee School of Nursing.

Krueger, J. (1978). Nursing administrators role in research: The WICHE program. *Nursing Administrator Quarterly, 2,* 27-31.

Lindeman, C.A., & Krueger, J.C. (1977). Increasing the quality of nursing research. *Nursing Outlook, 25,* 450-454.

Loomis, M.E., & Krone, K.P. (1980). Collaborative research development. *The Journal of Nursing Administration, 10,* 32-35.

Marchette, L. (1985). Developing a productive nursing research program in a clinical institution. *The Journal of Nursing Administration, 15,* 25-30.

McClure, M. (1981). Promoting practice-based research: A critical need. *The Journal of Nursing Administration, 11,* 66-74.

Miller, P. (1985). The nurse training act: A historical perspective. *Advances in Nursing Science, 7,* 47-65.

Munhill, P. (1986). Methodological issues in nursing research: Beyond a wax apple. *Advances in Nursing Science, 8,* 1-5.

Reynolds, M., & Haller, K. (1986). Using research in practice: A case for replication in nursing, Part 1. *Western Journal of Nursing Research, 8* (1), 113-116.

Spatt, L., Gonas, E., Hying, S., Kirsch, E., & Koch, M. (1986). Informational needs of families of intensive care unit patients. *Quality Review Bulletin, 12* (1), 16-21.

Strickland, O., Waltz, C., & Lenz, E. (1986). Measurement of research variables in nursing. In P. Chinn (Ed.), *Nursing research methodology: Issues and implementation.* Rockville, Md.: Aspen Publishers, Inc.

University of Maryland Clinical and Educational Measurement Project. University of Maryland School of Nursing. Baltimore, MD. 1983-85.

Werley, H., & Westlake, S. (1984). Impact of nursing research on public policy. *Journal of Professional Nursing, 1,* 19.

Zalar, M., Welches, L., & Walker, D. (1985). Nursing consortium approach to increase research in service settings. *The Journal of Nursing Administration, 15,* 36-41.

# Chapter 10

# Protection of Human Subjects

*Peggy L. Wagner*

*Protection of human subjects is a professional obligation no matter what the scope of the research. This chapter describes the development of ethical standards in the health professions, reviews key concepts, and describes modes of implementation. Human subject committees in a setting which promotes scientific investigations also enhance professional development and accountability for nurses involved in expanded quality assurance studies and other research.*

The growth of professionalism stimulates curiosity related to nursing; the natural outgrowth of inquiry is research. When nurses engage in research of any magnitude with patients or clients, it is their professional responsibility to protect the subjects of studies from physical or psychological harm. As staff nurses expand quality assurance or engage in other research, they have the opportunity to demonstrate their professional commitment by holding themselves and their colleagues accountable for protection of human subjects.

In institutions where such a supportive climate and structure is lacking, research may have negative consequences for patients. In such entities, nurses may not give consideration to human subjects' concerns, believing their research to be benign or inconsequential as to potential harm or risks. Consequences of such belief include negative or problem situations such as the following:

- A patient with myocardial infarction, as a precursor to an inpatient cardiac rehabilitation program revision, is interviewed by the primary

87

nurse soon after stabilization. A structured guide is used to determine learning needs. The interview is conducted without explanation and no time is allowed for patient questions. The 30-minute experience leaves the patient frustrated and severely fatigued.

- Patients on a medical floor are asked to complete a questionnaire giving their opinion as to the promptness of answering call lights. Although patients are assured that their answers will be kept confidential, the night nurse who is tabulating data in the nursing station is called away, leaving exposed a questionnaire that has complaints about one particular nursing assistant. As this nursing assistant passes the desk, her eye catches her name on the questionnaire and she reads it. The next time the patient calls, the nursing assistant struggles with passive anger that is evident to the patient.

- A graduate student is conducting a survey of employees regarding stressors on an oncology unit. Demographic data are collected, including the sex of the respondents. The only male nurse on the staff is quite candid in his opinions about the head nurse, feeling she is an inept manager and causes disorganization on the unit. When the head nurse receives her copy of the results she calls the male nurse into her office and confronts him with his answers.

Although these situations are fictional, they are not outside the realm of possibility in any nursing department that begins to engage in research without paying attention to the professional responsibility of human subject protection. These incidents bring up questions as to consent, risk, confidentiality and anonymity, and methodology that are germane to a discussion of the rights of human subjects. Nurses must understand the rationale and the full implications of such protection before designing their studies. A historical development with a description of standards of review follows.

## HISTORY

The development of protocols for protection of human subjects is relatively recent. Several key steps document the development of the current guidelines. Initial attempts to clarify human rights in research were an outgrowth of the Nazi prison camps and date to 1946. The Nuremberg code was the first formal declaration of the rights of subjects and emphasized voluntary consent. In 1948 the Declaration of Geneva, which forbade nontherapeutic research, was adopted by the World Medical Association. The first federal guidelines in the United States were approved in 1951. In 1964 the Declaration of Helsinki included statements on nontherapeutic research and proxy consent. In 1973, the then Department of Health, Education, and Welfare (DHEW) drafted policies and procedures for the protection of human subjects and in 1975 defined the essential components of informed consent.

The *Belmont Report* was developed by the National Committee for the Protection of Human Subjects in Biomedical and Behavioral Research in 1979 (OPRR, 1979). It dealt primarily with informed consent with vulnerable populations and summarized prior recommendations on guidelines for fetuses, psychosurgery, children, and institutionalized subjects of research (Bandman, 1985; Davis, 1981; Watson, 1982).

Codes of ethics for nursing researchers were established by the American Nurses' Association (ANA) in 1968. Its Human Rights Guidelines, published in 1975, established the role of the nurse as patient advocate in clinical research and state nursing associations as avenues for grievances alleging violation of human rights. Other specialty groups in nursing such as the American Association of Critical Care Nurses (AACN, 1984) have since established standards for nursing research.

## STANDARDS FOR REVIEW

### Federal Guidelines

The Federal Guidelines (OPRR, 1983) are the foundation for protection of human subjects in research. These mandate the structure and function of institutional review boards (IRBs). IRBs are committees charged with reviewing studies that are conducted by or receive funding from the Department of Health and Human Services. Protection of human subjects (POHS) committees are not accountable to the federal regulations. In any case, the Federal Guidelines constitute the most comprehensive and up-to-date standard for protection of human subjects.

Under these guidelines, IRBs are responsible for deciding whether the risk of a study is worth the benefit, assuring that the welfare of subjects is protected adequately, and determining the legality of informed consent (Abramson, Meisel, & Safar, 1981, p. 2; Benson, Roth, & Winslade, 1985, p. 1332). Issues related to these responsibilities include: (1) informed consent, (2) risks of research, (3) vulnerable populations and captive subjects, (4) effective functioning of IRBs, (5) qualifications of researchers, and (6) fiduciary relationships.

### Informed Consent

Informed consent is important in all research. Davis (1985, p. 40) identifies principles of informed consent: that humans have unique dignity and worth;

that humans are not to be used as a means, but always as an end; and that everyone has the right to life, liberty, and the pursuit of happiness. The basic components of informed consent include recognition of self-determination (i.e., the right to refuse) and comprehension of proposed participation (Hayter, 1979, p. 71).

A written document of consent should be made available to each subject and should include:

1. a statement that the study involves research; an explanation of the purpose, description and duration of subject's participation; and a description of the experimental procedures
2. potential risks and/or discomfort
3. benefits to the subject or to others
4. alternative treatments
5. confidentiality
6. compensation for injury
7. whom to contact regarding questions/concerns
8. voluntary participation and withdrawal without penalty (OPRR, 1983, p. 940).

Research on informed consent shows that patients do not have good recall of information in the consent and that they sometimes do not even remember giving consent (Kennedy & Lillehaugen, 1979). In fact, even after informed consent, patients have claimed not to know that they were participating in a research study, confusing treatment with research (Benson, et al., 1985). This may be a particular problem if the caregiver is the researcher or, in the case of nursing, if the patient does not understand that one role of nurses may be as researchers (May, 1979).

Silva and Sorrell (1984) identify the following factors as influencing understanding of informed consent:

• the amount, clarity, and complexity of information
• how the consent was explained and by whom
• the education and vocabulary levels of the subjects
• patients' health, patterns of recall (time elapsed/time of day), and attitude toward the research process.

Added factors include the patient's emotional state and relationship with the physician and the hospital (Kennedy & Lillehaugen, 1979). Older subjects may present additional barriers to informed consent because of distrust of the researcher, visual and auditory limitations, effects of senility, and fear of signing documents (Kelly & McClelland, 1979).

To assure true informed consent, in which the subjects understand their role in the study and consent willingly, the content and process of the consent must be scrutinized. Caregivers should be separated clearly from the research process when possible. Patients should be told as much as they want to know about the research in understandable terms (Davis, 1985). It is the responsibility of the researcher to determine what information the subject needs in order to give consent knowledgeably and yet balance total disclosure without information overload (Miller, 1982, p. 305).

To maximize understanding, Silva and Sorrell recommend that informed consent be a written statement that is clear, brief, and direct; that the amount of information be perceived as not too much or too little; that subjects have a day or longer to digest information before signing their consent; and that individuals such as those in poor physical or emotional health, the elderly, and persons with lower educational and vocabulary levels be given extra assistance to understand (1984, pp. 238-239).

Some nurse researchers believe that informed consent obstructs the research process and is not necessary for projects involving minimal risk (Noble, 1985). However, conscientious control over the process based on standards should not impede sound research conducted by qualified researchers. The serious business of protecting rights of clients is an ethical obligation of nursing professionals (Corah, 1977; Oberst, 1985).

In further defense of informed consent, Gardner (1978, p. 633) shows that the perception of control of participation reduces negative aftereffects of research and that the signing of the consent form results in a sense of commitment to the study. This is significant in view of documented feelings and reactions of informed research subjects: suspicion of deceit by the researcher, desire to please the researcher, and desire to undermine the researcher (Corah, 1977, p. 266).

## Risks of Research

The IRB or POHS committee has the responsibility of protecting subjects from research where risk outweighs benefits. Corah (1977, p. 267) believes that in most cases, if a study has some reasonable benefit and low risk, it should be done. Risk can fall on a continuum from none to life threatening (Kopelman, 1981).

The Federal Guidelines define minimal risk as when "the risks of harm anticipated in the proposed research are not greater, considering probability and magnitude, than those ordinarily encountered in daily life or during the performance of routine physical or psychological examinations or tests" (OPRR, 1983, p. 6). Risks can be physiological in nature—for example, in experimentation with new medications or procedures—or psychological, including the invasion of privacy, breach of confidence, overtesting, stigmatization, or loss of self-esteem (Kopelman, 1981, p. 5).

Risks inherent in everyday life do not need to be acknowledged on the consent form (Corah, 1977, p. 266)—for example, the risk of driving to the study site. Although ideally the benefits of study return directly to subjects (Levine, 1981, p. 63), they can be for the purpose of knowledge or human welfare or for the researcher (Corah, 1977, p. 266). Some caution is needed to be sure that the quality of the study is such that the time spent by the subject is worthwhile and, to that extent, the POHS committee must consider study methodology in assigning a risk/benefit ratio.

## Vulnerable Populations

Several populations have been referred to as being vulnerable. The Federal Guidelines (OPRR, 1983) define protected populations as including children, pregnant women, fetuses, and prisoners, and provide additional safeguards for review. Subjects with mental or psychological disorders; with physical illness, particularly those with chronic illness; the dying; and the comatose or brain dead have also been identified by several authors as needing additional safeguards for additional review (Fletcher, Dommel, & Cowell, 1985; Levine, 1981). Select elderly also are particularly vulnerable because of financial constraints, physical or mental impairment, institutionalization, and being without family (Davis, 1981).

Special issues arise as to the validity of consent for research involving emergency care (Abramson, Meisel, & Safar, 1981; Brody & Miller, 1981). State and federal laws also may restrict using the medical records of some populations, e.g., alcohol, drug and psychiatric-related admissions and those with developmental disabilities (Federal Drug and Alcohol Abuse Regulations, 1985; Wisconsin State Mental Health Act, 1985).

Captive populations such as hospitalized clients, employees (e.g., staff nurses), and students also deserve special consideration (Christakis, 1985). These readily available subjects may perceive that participation in studies is mandatory and that failure to comply will result in a different level of care or a poor evaluation or grade. As captive populations they also may be submitted to multiple studies (Lackey, 1986). Suggestions for protecting them are to recruit subjects in a group, rather than individually; to include their representative on a review board to speak as an advocate for these groups; to develop policies and procedures that define the extent of their participation; and to outline the research expectations as (for nurses and students) a condition of employment (ANA, 1975).

Most problems related to vulnerable populations can be handled according to a protocol developed by each individual institution, provided the researcher has justification for using the group and that sufficient groundwork has been laid either in literature or in previous research using other groups as subjects.

## Qualification of Researchers

Nursing researchers have varying degrees of preparation in a variety of fields. Hospitals may have research requests in the nursing department from clinical specialists, staff nurses, nurse managers, students, and a variety of researchers from other institutions or universities. The IRB or POHS committee must be assured that such investigators are qualified for their part in the study. Credentials must be verified. The reputation of a well-known investigator should not sway the committee from careful review of the protocol and monitoring of compliance (Pattullo, 1985, p. 7).

Although the committee does not want to perpetuate a reputation that instills fear into researchers, there are standards that must be enforced no matter who is the principal researcher. Students sometimes come poorly prepared, with questionable protocols and rigid time constraints (Robb, 1981, p. 29). The ANA (1975, p. 9) imposes the following restrictions on hospitals (or other sites) as to sponsorship of outside researchers:

1. agreement with aims, purpose, and importance of study
2. proposal translated into format required by IRB
3. minimal risk
4. no undue costs
5. faculty approval before submission
6. permission by disciplines involved
7. ample time between application for approval and data collection
8. adherence to IRB approval procedure.

This process of protecting human subjects should not hinder the search for new knowledge. It can be enhanced if the organizational system works collaboratively with universities and other institutions in accordance with predetermined standards.

## Fiduciary Relationships

The relationship between a researcher and a subject can be assumed to be "fiduciary" in nature, i.e., an inequality by virtue of power, skill, knowledge, or opportunity exists (Cupples & Gochnauer, 1985, p. 2). One of the pair necessarily is in a dependent position. Examples include a physician-patient or nurse-patient relationship, which can become confusing to patients as caregivers assume the additional role of researchers.

The integrity of the relationship relies on the fact that it is used for the benefit of the dependent person (Cupples & Gochnauer, 1985, p. 2). The nature of this relationship justifies the need for informed consent and an ability to withdraw without recrimination (Cupples & Gochnauer, 1985, p. 4); it also reinforces the necessity of the IRB to investigate and monitor research activity.

## Effective IRBs

The Federal Guidelines (OPRR, 1983) clearly outline the structure and function of IRBs. The committee is to be composed of members with varying backgrounds—i.e., not entirely men or women or members of one profession, at least one nonscientist, and one member not affiliated with the institution. Such a committee should provide a broader perspective on human subjects issues. The committee screens or reviews protocols according to criteria in the following categories: (1) no review, (2) review by a committee representative and exempt from full committee review, and (3) review by the full committee (OPRR, 1983).

Although exempt review of studies with minimal risk can expedite the functioning of the committee, there are exceptions in which discussion of the protocol by the entire committee is appropriate. These studies include: (1) greater than minimal risk, (2) sensitive information, (3) protected populations, (4) data that can be linked to the subject, and (5) information that could place the subject at risk of legal/financial liability.

Although many hospitals have IRBs, and their expectations are spelled out clearly, Gray (1975) finds that most committees are not active, i.e., do not revise/reject protocols and do not monitor compliance. In committees that are active, recommendations focus on incomplete consents, research design, safety of procedures, and means of obtaining informed consent.

Gulick (1981, p. 26) recommends that directors of nursing clearly define a process for review of nursing responsibility and that a single person not assume responsibility. Robb (1981) suggests that a nurse maintain membership on multidisciplinary IRBs to acquire increased appreciation of other members for behavioral research, to provide an alternative viewpoint, to prevent exploitation of nurses as uninformed data collectors, and to coordinate studies with nursing department activities.

## PROTECTION OF HUMAN SUBJECTS COMMITTEES

Many health care entities, such as community hospitals, do not have IRBs. However, implementation of a system for reviewing nursing research facilitates positive outcomes of inquiry at all levels.

### Models

Although the Federal Guidelines outline the structure and function of IRBs, many different models exist to fit and fill the needs of hospital, university, and other systems. Stopp (1985) in a study of IRBs in academic settings identifies three basic models: (1) the centralized IRB, which reviews every proposed research project involving human subjects; (2) the ad hoc IRB subgroup, whose members review specific projects, usually because of their expertise; and (3) dispersed independent groups, in which nonfunded and minimal risk projects are reviewed at the level of the department or school and others referred on to the IRB.

Many health care institutions with IRBs seem to function with a centralized board consisting primarily of physicians. An alternate system for nursing incorporating a dispersed independent group approach was developed at St. Michael Hospital. The Nursing Department has its own POHS committee, which reviews nursing studies involving minimal risk, including program evaluations, quality assurance studies, clinical research, and outside research. Any studies involving greater than minimal risk, sensitive information, or protected populations, or are multidisciplinary, are forwarded to the medical staff research committee, which functions as the hospital IRB.

### Structure

The membership of this Nursing Committee includes a chairperson with an advanced degree in nursing, the chairperson of Nursing Quality Assurance, the research facilitator (ex officio), a physician, a rotating member of the Medical Staff Research Committee, and the vice president for patient services. Community members include a priest, an attorney, a nursing faculty member, a minority representative, a university scientist (with experience in protection of human subjects), and a nonscientist. Members rotate through two-year terms on a varied schedule.

The diverse backgrounds of the members provide for excellent discussion from several points of view. In view of increased research using nursing staff members as subjects, an important addition to the panel would be a staff nurse.

**Exhibit 10-1**  Purpose and Objectives of the POHS Committee

*Purpose:* To protect the rights of patients and employees who are subjects of research conducted in the Department of Nursing at St. Michael Hospital in accordance with the federal guidelines.

*Objectives:*

1. To review nonexempt studies that involve minimum risk to the subject
2. To protect anonymity and confidentiality of subjects
3. To protect populations at risk
4. To assure voluntary participation and informed consent
5. To weigh the risk/benefit of studies
6. To identify studies with greater than minimum risk for referral to the Medical Staff Research Committee

## Process

The purpose and objectives of this POHS committee are listed in Exhibit 10-1. These are rooted in the Federal Guidelines and approved by the entire committee.

Studies and program evaluations are submitted to the POHS chairperson by the research facilitator, who works closely with researchers to refine protocols before committee review. Quality assurance studies are screened by the QA chairperson. Many studies do not meet review criteria, such as chart audits on existing data or anonymous surveys. Others are forwarded to the POHS committee.

Because of the nature of the studies reviewed, many protocols can be expedited, reviewed, and approved by the chairperson. The most common reason for committee review is confidentiality of data and anonymity of subjects. The POHS committee makes sure that questionnaires cannot be linked to subjects and that code lists identifying subjects are safeguarded. Once in committee, the majority of recommendations focus on revision of informed consent, validity of questionnaire items regarding rights of participants, and protection of data.

This system has worked well for a community hospital. Although it is time consuming, the review of quality assurance studies and program evaluations has raised consciousness about human subjects issues for all members of the professional staff. Subject anonymity and confidentiality are considered with each project. Identifiers are used on questionnaires only when needed and, if used, are coded and protected. Researchers examine the need for demographic information and eliminate all that is unnecessary; for example, the sex of nurse subjects often is unnecessary and revealing of identity. Patients and staff subjects are given the clear option to withdraw their informed consent without recrimination.

Although the outcomes are highly professional, the process is not without problems. The diversity of experience of those on the committee can cause more knowledgeable members to control discussion or a member can focus too long on one small part of a study that relates to that individual's specialty. Solutions to process problems are to choose a committee chair skilled in group process and to implement ground rules, such as parliamentary procedure. Education of members through discussion and literature equalizes knowledge bases and results in more constructive committee action. Adaptation of Federal Guidelines also has helped with group problem solving.

Volunteer community members are busy in their own professions and need ample notification of meetings as well as time to review protocols. Since a quorum is necessary for protocol approval, members are given a yearly schedule of meetings and asked to respond when agendas are distributed. Researchers must meet a submission deadline, allowing three weeks for secretarial preparation of materials and distribution to members. Support and respect for the contribution of each member is integral to committee functioning.

Many outside researchers find these standards for protection of human subjects high and the process rigorous. However, the committee is committed to its task.

## Issues

Several interesting issues or suggestions have arisen since the committee was formed.

*1. Are there limitations on the use of medical records for study?*

The question arose regarding what is covered on research in the routine consent form that patients sign on admission. Although criteria for use of the medical record were clarified, committee discussion stimulated development of an additional policy on handling a chart where the consent had been altered. State statutes on use of records and protection of vulnerable subjects were reviewed and incorporated into practice.

*2. Are program evaluations/quality assurance studies considered research and do they require review?*

It is difficult to distinguish these from clinical research, so mechanisms were developed to review all evaluation research for human subjects concerns. According to the Federal Guidelines, research is "any systematic investigation designed to develop or contribute to generalizable knowledge and may include research activities related to demonstration or service programs" (OPRR, 1983, p. 5). As the designs of evaluation research become more sophisticated and data or process more generalizable, researchers share studies at poster sessions as part of a research conference, research presentations, and in professional publications that support the review of such investigations.

3. *Is single-case study methodology research or advanced practice?*

One issue discussed at length revolved around course requirements that graduate students perform a series of single-case studies on a topic of interest to them (e.g., try a given type of relaxation strategy and test response). Although experienced nurses practice according to this model—diagnose a patient problem and test various interventions to achieve an outcome—the process the students were engaging in was questioned at numerous institutions from the standpoint of protection of human subjects.

After debate and checking with the faculty, the committee expressed its concern that the students were focused on testing a predetermined intervention and the nurses on solving individual patient problems—a conceptual difference that changed scientific-based practice into a series of small research projects subject to review and control in terms of protection of human subjects.

4. *What is appropriate protection of data stored on computer disks or tapes?*

This concern arose when an outside researcher asked head nurses to use computers for problem solving and guaranteed confidentiality of information on the disk. Safeguards controlled the identifiers used on the disk and involved an access code known only to the subjects and researchers. Since the initial question, other studies involving computer data have been reviewed, drawing on the standards that were used as precedent by the committee.

Implementation of a mechanism for protection of human subjects in the Department of Nursing has been challenging and rewarding. Concerns related to protecting clients have led to effective problem solving by a diverse committee of health professionals and community representatives.

## VALUE

The concept of protecting human subjects is germane to the development of nursing as a profession. Nurses' concern for the welfare of patients establishes the desire to monitor and be accountable for their own practice. Judicious informed consent also may raise the consciousness of the public regarding the content and value of nursing research.

Nurses can identify with protection of human subjects as a mechanism for implementing their role as patient advocates. Awareness of the issues assures knowledgeable response to problem situations and increases the nurses' value as members of the health care team.

Patients will benefit the most from incorporation of principles of protection of human subjects into nursing practice. The knowledgeable choice to participate in and withdraw from research is a consumer right that all potential subjects should be guaranteed as they negotiate the health care system.

The nursing human subject committee was an inevitable outcome of expanded research activities. As more quality assurance studies involved patient participation, such as family needs assessment, assessment of the postpartum mother, and the assessment of the learning needs of congestive heart failure patients, staff members saw the need to submit their study to the POHS committee. Through participating in the process and defending the proposal, they learned a great deal about the ethical considerations of research. Those who have been through the process once become excellent resources for their colleagues.

Staff members also have the opportunity to interact with faculty members who are submitting proposals to the committee. This leads to a newfound respect for each other as they meet colleague to colleague when discussing research. This again reinforces the discussion in Chapter 9 supporting research.

## REFERENCES

Abramson, N., Meisel, A., & Safar, P. (1981). Resuscitation research and human rights. *Topics in Emergency Medicine, 3,* 1-9.

American Association of Critical Care Nurses. (1984). *Ethics in critical care research.* Newport Beach, Calif.: Author.

American Nurses' Association. (1975). *Human rights guidelines for nurses in clinical and other research* (Publication #D-46). Kansas City, Mo.: Author.

Bandman, E. (1985). Protection of human subjects. *Topics in Clinical Nursing, 7,* 15-23.

Benson, P., Roth, L., & Winslade, W. (1985). Informed consent in psychiatric research: Preliminary findings from an ongoing investigation. *Social Science and Medicine, 20,* 1331-1341.

Brody, H., & Miller, B. (1981). Informed consent in critical and emergency care research. *Topics in Emergency Medicine, 3,* 11-17.

Christakis, N. (1985). Do medical student research subjects need special protection? *IRB: A Review of Human Subjects Research, 7,* 1-6.

Corah, N. (1977). Behavioral science research: Ethical and policy implications. *Community Dentistry and Oral Epidemiology, 5,* 265-269.

Council on Dental Research. (1985). Human subjects in dental research: Coping with the regulations. *Journal of the American Dental Association, 110,* 243-246.

Cupples, B., & Gochnauer, M. (1985). The investigator's duty not to deceive. *IRB: A Review of Human Subjects Research, 7,* 1-6.

Davis, A. (1981). Ethical considerations in gerontological nursing research. *Geriatric Nursing, 2,* 269-272.

Davis, A. (1985). Informed consent: How much information is enough? *Nursing Outlook, 33,* 40-42.

Federal Drug and Alcohol Abuse Regulations, P.L. 93-282, 1985.

Fletcher, J., Dommel, F., & Cowell, D. (1985). Consent to research with impaired human subjects. *IRB: A Review of Human Subjects Research, 7,* 1-6.

Gardner, G. (1978). Effects of federal human subjects regulations on data obtained in environmental stressor research. *Journal of Personality and Social Psychology, 36,* 628-634.

Gray, B. (1975). An assessment of institutional review committees in human experimentation. *Medical Care, 13,* 318-329.

Gulick, E. (1981). Evaluating research requests: A model for the nursing director. *The Journal of Nursing Administration, 11,* 26-30.

Hayter, W. (1979). Issues related to human subjects. In F.S. Downs & J.W. Fleming (Eds.), *Issues in nursing research.* New York: Appleton-Century-Crofts.

Kelly, K., & McClelland, E. (1979). Signed consent: Protection or constraint? *Nursing Outlook, 27,* 40-42.

Kennedy, B., & Lillehaugen, A. (1979). Patient recall of informed consent. *Medical and Pediatric Oncology, 7,* 173-178.

Kopelman, L. (1981). Estimating risk in human research. *Clinical Research, 29,* 1-8.

Lackey, D.P. (1986). A single subject in multiple protocols: Is this risk equitable? *IRB: A Review of Human Subjects Research, 8,* 8-9.

Levine, R.J. (1981). *Ethics and regulation of clinical research.* Baltimore: Urban and Schwarzenberg.

May, K. (1979). The nurse as researcher: Impediment to informed consent. *Nursing Outlook, 27,* 36-39.

Miller, P. (1982). A guide to informed consent. *Dimensions of Critical Care Nursing, 1,* 304-306.

Noble, M. (1985). Written informed consent: Closing the door to clinical research. *Nursing Outlook, 33,* 292-293.

Oberst, M. (1985). Another look at informed consent. *Nursing Outlook, 33,* 294-295.

OPRR (Office for Protection from Research Risks). (1979, April 18). *The Belmont Report* (U.S. National Commission for the Protection of Human Subjects of Biomedical and Behavioral Research). Washington, D.C.: Department of Health, Education, and Welfare.

OPRR (Office for Protection from Research Risks). (1983, March 8). *Protection of human subjects* [Federal Guidelines], 45 C.F.R. 46.

Pattullo, E.L. (1985). The wages of sin. *IRB: A Review of Human Subjects Research, 7,* 7-8.

Robb, S. (1981). Nurse involvement in the institutional review boards: The service setting perspective. *Nursing Research, 30,* 27-29.

Silva, M., & Sorrell, J. (1984). Factors influencing comprehension of information for informed consent: Ethical implications for nursing research. *International Journal of Nursing Standards, 21,* 233-240.

Stopp, G. (1985). The internal IRB structure. Models in academic settings. *IRB: A Review of Human Subjects Research, 7,* 9.

Watson, A. (1982). Informed consent of special subjects. *Nursing Research, 31,* 43-47.

Wisconsin State Mental Health Act, Wis. Stat. §51-30 (1985).

---

## BIBLIOGRAPHY

Angoff, N. (1985). Against special protection for medical students. *International Research Bulletin, 7,* 9-10.

Grodin, M., Azharoff, B., & Kaminow, P. (1986). A 12-year audit of IRB decisions. *Quality Review Bulletin, 12,* 82-86.

Irwin, M., et al. (1985). Psychotic patient's understanding of informed consent. *American Journal of Psychiatry, 142*, 1351-1354.

Jonsen, A. (1978). Research involving children: Recommendations of the National Commission for the Protection of Human Subjects of Biomedical and Behavioral Research. *Pediatrics, 62*, 131-136.

Knepper, J. (1982). Use of human subjects in experimentation. *Journal of the American Medical Research Association, 53*, 70-74.

Northrop, C. (1985). The ins and outs of informed consent. *Nursing 85, 15*, 9.

Porter, J. (1986). What are the ideal characteristics of unaffiliated/nonscientist IRB members? *International Research Bulletin, 8*, 1-6.

Sturges, J., & Sternberg, D. (1985). Family concerns about hospitalizing a patient in a psychiatric research unit. *Hospital and Community Psychiatry, 36*, 1187-1191.

# Part IV

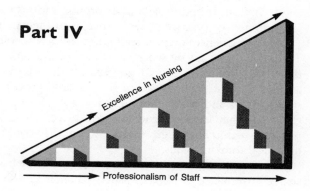

Excellence in Nursing

Professionalism of Staff

---

# Shared
# Governance

*Peggy L. Wagner*
Section Editor

The unit-based quality assurance structure provides staff nurses with several important experiences: working together as a staff group on their unit in an organized manner with purposeful direction and goals; opportunities to experience various group roles such as leader, facilitator, initiator, recorder, and technician (responsible for performing various tasks for the group); and an awareness of practice issues particular to their unit.

These experiences prepare staff nurses for a new role in shared governance. The skills they gain by working as part of a group could be transferred to their involvement in shared governance. In addition, the experience they acquire in critical thinking and the research process prepares them for responsibilities and accountabilities they face. Having learned to question and challenge, they could extend this skill to yet another structured, safe environment within shared governance where they could continue development of critical thinking skills.

This section focuses on preparedness for and beginning experiences in shared governance (see Book Model). Chapter 11 offers an overview of shared governance, followed in Chapter 12 by a review of organizational design with key indicators to be considered when planning a shared governance model.

Chapters 13, 14, and 15 present various components of such a model at St. Michael Hospital. What is important is that these three chapters were written by staff nurses who have had a big part in developing the system, both as chairpersons of the Staff Nurse Conference Group and the Nursing Practice Council. Their examples and perceptions are based on their experiences and are valuable for gaining insight into the significance of shared governance for staff nurses.

# Chapter 11

# An Overview of Shared Governance

*SueEllen Pinkerton*

*Shared governance is the organizational structure that provides an environment for autonomous staff nurse practice. It is the structure of the 1980s, the structure that accommodates professionals in a bureaucratic setting, the structure that tackles a history of subservience and dominance.*

This chapter presents a brief overview of the shared governance structure of the nursing department at St. Michael Hospital (SMH). This lays the groundwork for the substantive discussions on the process of implementation, the beneficial outcomes, and the perceptive insights of the staff nurses who were instrumental in helping to shape the system. Their accounting of the details of the process and of the shared governance system follows in Chapters 13, 14, and 15.

Shared governance is a model that helps with the transition from the traditional bureaucratic structure:

- It moves nurses from subservient to autonomous roles by giving them authority over practice decisions.
- It values the contributions of nurses in the changing health care system by recognizing their clinical expertise.
- It builds trust by teaching groups to work together in an environment of openness, self-disclosure, and inner honesty (see Chapter 2).

- It clarifies communication and reduces uncertainty by giving staff nurses direct access to information and access to persons who can clarify the information.
- It promotes quality performance and attitudes by giving the persons doing the major work of the organization (staff nurses) the authority for practice decision making.
- It results in high productivity, low absenteeism, and low turnover by creating a work environment where job satisfaction is high.
- It values and promotes advancement in and of the profession.

## FIRST STEPS

Several nurses have been forerunners associated with advanced systems of shared governance, including Lois Johnson (1983), Tim Porter-O'Grady (1986), Porter-O'Grady and S. Finnigan (1984), and Marlys Peterson and D. Allen (1986a, 1986b). Reports of the shared governance systems differ in that they are tailored to accommodate organizational readiness and variances and involve a process that will continue. Deciding to embark on a shared governance system is laudable. Each step of growth is marked by numerous achievements attesting to the depth and breadth of the dissemination of the concepts and the levels of commitment.

Based on edited works by Adams (1984) in *Transforming Work*, Peterson and Allen (1986a) outline the factors associated with needed changes in health care as it is experiencing the trauma of societal change: (1) lack of confidence in organizations due to layoffs and job insecurity with concomitant diminishing authority base of organizations due to the loss of power and stability of the organizations, (2) changed commitments of the workers to the organization with less identity of the worker with the organization and higher expectations of leaders in the organization, and (3) increased technology resulting in a need for complex systems and restructuring of organizations for communicating information. Peterson and Allen then present the need for transformation. "Old management attitudes and structures must give way to renewed commitment to the individuals who make up the organization. The underlying belief is that responsible participation can serve to empower the whole and create a work life that is meaningful and satisfying to everyone" (1986a, p. 10).

In implementing a shared governance system, a planning process is necessary. Literature, videotapes, consultants, workshops, and samples of bylaws all are available to help the individuals involved become familiar with the underlying concepts (autonomy, accountability, responsibility, authority, control, and critical thinking) and with the variety of structures. These ideas should be shared with the planning group, which must include staff nurses.

Peterson and Allen (1986b) describe implementation of a shared governance system as a transformation of the organization. Their strategies for transformation include:

1. Commitment of staff members to the philosophy of the transformation
2. Demonstrating beliefs of the system through actions
3. Publishing a decision making grid to accommodate staff input while avoiding having it become a cumbersome process
4. Timely communications
5. Openness to feedback
6. Helping staff members develop communication skills
7. Promoting accountability and responsibility of staff members
8. Establishing structures and systems for participation of all staff members in shared governance
9. Developing accountable, responsible, approachable, and visible leaders and managers
10. Teaching, guiding, and directing staff so they can effect change; this requires relinquishing control and developing trust in so doing.

## STRUCTURE

The structure of shared governance at St. Michael Hospital is depicted in Figure 11-1. It is divided organizationally into the management structure on the right and the practice structure on the left. Both make decisions using the philosophies and concepts listed in the center.

## PRACTICE STRUCTURE

Each type of nursing position at St. Michael Hospital has a conference group, governed by goals, objectives, and, in some instances, bylaws. This means there are five conference groups: director of nursing, clinical nurse specialist, head nurse, assistant head nurse, and staff nurses. Except for the staff nurses, all nurses in a specific-type of position are members of their conference group. The staff nurses elect a member for each nursing unit.

The conference groups are linked by a Nursing Practice Council (NPC) to make practice decisions. One member from each conference group, with the exception of the Staff Nurse Conference Group (SNCG), is elected to the NPC. All SNCG members are members of the NPC since this provides a more direct route to the nursing units and the staff nurses with whom they communicate. No other conference group entails such a large group of nurses.

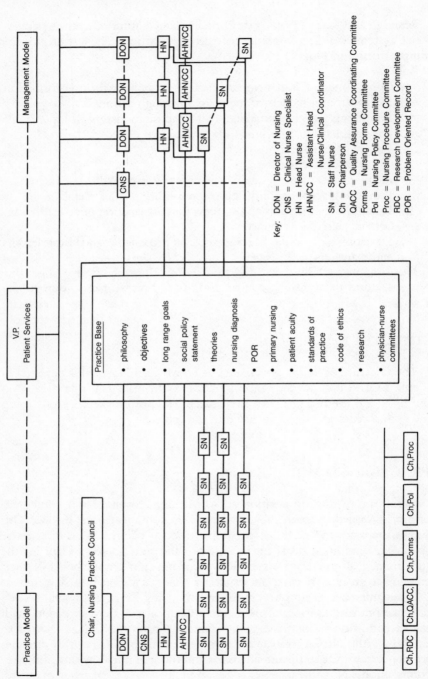

Key:  DON = Director of Nursing
      CNS = Clinical Nurse Specialist
      HN = Head Nurse
      AHN/CC = Assistant Head
               Nurse/Clinical Coordinator
      SN = Staff Nurse
      Ch = Chairperson
      QACC = Quality Assurance Coordinating Committee
      Forms = Nursing Forms Committee
      Pol = Nursing Policy Committee
      Proc = Nursing Procedure Committee
      RDC = Research Development Committee
      POR = Problem Oriented Record

**Figure 11-1** Shared Governance Model

The NPC is governed by bylaws (explained in Chapter 13). More details on the NPC and the SNCG are presented in Chapters 13, 14, and 15, along with explanations and examples of committee structure.

Four standing committees report to the NPC: Policy and Procedure, Quality Assurance, Forms, and Research. The NPC approves/disapproves policies, procedures, and requests from the committees. The NPC also may form task forces to investigate particular issues or problems.

## MANAGEMENT STRUCTURE

The management structure is in the traditional form with the exception that staff nurse input is sought for management decisions.

Achieving shared governance has not been without problems, but progress was continuing. There was (and continued to be) resistance at all levels, although persistent objectors learned to be more covert. In an open system such as shared governance, individuals are free to share, so their particular problems quickly become known or are obvious because of their behaviors or symptoms. Reaching the point where all participants are comfortable in their roles and are professional in their behaviors seemed like something that would never happen. However, it must be kept in mind that a history of conduct was being changed, and success in attaining such a goal in less than a decade would be phenomenal.

Peterson and Allen (1986a) describe similar experiences. They cite first-line managers as an essential link between beliefs and practice; they are also the group most challenged and most threatened by the system. An openness to feedback must be maintained to avoid barriers and the loss of vital information which needs to be communicated to managers. Being successful involves a supportive, open structure with a willingness to teach and learn.

The role of vice president for patient services has been traditional in the management structure at St. Michael. In the new governance, the vice president has acted as an adviser to the NPC and as a nonvoting member of SNCG. This has countless benefits from the perspective of gaining valuable insights and observing staff nurse perceptions. Participation enhances communication and credibility and provides an opportunity for input into professional development.

Johnson (1987) describes signs of success of the shared governance system at Rose Medical Center in Denver, with an annual attrition rate of less than 12 percent and a significant five-year retention rate. These factors, translated to money, mean fewer dollars spent on recruiting and orienting new personnel, and more experienced nurses present on nursing units to care for patients. Johnson also cites greater than average satisfaction with general working conditions and positive comments from physicians acknowledging that the quality of nursing care is a key reason for admitting patients to Rose.

In a program designed to promote professional nursing accountability through a model which incorporated self-governance, Ethridge (1987) reports decreased nurses' job stress and increased job satisfaction as measured in 1983, 1985, and 1987. Turnover rate of nurses also decreased from 15.2 percent in 1983 to 5.4 percent in 1987. Again, this saves dollars on recruitment and orientation of new nurses.

Ethridge also attributes a decreased length of hospital stay for Medicare patients to professional nurse case managers, thus increasing the profit under the DRG reimbursement system. She also indicates that there is a definite link between nursing centers, which have been established in the community to extend care to persons and families, and the increase in hospital census. For the numerous programs implemented at St. Mary's Hospital and Health Center in Tucson which have been designed to promote professional nurse accountability, actual savings have exceeded $500,000.

At St. Michael Hospital, a study to measure change as a result of the shared governance system showed no change in nine months (Pinkerton, 1985), a fact not so surprising since the time factor was so short.

In a study completed by Kramer (personal communication, June 30, 1986) at St. Michael Hospital as part of a national study, several interesting results were reported by her which supported confidence in staff nurses' accountability and responsibility:

1. Very high autonomy scores for staff nurses (90, with 100 being very high and usually a score associated with nurses in education, nursing service leadership positions, and academic settings).
2. Patient rights scores of 59, with high scores beginning at 60.
3. Rejection of traditional role limitations reported at 51, with high scores beginning at 52.
4. Internal locus of control scores at 37, with high scores beginning at 37.
5. Results of role behavior testing indicate that nurses at St. Michael Hospital need to work more on balancing the professional and bureaucratic conflict; their scores tended to be higher toward a bureaucratic role conception.
6. The measurement of their self-concept showed them low in care but high in cure, coordination, and personal and professional development. They scored moderately high on self-esteem, meaning that as a group they think well of themselves.

These facts support a professional rather than bureaucratic structure for the practice of nursing. Shared governance may be enacted differently in different organizations, but the underlying concepts remain constant. These concepts are empirically supported and provide direction and courage for the future.

**REFERENCES**

Adams, J. (1984). *Transforming work*. Alexandria, Va.: Miles River Press.

Ethridge, P. (1987). Nurse accountability program improves satisfaction, turnover. *Health Progress, 68,* 44-49.

Johnson, L.M. (1983). A model of participatory management with decentralized authority. *Nursing Administration Quarterly, 13,* 30-36.

Johnson, L.M. (1987). Self-governance: Treatment for an unhealthy nursing culture. *Health Progress, 68,* 41-43.

Kramer, M. (June 30, 1986). Personal communications.

Peterson, M.E., & Allen, D.G. (1986a). Shared governance: A strategy for transforming work, Pt. 1. *Journal of Nursing Administration, 16,* 9-12.

Peterson, M.E., & Allen, D.G. (1986b). Shared governance: A strategy for transforming work, Pt. 2. *Journal of Nursing Administration, 16,* 11-16.

Pinkerton, S.E. (1985). *Evaluation of Shared Governance in a Nursing Department*. Milwaukee: St. Michael Hospital.

Porter-O'Grady, T. (1986). *Creative nursing administration: Participative management into the 21st century*. Rockville, Md.: Aspen Publishers, Inc.

Porter-O'Grady, T., & Finnigan, S. (1984). *Shared governance for nursing*. Rockville, Md.: Aspen Publishers, Inc.

# Chapter 12

# Assessment of Organizational Structure for Readiness to Decentralize

*Margaret Meyer*

Decentralization, in terms of decisionmaking power within an organization, exists to the extent that power is dispersed among many individuals (Mintzberg, 1979). When an organization is composed of professionals, it is assumed that it has within it a high degree of individual expertise available for decisionmaking. Decentralization may take place formally, if the executives merge this expert power with formal authority; it also may occur less formally but with concomitant difficulties.

This chapter describes the components of organizational structure and development, comparing traditional and professional bureaucracies. It also discusses indicators of professionalism among the nurses in a nursing department that reflect their readiness to decentralize decisionmaking.

It is inherent in the role and responsibilities of leaders to recognize the needs of an organization and its members. Salmond (1985, p. 296) indicates that leaders may choose between preparing members of an organization to anticipate and accept the change to a more decentralized structure or implementing the change and supporting the members after change takes place. Either course requires planning of the strategies to be used to assure the highest probability of success. An understanding of organizational structures and organizational development is essential in analyzing corporate cultures in planning for change.

# STRUCTURE, DEVELOPMENT, AND EVOLUTION

## Typical Structures

The structure of an organization is defined by Mintzberg (1979, p. 2) as the total of the ways in which an entity divides its work into distinct tasks and then achieves coordination among them. When tasks and workers are few, the organizational structure may be simple. As the nature of the tasks becomes more involved and the number of employees increases, the structure becomes more complex—a blend of formal and informal mechanisms for coordination of the work.

A typical organizational structure that delineates the official lines of communication is composed of an operating component, or operating core, consisting of workers who produce goods or services, and an administrative component, or strategic apex, consisting of top-level strategic managers and middle managers. The various levels of managers comprise the formal chain of command from the strategic apex to the operating core. However, workers also establish an informal mechanism of authority and communication within the structure. Decisionmaking then occurs within this framework of formal and informal processes, both of which must be understood and recognized by all members of the organization.

Gibson, Ivancevich, and Donnelly (1982, p. 353) identify the elements of organizational theorist Max Weber that compose the ideal bureaucratic structure: (1) division of labor; (2) control by rules so that official decisions assure uniformity, predictability, and stability; (3) chain of command; (4) impersonal relationships so that control over people and activities can be established more efficiently; (5) career orientation.

## Professional Bureaucracy

Professional nurses, educated to function autonomously, may find it difficult to adjust to the hospital bureaucracy with its regulations, hierarchy of authority, and segmentation of work (Ketefian, 1985, p. 249). Professional work involves service to people and a human relations model, rather than the output of uniform products or a bureaucratic model. Human relations skills and the ability to deal with nonuniform events are requisites for professionals. Litwak (1961, pp. 181-184) developed a model of a bureaucracy that incorporates elements of the typical bureaucracy and the human relations model. This structure is termed the professional bureaucracy.

Table 12-1 compares the structural elements of traditional and professional bureaucracies. Traditional organizational structures may demonstrate attainment of a number of the attributes of a professional bureaucracy. Differences between

**Table 12-1** Comparison of Bureaucratic Structures

| Traditional Bureaucracy | Professional Bureaucracy |
|---|---|
| **Specialization of Tasks** | |
| • Narrow scope of activities | • Broad scope of activities (horizontal specialization) |
| • Unskilled or semiskilled | • Highly skilled |
| • Tasks learned on the job or in technical programs | • Education in institutions of higher learning, followed by extensive orientation following employment |
| • Completion of tasks that depend on close cooperation with others | • Work performed independently of colleagues, but in close relationship with clients |
| **Rules and Regulations** | |
| • Standards determined by technical experts | • Standards determined by professional associations outside organization |
| • Uniformity assured | • Complexity allows considerable variation in application of skills by individuals |
| | • Some tasks outlined in written procedures |
| • Coordination achieved through rigid definition of tasks | • Coordination achieved by knowledge of what to expect from others |
| • Outputs measurable | • Outputs not easily measurable |
| **Chain of Command** | |
| • Direct supervision of work | • Close relationship with clients that impedes direct supervision |
| • Rules and regulations enforced by line managers | • Managers administer secondary activities, the means to provide the major activities carried out by professionals |
| • Authority of hierarchical nature: Legitimate power | • Authority of professional nature: Expert power |
| **Interpersonal Relationships** | |
| • Emphasis on quality of product | • Emphasis on relationship with client to assure quality of service |
| **Career Orientation** | |
| • Based on technical qualifications | • Based on formal education in profession; licensure and/or certification required |
| • Promotions based on seniority and achievement | • Promotions based on expertise; may include seniority factor |
| • Viewed as lifelong career in the organization | • Considerable mobility when skills are in demand |

**Table 12-1** continued

| Traditional Bureaucracy | Professional Bureaucracy |
| --- | --- |
| • Loyalty to organization | • Loyalty to profession may supersede loyalty to organization |

*Sources:* From *Organizations: Behavior, Structure, Process* by J.L. Gibson, J.M. Ivancevich, and J.H. Donnelly, 1982, Plano,Tex., Business Publications, Inc. Copyright 1982 by Business Publications, Inc.; and *The Structuring of Organizations* by H. Mintzberg, 1979, Englewood Cliffs, N.J.: Prentice-Hall, Inc. Copyright 1979 by Prentice-Hall, Inc.

the two models are most apparent in the areas of interpersonal relationships and chain of command. Cleland (1982, p. 392) indicates that communication flow from the top of traditional organizations makes it difficult for ideas generated by staff (at the opposite end) to be shared with upper levels of management.

Contemporary nursing leaders face the challenge of changing the traditional hierarchical nursing department to a professional model. Designing an organizational structure to facilitate this change involves four decision processes that will determine the fixed relationships among the jobs in the organization— division of labor, departmentalization, span of control, and delegation.

The first decision involves the division of labor, by which the work is divided or specialized among workers. Clifford (1982, p. 106) describes the change process toward decentralization at Beth Israel Hospital in Boston. The team-functional method of nursing care delivery (high work specialization) was replaced by primary nursing in order to provide continuity of service and accountability for nursing care by practitioners. In primary nursing, specialization is low because of the complexity of the work.

The second design decision, departmentalization, determines the way in which jobs are grouped together. Common bases for combining jobs are function, geography, product or service, customer or client served, and mixtures of these. In hospitals, nursing usually is a separate department by virtue of function, but nurses work in areas where the geography (4 North, 2 West), service (surgery, maternity), and clients (outpatient, oncology) help determine departmentalization. Support services such as pharmacy, housekeeping, and medical records usually are grouped functionally. McClure and Nelson (1982, p. 70) describe a problem this presents to nurses since they have the knowledge to integrate patient services but frequently lack authority over the functions of the support services.

The third design decision determines the size of the group reporting to one superior, or span of control. Issues affecting this decision are the amount of contact required between supervisor and subordinate, the level of education and training of the subordinate, and the ability of the superior to communicate effectively. Gibson et al. (1982, p. 301) indicate that supervision of workers with complex jobs requires more frequent and in-depth contacts, necessitating a smaller span of control.

However, Mintzberg (1979, p. 143) concludes that in professional work that is independent, with individuals serving their own clients, there is less need for consultation and communication. This provides a larger span of control for managers in professional organizations. Cleland (1982, p. 384) finds that head nurses frequently have responsibility for 30 to 60 employees, including increasing numbers of part-time nurses, which indicates a large span of control of a professional group.

The fourth design decision, delegation, describes the method by which decisionmaking authority is distributed among jobs. Dennis (1983, p. 54), in her review of the literature on the power of nursing in the organization, reports that decentralized decisionmaking structures for nursing have been advocated, but little research has resulted to verify or refute decentralization as the ideal structure.

Each of the four design decisions may be conceptualized as existing on a continuum. Gibson et al. (1982, p. 291) note that organizations will tend toward one end or the other along each continuum. Those with high specialization, homogeneous departmentalization, small span of control, and centralized authority are described as structured, formalistic, bureaucratic, and mechanistic. Organizations with low specialization, heterogeneous departmentalization, large span of control, and decentralized authority are described as unstructured, informalistic, nonbureaucratic, and organic.

Aydelotte (1985, pp. 397-398) discusses a number of generalizations, based on the work of several authors, that she considers appropriate when making choices for the design of a professional nursing department. The decisions made should allow nurses more control over their work, the ability to adhere to their own professional standards rather than those imposed by the entity, recognition of their influence within the organization, and accountability for their work through an administrator who also is a professional. Choosing a structure that addresses these issues decreases the alienation of professionals working in a typical bureaucratic organization. These choices allow the selection and development of a decentralized structure for professional nurses.

## Organizational Development

Organizational development is described by Mintzberg (1979, pp. 241-243) as a process. Traditional organizations may begin as craft structures, with a single, informally organized group of workers whose managers work along with them, performing similar tasks. As this simple organization grows, informal communication no longer is adequate to coordinate the work.

Additional levels of management are created, resulting in a vertical division of labor. This entrepreneurial structure centralizes decisionmaking in a single leader, with little middle management between leader and workers. With further growth and elaboration, the transition to bureaucratic structure is necessary for an organization to survive.

Hampton, Summer, and Webber (1982, p. 73) indicate that the most essential structural difference between the traditional and bureaucratic organizations is in the middle level. They report that the number of managers and specialists per 100 workers in organizations has increased in all industrialized nations. Thus, as organizations grow in size, they tend to add middle managers.

The typical bureaucratic organization has a highly centralized structure, with formal decisionmaking power vested in the chief executive at the strategic apex. Vertical decentralization occurs as this power is delegated down the chain of command. In the system of formal authority, informal decisionmaking power may remain with line managers or it may be shared with others, such as specialists, or the workers themselves. Horizontal decentralization describes the extent to which nonmanagers have the autonomy to control decision processes themselves (Mintzberg, 1979, p. 194).

For example, professional nurses make many independent decisions about planning and implementing the care they give to patients. Centralized decisionmaking in a traditional structure is readily apparent in team/functional nursing care delivery systems. A professional nurse makes the decisions on patient care for a number of other caregivers who, most often, are not professionals. In traditional structures without decentralized, unit-based quality assurance, decisionmaking about factors to evaluate may be centralized in persons with little or no involvement in actual patient care.

## Organizational Evolution

Citing Toynbee's theory of civilization, Hampton et al. (1982, pp. 813-820) delineate the stages of the evolution of an organization: (1) inception/birth, (2) growth/development, (3) a period of conflict, leading to either (4) realignment/growth or (5) stagnation/decline. They identify the theory of organizational evolution as having three central concepts—organization, environment, and strategic choice:

1. Nursing leaders must assess an organization, in the context of its environment, in order to make strategic choices to ensure the continuing realignment and growth necessary for its survival.
2. The environment or society is unique for each organization. Resources (clients and materials), political support, and consumer recognition of its legitimacy are elements in the environment of a contemporary organization.

3. Evolution of an organization leads to the third central concept, strategic choice, which becomes the process used by the influential managers to maintain alignment between the organizational structure and society.

Aydelotte (1985, pp. 394-396) synthesizes the environmental changes influencing professional nurses that were considered by the National Commission on Nursing in 1983:

1. Advances in technology and scientific knowledge require physicians to acknowledge the unique knowledge and skill essential to the role of the nurse and the need for more collaborative role relationships.
2. Consumers are more knowledgeable about health care and its cost and are more involved in making decisions.
3. Emphasis on cost effectiveness is increasing.
4. More women are working in lifetime careers and entering traditionally male professions.

The National Commission on Nursing recommended that changes be made in nurses' relationships with physicians, with hospital administrators and trustees, and among nurses themselves based on the environmental issues identified. It recommended that nursing be recognized as a clinical practice discipline with authority over its management process. This change would require replacing the bureaucratic structure with a professional model.

McClure and Nelson (1982, pp. 60-68) describe environmental changes in hospital nursing: high patient acuity; advanced technology; more elderly with multiple health problems; shorter lengths of stay; more complex, sophisticated care requiring more professional nurses; and the shift to a primary nursing system, highly valued by nurses, in which they have responsibility, accountability, and autonomy in practice.

Nursing researchers have demonstrated awareness of the environmental and societal issues that will influence the evolutionary process in nursing organizations. Strategic choices must be made that will assure realignment and growth in accordance with environmental changes.

A concept essential to the process of strategic choice is power. Dennis (1983, p. 47) defines power as "the ability to exert influence, to compel others to do what they may or may not want to do, and to persuade others in ways that may further one's own interest." It is the capacity to affect the behavior of others and to control valuable resources. She also asserts that the strongest base of power for a professional is knowledge, which affects client outcomes and is essential for professional control within an organization.

Cipriani (1985, p. 13) describes the power of the staff nurse as based on the professional credibility and scope of nursing. Both are related to current knowledge and continuing education in nursing practice. Aydelotte (1985, p. 409) relates power to the knowledge and expertise that traditionally have given professionals the right to governance.

Camilleri (1985, p. 574) defines governance as "a term applied to the decisionmaking arrangements which groups develop for the management of their affairs." Both structural elements and processes compose the system of governance within organizations. A possible strategic choice, based on recognition of nursing's expert power base, is to design an organizational structure that allows the best use of that expertise by professional nurses.

One of the environmental features of magnet hospitals that allows them to retain satisfied professional nurses is the recognition that these nurses are professionals, with control over their work, in a system that allows the authority and responsibility for decisions affecting them to be decentralized to nursing staff on nursing units (Aydelotte, 1985).

## READINESS TO DECENTRALIZE

The organizational design elements just discussed are reflected in several factors that indicate the level of professionalization of the nursing staff. These may be considered in assessing readiness to decentralize:

- Primary nursing and nursing diagnosis are indicative of practice decisionmaking vested in individual professional nurses and are a measure of low specialization.
- Peer review allows professional nurses to evaluate each other's practice, another departure from hierarchical, centralized authority.
- Shared governance and collaborative practice committees enable professional nurses to make decisions about their practice issues with other professionals in a decentralized forum.
- Unit-based quality assurance is another example of decentralization in which professional nurses themselves select standards of the care to be monitored, which may be customized to meet their unit's needs.

Assessment of a nursing department will measure the degree to which each of these elements has been recognized. A department ready to decentralize will have acknowledged these as desirable goals, begun active planning or implementation, or have implemented them.

A nursing department in which some or all of these are absent will need to determine the reasons. These may include lack of awareness, perceived or actual financial or human resource deficits, or overt political opposition from within the organization at some level. Decisions then may be made as to the desirability and feasibility of a decentralized structure within that organization.

### Problems/Resolutions

Changes that create a decentralized nursing department to enhance professional autonomy may be accompanied by problem situations. These may be minimized if anticipated and if measures are taken to reduce their potential impact.

One financial impact of a decentralized system is the cost of meeting and committee time. It is possible to budget a specified amount of time for each nursing unit or even for each staff person in order to monitor the cost and productivity of indirect time. It also should be recognized that participation in the activities that have an impact on patient care programs and the quality of that care are some of the factors cited by Sovie (1984, p. 87) as contributing to staff retention in magnet hospitals.

Having staff members invested in the issues makes the change process easier. Money spent on indirect activities may be much less than the cost of more frequent staff turnover and replacement. Alternatives to meeting time also should be considered. Surveys and a modified Delphi technique [which involves several rounds of questionnaires with feedback from the previous questionnaire incorporated into the new questionnaire as described by Polit & Hungler (1978)] to solicit input from many participants is one option. Staff members also may work on projects whenever they have time during their workdays, or project leaders can talk with them during work hours to obtain input, instead of establishing an arbitrary meeting time that results in overtime or other excessive costs.

Another category of problems is more political in nature. Changes in the traditional chain-of-command roles of managers and staff may be difficult to accept. Fanning and Lovett (1985, p. 21) advocate preparation and education of those to be affected by a change in structure. They also cite the value of "positive attitudes, high motivation, and problem-solving abilities of the nurse managers" as critical to the success of their decentralization process (p. 23).

This is supported by New and Couillard (1981, p. 17), who state that "change ultimately requires altering the attitudes and behaviors of individuals." Mintzberg (1979, p. 376) identifies a problem with innovation in a decentralized structure: With many people empowered to make decisions, change occurs slowly and only after considerable negotiating with the numerous professionals involved. They may even view the cooperation required for making a change as threatening to their autonomy.

Jacox (1982, p. 95) describes a problem issue that threatens the autonomy of nurses. Resisting the attempts of hospital administrators to influence their practice, physicians continue to exercise major authority. At the same time, hospital administration seeks the alliance of physicians who will support decisions made on the basis of what is best for the total institution.

Nurses are in the middle, expected to be loyal to and protect the interests of both groups. One approach to extracting nurses from this position is to promote significant nursing representation in both hospital governance and collaborative practice committees. This promotes collegiality and minimizes the image of dominance over nursing by administration and physicians.

## Significance

Decentralized decisionmaking in a nursing department brings into focus the autonomy inherent in professional nursing. The increased accountability for practice stimulates nurses to be more aware of issues that have an impact on the future of the profession. The changes that have influenced health care in recent years may give additional momentum to the efforts to enhance the professional status of nursing. Financial systems that determine the cost of nursing care will do more than bring it out of its hiding place in the room charge. Sophisticated classification systems to measure patient acuity will allow nursing to demonstrate its knowledge and skills and determine appropriate reimbursement.

Recognition of the potential economic power and autonomy in this level of knowledge may promote the demand for baccalaureate and higher degrees among nurses as no other force has yet accomplished. The skill of critical thinking will be essential, as nurses are challenged to work with complex patients in rapidly changing health care systems. In addition to nurses with clinical skills, those with business and management ability will be increasingly valuable to the profession. As they are able to demonstrate their ability to generate revenue according to the level of care provided, nurses may seek and be granted fiscal accountability for their departments.

Nurses will benefit from their emergence to more independence and accountability. The more knowledgeable, skilled, and economically and politically sophisticated nurses become, the better the growth and survival of the profession is assured. This is modeled after the most successful of the independent professionals, who are recognized and compensated for their exceptional abilities.

Relationships with physicians must change. More collaboration and recognition of the mutual dependency between physicians and nurses will be necessary, extricating nursing from a subservient role.

Patients will benefit from nurses who are better educated and more skilled. Direct reimbursement for professional nursing care, from patients or third party payers, will have the effect of increasing nurses' accountability for the quality of that care.

Innovative health care programs will continue to be developed as institutions compete for patients. The health care system itself, as well as patients, will be the beneficiaries of the positive effects of such programs.

Finally, as nurses learn to negotiate in corporate settings, they also will learn to challenge the political systems that influence health care and the future of nursing.

## REFERENCES

Aydelotte, M.K. (1985). Structure of nursing practice departments: Governance and professionalism. In J. McCloskey & H.K. Grave (Eds.), *Current issues in nursing* (2nd ed.) 394-404. Boston: Blackwell Scientific Publications.

Camilleri, D.D. (1985). Health care governance in the 1980s: A systems review. In J. McCloskey & H.K. Grace (Eds.), *Current issues in nursing* (2nd ed.) 573-585. Boston: Blackwell Scientific Publications.

Cipriani, P.A. (1985). Staff nurse power can solve problems. *Nursing Success Today, 2,* 13-16.

Cleland, V. (1982). Nurses' economics and the control of nursing practice. In L.H. Aiken (Ed.), *Nursing in the 1980s: Crises, opportunities, challenges.* Philadelphia: J.B. Lippincott.

Clifford, J.C. (1982). Professional nursing practice in a hospital setting. In L.H. Aiken (Ed.). *Nursing in the 1980s: Crises, opportunities, challenges.* Philadelphia: J.B. Lippincott.

Dennis, K.E. (1983). Nursing's power in the organization: What research has shown. *Nursing Administration Quarterly, 8,* 47-57.

Fanning, J.A., & Lovett, R.B. (1985). Decentralization reduces nursing administration budget. *The Journal of Nursing Administration, 15,* 19-24.

Gibson, J.L., Ivancevich, J.M., & Donnelly, J.H. (1982). *Organizations: Behavior, structure, processes.* Plano, Tex.: Business Publications, Inc.

Hampton, D.R., Summer, C.E., & Webber, R.A. (1982). *Organizational behavior and the practice of management.* Glenview, Ill.: Scott, Foresman.

Jacox, A. (1982). Role restructuring in hospital nursing. In L.H. Aiken (Ed.), *Nursing in the 1980s: Crises, opportunities, challenges.* Philadelphia: J.B. Lippincott.

Ketefian, S. (1985). Professional and bureaucratic role conceptions and moral behavior among nurses. *Nursing Research, 34,* 248-253.

Litwak, E. (1961). Models of bureaucracy which permit conflict. *American Journal of Sociology, 67,* 177-184.

McClure, M.L., & Nelson, M.J. (1982). Trends in hospital nursing. In L.H. Aiken (Ed.), *Nursing in the 1980s: Crises, opportunities, challenges.* Philadelphia: J.B. Lippincott.

Mintzberg, H. (1979). *The structuring of organizations.* Englewood Cliffs, N.J.: Prentice-Hall.

New, J.R., & Couillard, N.A. (1981). Guidelines for introducing change. *The Journal of Nursing Administration, 11,* 17-21.

Polit, D.F., & Hungler, B.P. (1978). *Nursing research: Principles and methods.* Philadelphia: J.B. Lippincott.

Salmond, S.W. (1985). Supporting staff through decentralization. *Nursing Economics, 3,* 295-300.

Sovie, M.D. (1984). The economics of magnetism. *Nursing Economics, 2,* 85-91.

## BIBLIOGRAPHY

Bergman, R. (1985). Nurses as a social force. *Journal of Advanced Nursing, 10,* 197-198.

Dear, M.R., Weisman, C.S., & O'Keefe, S. (1985). Evaluation of a contract model for professional nursing practice. *Health Care Management Review, 10,* 65-77.

Fagin, C.M. (1982). The national shortage of nurses: A nursing perspective. In L.H. Aiken (Ed.), *Nursing in the 1980s: Crises, opportunities, challenges.* Philadelphia: J.B. Lippincott.

## Chapter 13

# Implementing Shared Governance: A Process for Growth

*Alice Eckes*

*Decisionmaking in nursing practice can be actualized through a system of shared governance. Shared governance transfers decisionmaking from theory to reality.*

The formation of a nursing practice council brings together staff nurses and managers to share knowledge, foster trusting relationships, and make decisions. Such a council provides an opportunity for discussion of issues that affect the practice of nursing. Staff nurses bring to it their expertise in practice and managers have the opportunity to seek input and advice from them.

## COUNCIL STRUCTURE AND BYLAWS

Such a council can be created by a joint effort of both staff and managers. This involves developing bylaws that define the council's purpose, objectives, meeting protocol, membership, reporting relationships, and decisionmaking power. Each of these subjects becomes a separate article in the bylaws that then can be ratified by participants.

The bylaws should begin with a clear statement of purpose, including concepts such as autonomy, accountability, interprofessional collaboration, and trust. The bylaws guide the council's functions. It is in its objectives that the council's power base can be defined in that they state clearly its right to make decisions on practice issues.

Meeting protocol is defined by the bylaws. Frequency of meetings, minute taking, attendance, communication, agenda, chairperson, and adviser from nursing administration are addressed, along with membership, which can be one of the most controversial areas to define. Membership should include nurses holding different job classifications in the department—head nurses, assistant head nurses, clinical nurse specialists, and directors—but the majority should be staff nurses.

A staff nurse from each unit is ideal to facilitate communication to all staff members throughout the hospital. Staff nurse members can be elected by their respective units and serve for a designated time. Alternates for all members help achieve 100 percent attendance at all meetings.

The chairperson is elected by the council, which can appoint an adviser from nursing administration. This adviser has no voting or veto power but provides guidance and perspective in discussions. The adviser is responsible for offering input in decisions that the council members may not be able to supply.

The bylaws define nursing department committees' reporting relationships with the council. This establishes the council as an arena for the communication of nursing practice issues. Standing committees such as policy, procedure, research, and quality assurance can report their activities to the council and seek decisions. Conference groups that represent different job classes, such as staff, head nurses, clinical nurse specialists, and directors take issues to the council and serve as channels of communication for it. The nursing practice council also has responsibility for the ad hoc committees that it creates for specific issues. These committees report to the council on a regular basis.


## IMPLEMENTATION

The implementation of shared governance should be viewed as a process—a series of changes that lead to an end goal of shared decisionmaking. If shared governance is regarded as a process, the hospital system will change to meet the needs of the participants as they mature within it. This change process is said to take anywhere from three to ten years. Bureaucratic behaviors are slow to adjust and the process in itself can bring about turmoil, conflict, and resistance. However, if it is kept in mind that shared decisionmaking can lead to better problem resolution, greater job satisfaction, and increased commitment to decisions, the energy needed to implement shared governance will be worthwhile (Dressler, 1983, p. 173).

Shared governance takes time to evolve and implementers need to be aware of the changes and conflicts it will produce in an institution. If these problems are acknowledged, they can be dealt with creatively. Problems should be anticipated and viewed as part of the change process, not as failures of shared governance. It is important to acknowledge successes that occur because of participative decisionmaking so that these forces can be used to drive the organization's system toward success. These successes take time to appear, and such factors as quality of decisionmaking, knowledge sharing, job satisfaction, and professional growth are hard to assess immediately.

Decisions in a shared governance system take longer to make than in a traditional bureaucratic system. There is no denying that bureaucracy usually is more efficient. However, the end result is nurses' increased commitment to better decisions and their implementation because of the input from so many sources.

The slow decisionmaking process can be frustrating to participants. They continue to look for an autocratic leader who will make quick, on-the-spot decisions. When this no longer happens in shared governance, participants verbalize lack of confidence in the leader by remarks such as, "I don't know where to take this problem anymore," "This system is so confusing," "It will take months to get an answer." In the initial stages of implementation of shared governance, much time will be spent on who is the right person to make a decision rather than on what is the best way to solve a problem.

Staff nurses at the outset tend to lack confidence in their ability to make decisions and lack experience in group decisionmaking. They are reluctant to make decisions without consulting peers. Leaders think of themselves as the experts and tend not to believe that staff members have anything significant to contribute. As staff nurses work within the system, they develop confidence in their knowledge of their practice and are more willing to share their ideas.

Managers begin to see that staff nurses do have a unique body of knowledge that contributes to decisionmaking. Granted, either group might come to the same decision independently, but the collaboration is the most important part of the process.

The council often is misunderstood and is regarded as solely a decisionmaking body. If this attitude becomes pervasive, the council becomes just another authoritarian figure. It does have the right to make decisions, but that is not its sole function. If staff nurses expect the council to function as a decision making body, it is up to the chairperson of the council to direct decision making to the appropriate level and to keep agenda items appropriate. The guiding factor for the chairperson should be to keep decisionmaking at the level where the decision is needed since it is the input of those individuals which will be most relevant. Managers who make decisions about practice are making them one step removed from the practitioners. This can lead to incorrect decisions (which eventually have to change) and to a lack of support of the decision by the practitioner since it may be an inappropriate decision.

The council also is a forum for the exchange of ideas and for communication. With this exchange comes a sharing of power, accountability for practice, and a sense of ownership of the decisions. Shared decisionmaking acknowledges the fact that staff nurses are the best resource in the practice of nursing.

## THE ROLE OF LEADERS AND MANAGERS

Competition for power does occur during the implementation of shared governance. Leaders may find it difficult to share their power with the staff. They fail to realize that they can strengthen their own power base by seeking advice from staff nurses who practice daily.

Managers need to consider making decisions with input from available resource persons. Collaboration is an excellent way of achieving personal power, and shared governance puts participants in situations that make possible this type of behavior. Power struggles often are manifested by nurses' or leaders' withholding information. They can refuse to bring issues to the council and deny that problems exist that the group can handle. This is a normal response of individuals when they are threatened by the fact that people other than those on the unit will know that they have operational problems. Power negotiation occurs during the group process at the meetings. Staff nurses imply that managers cannot relate to their situation and managers respond defensively. Leaders feel that the staff needs their expertise and guidance and staff nurses view this as lack of trust in their knowledge.

A "we-they" situation can develop, with managers and staff competing for status. Staff nurses often fail to realize that their power and knowledge are worthwhile. As both sides interact during meetings, they begin to appreciate and understand each other's expertise and are relieved to hear that every unit has some problems.

Some criticism of shared governance is based on a fear of loss of power. Criticism unfortunately is not always given in the spirit of trying to improve the system but rather in attempting to subvert it and restore the old bureaucracy which is familiar and comfortable. Supporters need to take a strong stance that shared governance is here to stay and help participants work through their feelings by focusing on constructive ways to resolve problems within the new system. Inservice workshops and discussions on shared governance, power, and trust can help ease fears of change and of power loss.

## TRUST AND MISTRUST

Behaviors that appear in power struggles are similar to those in situations in which trust is low. It is important to create an open climate that fosters trust so shared governance can flourish. A trusting climate cannot be assumed. Achieving trust takes conscious effort as is described in Chapter 2. Trust is not just the ability to get along socially. It is confidence in the abilities and intentions of another person. It is demonstrated when a person reveals information that need not be disclosed, seeks advice from peers or subordinates, and delegates tasks or decisions to others. Trust can stimulate creativity, feelings of security, and openness.

Mistrust leads to defensiveness and lack of disclosure. Mistrust breeds mistrust and is cyclical. However, the cycle can be broken if common interests are emphasized and open communication skills are taught and used, with an emphasis on listening. Problem solving then becomes the main issue, with less concern for power.

Shared governance helps create an environment in which trust is possible. It promotes collaboration that is essential to the development of trust. A nursing department philosophy and administration that speak to the value of individuals and their worth in the institution will help create a trusting environment. Open discussions about trust can assist in developing a common understanding of its meaning, and the effects will be helpful at council meetings (Zand, 1981, pp. 38-39, 44).

Motivating staff nurses to participate in shared governance is a challenge. At the outset, they will not trust the system and will not believe that they have the power to initiate change based on their past experience. They express feelings of being overwhelmed with day-to-day responsibilities and sometimes encounter lack of support from their first-line managers for time spent on council business. Management needs to support the staff nurses' efforts and to view council membership as an extension of their practice.

Support can be provided by the head nurse by budgeting time, facilitating coverage, and assisting with time management skills. Once a staff nurse begins to receive rewards for participating, motivation will increase. Such rewards include recognition, status, a sense of belonging, and a sense of accomplishment. The nurses begin to trust the system, actualize their potential, and become effective and skilled contributors in the council.

## COMMUNICATION: A KEY ELEMENT

Effective communication is vital in shared governance, as it is in any system. Since the council includes members from all units (a head nurse, assistant head nurse, clinical nurse specialist, and director) it provides an excellent opportunity for communication and the dissemination of information. Chairpersons of standing committees such as policy, procedure, quality assurance, and forms report accomplishments at each meeting.

The council in turn shares concerns and provides advice on decisions (see Figure 11-1 in Chapter 11). Conference groups that represent different types of jobs are afforded opportunities to communicate concerns and share accomplishments, minutes of meetings are posted on units, and reports of council activities are given at unit meetings. General areas of interest also are communicated via the department newsletter.

To promote the success of shared governance, accomplishments and changes in behaviors should be applauded. Members who work to advance shared governance should be recognized. A posting of accomplishments is helpful in fostering change. When staff nurses begin to chair committees that previously were presided over only by managers, growth becomes apparent. Not only do nurse managers begin to trust the abilities of staff nurses, but nurses themselves gain confidence in their abilities to institute change.

Evidence of growth is seen in improvements in patient care resulting from council decisions. These bring about change because staff nurse involvement in decisions adds their commitment to the success of the outcome. The adoption of the American Nurses' Association Social Policy Statement (1980) as a philosophical base for nursing and its integration into daily staff practice can mark the council's maturing in its handling of complex issues.

As trust develops members learn to take risks and handle issues such as the self-worth of staff nurses and their responsibility and accountability for their practice. These types of accomplishments enable shared decisionmaking to produce growth in nurses. "Professional status can be achieved and maintained only when nurses can determine their own goals, course of action, evaluation, and the modification of its action" (St. Michael Hospital, Department of Nursing, Statement of Philosophy, 1985).

Shared governance creates an environment that enhances professional creativity through interprofessional collaboration. It results in the growth of the professional, and it is through such growth that the profession of nursing will be able to achieve more in the future.

## REFERENCES

American Nurses' Association. (1980). *Nursing: A Social Policy Statement* (ANA Publication Code: NP-63 35M 12/80). Kansas City, Mo.: Author.

Dressler, G. (1983). *Human behaviors: Improving performance at work.* Reston, Va.: Reston Publishing.

St. Michael Hospital. (1985). Department of Nursing, Statement of Philosophy.

Zand, D.E. (1981). *Information, organization and power.* New York: McGraw-Hill.

## BIBLIOGRAPHY

Cipriani, P.A. (1985). Staff nurse power can solve problems. *Nursing Service Today, 2,* 13-16.

Jordan, C.H. (1982). Sharing decision making with staff. *AORN Journal, 36,* 391-398.

Porter-O'Grady, T., & Finnigan, S. (1984). *Shared governance for nursing.* Rockville, Md.: Aspen Publishers, Inc.

**Chapter 14**

# Realization of Staff Nurse Power Base

*Maureen Marcouiller*

*Success in a shared governance model requires a realization and strengthening of the power base of staff nurses. Progress in the development of such a power base can be tracked through examples that demonstrate the nurses' influence within the system.*

The foundation of a staff nurse power base in the shared governance system at St. Michael Hospital was laid with the selection of four staff nurses to represent all of their peers at the newly formed Nursing Practice Council (NPC), which met for the first time in January 1983. The names of these four nurses were drawn from boxes containing the names of those on each nursing unit who had expressed an interest in the council.

The names had been divided into the areas of responsibility of each of the four directors of nursing: Specialty Units, Medical-Surgical Units, Medical–Critical Care Units, and Specialty Surgical Units. It would be the responsibility of these four staff nurses to attend the NPC meetings and report back to the 16 nursing units in the hospital. The information was to be communicated to other staff nurses at unit meetings.

## PROBLEMS EMERGE

Problems arose at once because each staff nurse member had to attend four unit meetings a month to report on the NPC sessions, and so ran into

129

difficulties with scheduling time and with schedule conflicts. This led to a meeting of a staff nurse from each unit who had expressed interest in the NPC and had been an unsuccessful candidate for one of the four positions. The four elected nurses proposed setting up a network with the units to provide better communication and felt that this could be accomplished best by working with the nurses who had been interested at the outset.

Staff nurses had not participated in such meetings under the previous governance system in the nursing department. The invitations went to the individual unit representatives, who negotiated with their head nurses for time away from the unit. One head nurse expressed concern about the propriety of the meeting lest it might be construed as an attempt to unionize the nursing staff. Because of this concern and a desire that nothing about the meeting be secret, one of the four staff nurse representatives asked the approval of the hospital's vice president of patient services. Not only was approval given, support was offered the staff representatives in their efforts to set up the meeting.

At the meeting, in March 1983, the staff nurses decided to petition the Nursing Council for recognition as a conference group similar to the existing Head Nurse Conference Group, Assistant Head Nurse Conference Group, Administrative Supervisors Conference Group, Clinical Nurse Specialist Conference Group, and Directors Conference Group. The staff nurses also decided to draft a purpose for meeting on a regular basis.

The petition for recognition was approved at that March meeting. This made the Staff Nurse Conference Group a valid entity in the nursing department.

At the first meeting of the Staff Nurse Conference Group (SNCG) in April 1983, ten staff nurses were present, including the four on the Nursing Council. The minutes of that meeting record that:

1. a chairperson and a secretary were chosen
2. minutes of the conference group meetings were to be kept on each unit, along with the minutes of the NPC meetings
3. nursing personnel not affiliated with a specific nursing unit (float and on-call personnel and home care coordinators) were sent a letter explaining the existence of the group and extending an invitation to select and send a representative
4. the Staff Nurse Conference Group was to formulate a purpose and objectives to guide its work.

A subcommittee was appointed to establish a rough draft that would be discussed at the next meeting. The need for an administrative adviser was discussed and the group chose to invite the vice president of patient services to join in that capacity. The minutes of the NPC also were reviewed.

The minutes of the first meeting of the SNCG are important in that:

1. They reflect the formation of an organizational structure and recognition of the need for written purpose and objectives to confirm its existence.
2. The group recognized the need for administrative advice and direction.
3. The group was beginning to divide its work through formation of subcommittees.
4. The group was acting as a communication link between the nursing staff and the NPC.

## OPERATION OF THE SNCG

In the next few weeks, the SNCG exercised its power base in the selection of a replacement representative to the NPC because one of the original four transferred to another unit and vacated her position on both the SNCG and the NPC. The conference group elected one of its members as the new representative and instructed the former representative's unit to select a new member. This was an exercise of power in that the original representatives were selected from the director's area of responsibility and the nurse elected to fill the vacancy was elected from the conference group's members as a whole. The group filled its own vacancy without relying on management to do so.

Although the SNCG's membership is composed of, and its internal governance is by, staff nurses, it is not an isolated group. In the shared governance system at St. Michael Hospital it functions as a component of the NPC, working to carry out the Council's purpose and objectives:

> The NPC serves to develop and strengthen shared and trusted relationships by expanding the communication network within the Department of Nursing. It serves as a forum for intraprofessional collaboration and/or decisionmaking regarding practice-related issues.

The power base for staff nurses has grown in the SNCG and NPC as a result of participation in the meetings and through the work of conference group and NPC committees and task forces.

Hospital staff nurses now have a way to make their concerns heard. Problems are given to the unit representative to the SNCG or NPC or are referred to one of the hospital standing committees, which report to the NPC.

Practice concerns presented to the SNCG are discussed by the whole group and are either resolved, referred to the appropriate conference group in the NPC, or placed on the NPC agenda for discussion by the entire Council.

One concern dealt with in this manner involves the hospital's professional staff evaluation form. A competency-based form had been put into use in the Department of Nursing. By October 1983, the staff nurses all had been evaluated and had a number of concerns. These were carried to the SNCG by the unit representatives and were discussed by the group, which felt that there were inconsistencies with the form:

1. Staff nurses felt there was an overemphasis on committees and extra-curricular activities instead of the day-to-day practice necessary to maintain status on a specific level of the department's professional clinical ladder. The nurses felt that "good nursing care" was not given enough emphasis to maintain particular job levels.
2. The nurses expressed concern about not being able to fulfill all of the duties, including extracurricular activities and committee work, within shift hours, requiring them to come in on days off and to work overtime to meet these demands.
3. Staff nurses felt that the form did not reflect unit needs and should be changed to do so.
4. Much of the evaluation was regarded as not applicable to all shifts. Nurses working primarily nights or part-time felt they could not fulfill the requirements to keep their clinical level.
5. Nurses voiced concern about individual interpretations of the form by the evaluators (the head nurse or assistant head nurse) and whether it was or was not being filled out consistently by the particular evaluator.

The SNCG decided that these concerns should be addressed in a letter to the Nursing Directors Conference Group. After considering the letter, the directors referred the issue to the Head Nurse Conference Group, which set up a task force to revise the form.

By December 1984, the Competency-Based Evaluation Task Force had completed much of its work and its chairperson updated the SNCG on the revisions. Copies of the first draft of the new form were reviewed and the representatives discussed the revisions and any additional concerns.

## THE REVISED FORM

The task force completed its work by August 1985. The new Revised Professional Nurse Performance Evaluation form was printed. It was presented to the NPC, which recommended to the nursing management group that it be approved and used. Extensive unit training was given on the revised form, first for the unit leadership groups, then for staff nurses, who had the opportunity to question changes and learn how they could meet the competencies for their level of clinical performance. For additional information about the form, see Chapters 22 and 24.

It is important to note in this example of the growth of a power base in shared governance that staff nurses had an opportunity to initiate change that affected them personally and professionally. They were a vital link in the communication system on the revisions at both unit and conference group meetings.

It would be heartening to report that all of the evaluation problems were resolved, but they were not. At this writing, staff nurses were undergoing their first evaluations with the new form and were expressing new concerns, especially in regard to being able to meet the expectations for the higher levels of the clinical ladder. The Assistant Head Nurse-Clinical Coordinator Conference Group worked on clarifying some of the criteria, after which individual units were to decide on new training in use of the form.

Through participation on groups such as quality assurance, policy, procedure, and physician-nurse committees, being active within the SNCG, and working on NPC committees and task forces, staff nurses were developing an awareness of their own political skills. They were developing strategies for making change and gaining knowledge of the political mechanics involved. Exhibit 14-1 lists accomplishments of the SNCG.

An example of developing political skills is the SNCG's bringing about an increase in the number of its representatives to the NPC. By December 1985, the SNCG had five staff nurse representatives on the NPC but saw a need to increase that number to include members from each hospital unit. It was felt that this would result in: (1) a more fair representation of all staff nurses at St. Michael Hospital; (2) a more effective network to communicate professional staff nurse concerns to NPC or higher level of authority, and vice versa; (3) an expanded opportunity for shared decisionmaking on nursing practice issues, and (4) encouragement for all of the hospital's staff nurses to participate in the professional nursing structure.

After much discussion, the group decided to present a proposal to increase staff representation to the NPC and formed a committee to draft the plan. That committee based the proposal on (1) the concept of shared governance, (2) the objectives of the NPC itself, and (3) the purpose and objectives of the SNCG.

The group also decided to inform each of the conference groups of the proposal so that they would be able to discuss it before the NPC meeting. A memo was distributed to the conference group chairpersons: (1) stating the intent of the proposal, (2) explaining the reasons for it—improved communication among staff nurses and expansion of the shared governance concept, and (3) seeking support for the petition. A copy of the proposal was included with the agenda for the NPC meeting so there would be no surprises.

**Exhibit 14-1** Accomplishments of the Staff Nurse Conference Group

- Guidelines for staff nurse reassignment

- Maps of each unit to assist reassigned personnel

- Mandatory CPR certification for all nurses, with annual recertification

- Changes in IV administration of vitamin K

- Start of process resulting in changes in identifying no-resuscitation status of patients (use of blue armbands)

- New name tags for all employees that patients can read more easily

- Write-in time cards for all nursing units (rather than punching the time clock)

- New policy on uniforms

- New nursing data base and nursing fact sheet

- Changes in system for checking crash carts

- Development of a shared governance videotape

- Formulation of guidelines for recommendations for appointments to physician/nurse committees

- Changes in method of reporting isolation status of patients being transported from one unit to another

- Establishment of peer review process

- Staff representation on product evaluation committee

- Discussion of staff morale issues

- Formation of guidelines for transfer of patients to critical care areas from general units

- SNCG representatives' participation in coauthoring this book.

The SNCG committee members presented the proposal to the council, aware of support from staff nurse unit representatives sitting in as observers. There was general council support for the proposal, but one representative sought to defer a vote until individual conference groups could discuss it further. The motion was defeated, as the majority felt there already had been sufficient discussion. The motion on increased staff nurse representation to the council then passed, and it was decided to have the change take place immediately.

## TIME OFF FOR MEETINGS

Another example of staff nurse growth in utilizing political skills in shared governance can be seen in the negotiations between the representatives to the SNCG and the Head Nurse Conference Group on scheduled time off for meetings.

Staff nurse representatives to the SNCG and NPC were encountering difficulty meeting unit expectations for staffing on the days that the conference group and council were scheduled. Leaving the unit for the meetings was causing friction with co-workers, who had to cover patient assignments for the representatives and care for their own patients. A majority of the representatives also were involved on additional subcommittees, task forces, and special projects reporting to the conference group and council, which involved more time away from the unit.

The problem was discussed at a SNCG meeting, and several representatives volunteered to write a memorandum to the Head Nurse Conference Group requesting scheduled preparation time for the SNCG/NPC representatives. The memorandum listed the amount of time involved in preparation for and attendance at the meetings, and gave the following reasons the SNCG/NPC staff representatives felt scheduled time off the unit was essential: (1) to decrease overtime, (2) to provide more fair distribution of unit workload while representatives were at meetings, (3) to increase quality involvement in the shared governance system, and (4) to enhance quality of communication on both unit and committee levels.

The chairperson of the SNCG was invited to a meeting of the head nurses to discuss the request. As a result of that session, the individual representatives were assigned the responsibility of noting requested preparation time in their unit request book; the head nurse considered this in drafting the schedule. The head nurses have been supportive of their unit representatives on this issue.

As a result of the growth of a power base and the development of political skills in the shared governance system, professional nurses are participating in decisionmaking, exercising control over practice, taking responsibility for their practice, and growing both personally and professionally.

## Chapter 15

# Committee and Communications Structure

*Doug Haley and Susan Matyas Black*

*Communication in a shared governance nursing structure is of paramount importance for sound decisionmaking. One of the most important functions of committees is to provide that essential communication link within the organization. In addition, staff involvement on committees provides a forum for development of leadership skills that have a positive effect on a nurse's personal feeling of professionalism.*

A shared governance system brings with it the enormous task of obtaining, processing, and disseminating information to a number of persons in an effective, efficient manner. The acquisition of input and ideas from staff members and collaborative problem solving among all levels requires development of sound communication skills. The intent of this chapter is threefold: (1) It highlights the importance of committee growth and the need for an organized communication network in a shared governance model. (2) It describes the development of a staff nurse committee to facilitate the communication and decisionmaking process required by a shared governance structure. (3) It supports the concept that participation in the committee process contributes to staff nurses' sense of accountability, professionalism, and feelings of autonomy.

## HISTORICAL PERSPECTIVE

Historically, women's roles and bureaucratic structures have affected communication in nursing. In the early twentieth century, women in society were subservient to men. Women were thought to be emotional, dependent, and incapable of assuming major responsibilities, such as decisionmaking. With nursing seen as a women's occupation, nurses were labeled as possessing the same characteristics in their professional capacity. Their role in hospitals thus was clearly defined and structured (Affiliated Dynamics, 1984, p. 4).

The bureaucratic hospital organization in which nurses practiced was another factor that influenced their role. The bureaucratic model is a physical representation of McGregor's Management Theory X. It delineates a specific hierarchy of areas of authority and responsibility. The major communicative emphasis of this theory is up and down the management ladder. This model perceives the employee as being inherently lazy, with an actual tendency to avoid work. This structure requires the manager to coerce the employee to meet organizational goals.

On the other hand, McGregor's Theory Y holds that with the proper motivation and opportunities, employees will strive to meet organizational and personal goals. The will to improve comes from within (McGregor, 1960, pp. 33-57). The bureaucratic structure reduces the amount of input nurses have into their practice, thereby lowering their personal feelings of professionalism. Shared governance is a shift in management attitude from Theory X to Theory Y.

The types of communication processes that prevailed in nursing have been affected by society's male/female role stereotypes and by the organizational system in which they practice. In the past, nurses' communication tended to be patient oriented, information relaying, and subservient to physicians and administrative superiors. Now, with increased emphasis on professionalism and autonomy, nurses are more involved with decisionmaking and problem solving, requiring skill in group dynamics and assertiveness in communication.

## THE NURSING LITERATURE

The nursing literature provides an abundance of information on types of communication, effective communication strategies, pitfalls, and communication within committees. For purposes here, communication is not just the flow of a message from sender to receiver via a channel; it is a process that unites an organization. This flow of information is essential for the survival of a group. All levels of nursing depend upon the availability of reliable, accurate, and current information. Feedback, both positive and negative, is essential in maintaining system performances (Cherry, 1966, p. 36).

Literature is lacking on communication in a shared governance system because of its relative newness. Shared governance is based on the communication of ideas and information among peers as well as levels of nursing.

A breakdown in communication at any one of these points could result in ineffective, poorly made decisions.

## Committees

Hospitals traditionally have used two types of committees, with varying degrees of success. Standing committees generally are defined in organizational bylaws, have well-outlined duties, scopes, and authority, and are permanent or of long duration. Ad hoc committees are temporary or special-purpose groups. They usually have one specific task and are of short duration, often working on a fixed deadline (Snook, 1984, pp. 39-49).

Whatever the type, committees perform a variety of purposes and functions. Two common reasons for forming a committee are: (1) to communicate diverse viewpoints and areas of expertise and (2) to utilize the "group think" process for decisionmaking and problem solving (Snook, 1984, pp. 39-49). Probably the most important function in a decentralized or shared governance system is communication. Horizontal and vertical flow of information is essential, so the communication function becomes the premise of shared decisionmaking.

## Growth of a Professional

In 1982, *Nursing in Transition: Models for Successful Organizational Change* was published by the National Commission on Nursing. This work identified characteristics common to a profession and emphasized that nurses were becoming more professional, thus "requiring more input regarding clinical and managerial decisions" in addition to seeking a "more active role in policy development, implementation, and evaluation."

By virtue of their educational background, nurses are more qualified for leadership roles and are actively pursuing input into their professional practice that traditionally was reserved for hospital or nursing administrators, resulting in their increased professionalism. "The key to success is participation in decisionmaking. Shared power means more power" (National Commission on Nursing, 1982). The key to participation is communication.

## Description of the Structure

Implementation of shared governance requires input from all levels of nursing organization. The structure also must provide for feedback channels and an identified entry point for new topics. This can be accomplished through the development of a nursing practice council with members from all levels and the identification of reporting mechanisms among established committees, task forces, and other groups. This nursing practice council has decisionmaking authority for all practice-related issues.

Figure 15-1 illustrates the Nursing Practice Council (NPC) committee structure established at St. Michael Hospital in 1983 and the communication channels associated with the various committees. The shared governance structure consists of the NPC and four conference groups. Conference groups are collections of members from specific job positions, i.e., head nurse (HRN), assistant head nurse (AHRN), clinical nurse specialist (CNS), director of nursing (DON), and staff nurse conference group (SNCG). The conference groups discuss issues pertinent to their respective level. The double-ended arrows in Figure 15-1 represent the communication flow and reporting mechanisms within the structure. Standing hospital committees and ad hoc committees established by the NPC report directly to the Council. This information then is disseminated to the nursing staff at the unit level via the unit member of the SNCG.

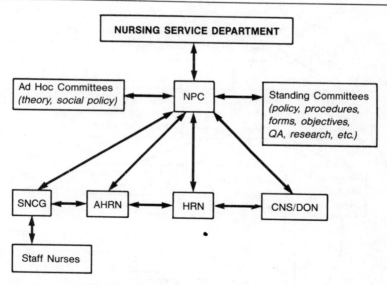

Key: AHRN = Assistant Head Registered Nurse
     CNS/DON = Clinical Nurse Specialist/Director of Nursing
     HRN = Head Registered Nurse
     NPC = Nursing Practice Council
     SNCG = Staff Nurse Conference Group

**Figure 15-1** Committee Structure for Decisionmaking

The core of the shared governance process is the conference groups. They all act on an agenda item in similar fashion by collaborating and providing diverse input related to their respective roles. Using the Staff Nurse Conference Group as a model, Figure 15-2 represents the process of acting on

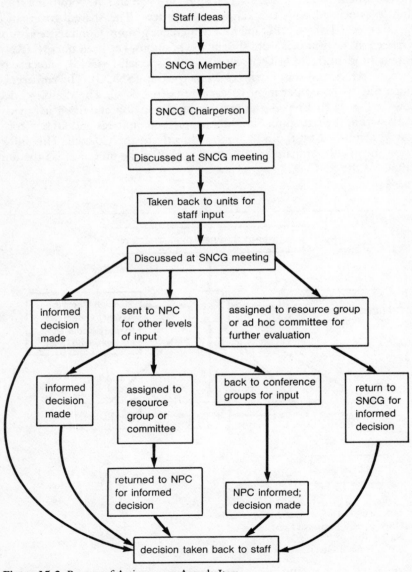

**Figure 15-2** Process of Acting on an Agenda Item

an agenda item presented to the SNCG and illustrates the feedback channels needed for shared decisionmaking and the increased accountability of the staff nurses. Any conference group or staff member can request that a topic or issue be discussed at the SNCG. In turn, staff nurses may request a discussion in another conference group by recommending it to the SNCG.

A specific example illustrates the process described in Figure 15-2. Staff nurses identified a chronic problem of inadequate charting of intake and output on patients during the intraoperative and postanesthesia periods. The staff found the charting often was incomplete and, in some cases, no intake or output was charted for the entire period that a patient was off the unit and in surgery. Exhibit 15-1 illustrates the steps taken to rectify the problem. Six months after implementing the format, the SNCG was notified of a great improvement of intake and output documentation during surgery. Some inconsistencies still were found but these were handled at the unit level. This helps illustrate the interrelationship of the SNCG, NPC, and other established hospital-based committees.

Obtaining input from the staff and communicating decisions is the most important factor if decisionmaking is to be truly shared. Careful consideration must be given to the actual mechanics of this communication channel to prevent breakdowns, resulting in poorly informed staff or inadequate input of staff ideas. The responsibility for maintaining the communication channel lies with the units' SNCG members. One system effective in disseminating information and acquisition of input from the staff level is a combination of written and verbal channels.

The written component uses a communication logbook on each nursing unit that contains the agenda and minutes of the SNCG and NPC meetings.

**Exhibit 15-1**  Steps in Rectifying Charting Problem

---

1. Staff nurse presents intake and output problem to the Staff Nurse Conference Group. Discussion follows.
2. Decision is to take these concerns to the operating room and postanesthesia recovery unit quality assurance groups.
3. There groups develop a format for charting that includes the following: (a) the OR circulating nurse is responsible for measuring and documenting intake and output while with the patient, (b) the anesthesiologist is responsible for documenting intake and output on a flow sheet while in the OR, and (c) the circulating nurse is responsible for charting the intake and output on the record.
4. Format is presented to the Staff Nurse Conference Group and reviewed.
5. Format is submitted to hospital policy committee.
6. Format is reviewed and approved by Nursing Practice Council.
7. Format is included in all policy unit texts.

The staff nurses are responsible for reading the agendas and minutes, providing input in writing where needed, and initialing the log.

The verbal component uses a prearranged amount of unit meeting time for discussion of topics requiring staff input. The staff nurse member of the SNCG and NPC is responsible for keeping logbooks current, arranging for and leading discussion of NPC issues at unit meetings, and relaying this information back to the SNCG or NPC. By using a combination of unit meeting time for discussion and a communication logbook, the unit representatives can disseminate the information efficiently. The logbook also provides an opportunity for staff members on all shifts to be a part of the system.

Other systems also can be developed to assure communication flow, such as: (1) holding occasional meetings on the unit for discussion of significant NPC issues, and (2) reporting NPC issues in a hospital bulletin or newsletter. The type of system selected should be consistent from unit to unit and should be flexible, allowing changes as necessary, depending on the needs of staff management.

## Growth of Accountability

From analyses of Figures 15-1 and 15-2, it becomes evident that a great percentage of the accountability for practice-related decisions rests at the staff nurse level. Staff nurses who are members of the SNCG have accountabilities, including: (1) keeping abreast of the current topics of discussion, (2) relaying staff concerns or suggestions through appropriate channels and keeping their units informed of discussions and decisions, (3) using their votes on the NPC to demonstrate the view of the staff nurses in their unit, (4) being active members of select hospital committees and task forces.

Many practice-related issues require further input from all levels of nursing. These may be handled effectively in committees. For example, if transporting patients within the hospital in a more efficient fashion were discussed, input would be needed on cost feasibility, ancillary assistance, and implementation strategies. Input would be valuable from head and assistant head nurses, clinical specialists, and directors of nursing, thus producing a more comprehensive approach to the problem.

## DEVELOPMENT OF A CONFERENCE GROUP

The essential role of a conference group is sharing information, ideas, and concerns from its level of nursing and developing a channel of communication to all conference groups.

Several steps are required in organizing a conference group: (1) The group must be able to define its needs and purposes. (2) The participants must believe in the strengths of the needs and purposes; value to the institution also must be demonstrated, with a strong sense of accountability to both peers and clients. (3) Membership must be determined and peers organized. (4) A chairperson must be chosen and that role defined. (5) The role of the staff nurse members of the conference group must be defined.

### Determination of Membership

It is essential to have the support of the Department of Nursing for the successful establishment of a staff nurse committee/conference group. The idea of a shared governance model should have the support of all levels in the organizational structure. Head and assistant head nurses should be supportive of staff nurse time off the unit, clinical nurse specialists need to be available as resource personnel, and directors should support staff nurses in making practice-related decisions.

The number of members of an SNCG may influence staff representation on the NPC. If there are too few staff nurses, input is inadequate, it is difficult to disseminate information, and a degree of discomfort develops because of the limited peer support for communicating information to the NPC. If there are too many staff nurse members, the results are chaotic, with unmanageable meetings, difficulty in obtaining time off the units for the meetings, and delays in decisionmaking on agenda items because of long and perhaps repetitive discussion.

### Problems and Problem Solving

Problems identified in organizing peers for the development of a SNCG include: (1) gaining support of the staff, (2) arranging for time off the unit, (3) changing membership, and (4) dealing with feelings of skepticism.

Gaining the support of peers is essential for a strong organization. This can be accomplished by inservice training for the staff on shared governance, its structure and process, and how it benefits them. The staff must be aware of the time commitment required for SNCG members and their role in the system. As the staff nurse's knowledge level on shared governance improves, support to the other SNCG members will increase by all SNCG members taking on more responsibility.

Arranging for time off units for the SNCG members can be difficult because of patient case load and staffing needs. Units can facilitate the SNCG member's time away by: (1) identifying one staff nurse to take over the patient responsibility, (2) dividing the SNCG member's caseload among other staff members, or (3) having an additional staff member available for that block of time. Time away from the unit needs to be arranged with the unit manager well in advance so that overtime can be minimized.

Membership changes on the SNCG also can affect staff nurse cohesiveness. Frequent membership changes disrupt efficient processing of agenda items. Such changes must be addressed specifically in the group's bylaws, identifying the process for recruiting new members when others leave. Consistency in leadership can minimize the disruption produced by frequent changes.

Feelings of skepticism about the effectiveness of a shared governance system also affect group process. Skepticism resolves itself as part of the growth process, and can be minimized by providing inservice training for the staff. Skepticism also can be reduced by highlighting accomplishments of the group and using failures as learning experiences.

As a group matures and becomes more stable, leaders emerge. Each member brings to the group a unique body of knowledge, differing viewpoints, and varying degrees of leadership skills. It is important for the group to identify individuals with good leadership skills and to use them as role models for less experienced members. Many staff nurses are not aware of their leadership capabilities. Exposure to a good role model in a group allows them to adopt such skills in a nonthreatening environment.

## THE CHAIRPERSON

The chairperson should be able to communicate effectively with the group and facilitate its business while providing an opportunity for a balanced discussion. The chairperson also must possess the respect of peers and have some background in the organization's activities.

The primary task of the chairperson is to facilitate orderly progress through the business agenda. The individual should be familiar with *Robert's Rules of Order* and group process to produce effective discussions. The chairperson also should be able to maintain a focus on the topic at hand. Discussion often can become caught up in other topics, so it is important for the chairperson to help keep the group focused.

One of the more difficult duties of the chairperson is to see that certain members do not dominate discussions or manipulate group thought. One way to prevent this is to ask such questions as, "How do the critical care units handle this problem?" or, "Do the smaller units experience these same difficulties?" or, "Maybe we should hear how orthopedics deals with this problem." These types of questions help focus the discussion and increase input.

Communicating with other groups in the organization and being the liaison to other conference groups also is a task of the chair. The chairperson of the staff group is a spokesperson for the rest of the staff nurses.

Being a timekeeper is essential in chairing a group. If there is difficulty with running overtime and not completing agenda items, the chairperson must be more rigid in setting limits on topics, deferring long discussions, and reordering the agenda.

The chairperson should not be responsible for secretarial duties. A secretary to take minutes should be appointed at the first meeting. Ideally, the secretary also should be available to assist with the agenda, but it can be difficult to coordinate a premeeting session between the chairperson and secretary because of unit obligations.

The agenda becomes the primary way the committee (1) communicates the issues for discussion, (2) organizes the flow of the meeting, and (3) allows members to prepare, beforehand, to facilitate business. It is the most time-consuming premeeting activity because it involves sorting communications and determining whether business from past meetings has been completed. The chairperson must know the resources available within the organization, e.g., secretaries in nursing service for typing or staff nurses willing to assist with follow-up on old business. The agenda is so important to the success of the group that the chairperson should send it to the members well in advance, allowing time for their review.

## RESPONSIBILITIES OF AN SNCG MEMBER

Today's staff nurse as a member of a shared governance system has a new role, with great autonomy and accountability to various groups. Traditionally, the responsibility in a bureaucratic health care system was to function according to the standards set by management. This allowed little collaboration among administrators, managers, and staff nurses. The accountability for determining policies for practice remained with administration. Participants in committee work included persons removed from direct patient care, and individuals with the most experience in such work had little or no input in decisionmaking (Sorenson & Wheeler, 1982).

Being an accountable member of a decisionmaking group is a new role for the staff nurse, a role that with a little experience can become as comfortable as patient care. The role also involves interaction with those in authority. Some staff nurses adjust to the role quickly and feel comfortable, but others do not. It should be understood that not all staff nurses want to be part of the direct decisionmaking process. Therefore, the staff must choose as its representative a member whom peers can relate to comfortably.

Members of the SNCG must be aware of their responsibilities: (1) full knowledge of the group's bylaws, purpose, and objectives; (2) commitment to attendance at meetings; (3) preparation for meetings; and (4) articulation and communication of staff nurse input.

Members are required to negotiate individually with their units to arrange for the time to prepare for and to attend meetings.

A sense of trust, or the feeling that the staff members are working together and not against each other, is strongest within the SNCG itself. It is part of the growing process to expand the trust to all staff nurses. It is accurate to say that those not actively involved question the support of nursing administration to staff nurses. For that reason, the role of communicator is important.

## Benefits of Increased Communication

Benefits to nursing practice can be seen as a result of involving staff nurses in the decisionmaking process. Increased feelings of accountability, responsibility, and professionalism are reflected in the day-to-day care of patients. Employees' feelings of self-esteem increase when their input is valued.

Working within the shared governance system provides the staff nurse with a greater understanding of how it operates and can increase feelings of loyalty toward it. It also provides further avenues for personal goal development and maturity. It fosters improved communication techniques with peers and management and improves time management skills. These obviously are additional benefits but any that improve staff morale contribute to better patient care.

## Obstacles to Collaborative Communication

Despite all that shared governance has to offer to a nursing organization, there still are obstacles that must be overcome if the system is to function effectively. Some common obstacles are resistance to change, feelings of discouragement and doubt by staff and leaders, apathy among staff and leadership, lack of acceptance by management of shared decisionmaking, and a knowledge deficit at all staff levels as to the shared governance system itself and how it works.

Many of the common obstacles can be removed by an inservice program, consistent support by administration, and increased involvement by staff and leadership personnel in shared governance.

Problems arise in committees involving group dynamics: insecurity of group members, poor attendance, skepticism, feelings of powerlessness, and poor communication. The frequency of such problems can be reduced by educating members in group process and group dynamics. Their familiarity with the change process helps provide insights into problems. Regardless of the behaviors they might demonstrate, consistent support and encouragement from the administrative staff help to sustain the new structure and provide early recognition of issues as they develop.

Another potential problem is the amount of time necessary to make decisions. Obtaining input from appropriate levels in the organization may be delayed or be slower than a bureaucratic system, but the results of decisions supported by the staff are worth the effort.

Many of these roadblocks will be encountered, and dealing with them successfully should make the group stronger. However, a group should continue to work to increase its power base and make a point of acting on issues promptly and professionally.

In summary, the use of a shared governance system for decisionmaking increases the need for greater communication and committee use. Committee roles and functions must be identified clearly and communication channels and reporting mechanisms must be established to facilitate dissemination of information and acquisition of diverse input. The staff nurse's role is expanded, and participation in shared decisionmaking increases feelings of professionalism, autonomy, and accountability—concepts essential to the provision of quality health care.

## REFERENCES

Affiliated Dynamics, Inc. (1984). *Shared governance for the nursing organization* (An Affiliated Dynamics Nurseguide). Norcross, Ga.: Affiliated Dynamics, Inc.

Cherry, E.G. (1966). The Communication of Information. In A. Smith (Ed.), *Communication and culture*. New York: Holt, Rinehart, & Winston.

McGregor, D. (1960). *The human side of enterprise*. New York: McGraw-Hill.

National Commission on Nursing (1982). *Nursing in transition: Models for successful organizational change*. Chicago: The Hospital Research and Educational Trust.

Snook, I.D. (1984). Advantages and disadvantages of committees. *Health Care Supervisor, 2,* 39-49.

Sorenson, M.A., & Wheeler, K. (1982). On the scene: Saint Joseph's Hospital. *Nursing Administration Quarterly, 7,* 27-60.


## BIBLIOGRAPHY

Althaus, J., Hardyck, N., Pierce, P., & Rodgers, M.S. (1981). *Nursing decentralization: The El Camino experience*. Waterfield, Mass.: Nursing Resources.

Binger, J.L., & Huntsman, A.J. (Eds.). (1981). *Communicating effectively*. Wakefield, Mass.: Nursing Resources.

Bradford, L.P. (1976). *Making meetings work*. San Diego: University Associates.

Brunner, N.A. (1977). Communications in nursing service administration. *The Journal of Nursing Administration, 7,* 29-32.

Bullough, B. (1975). Barriers to the nurse practitioner movement: Problems of women in a woman's field. *International Journal of Health Services, 5,* 225-233.

Clark, C.C. (1977). *The nurse as group leader*, Vol. 3. New York: Springer.

Cleland, V.S. (1978). Shared governance in a professional model of collective bargaining. *The Journal of Nursing Administration, 8,* 39-43.

Easterling, J.F. (1983). Autonomy, professionalism, and collective bargaining. *The Michigan Nurse, 56,* 6-7.

Edelstein, R.R.G. (1979). Self-management in American nursing. *International Nursing Review, 26,* 78-83.

Elpern, E.H., White, P.M., & Donahue, M.F. (1984). Staff governance: The experience of one nursing unit. *The Journal of Nursing Administration, 14,* 9-15. .

Haggard, A. (1984). Decentralized staff development. *The Journal of Continuing Education in Nursing, 15,* 90-92.

Mathews, J.J. (1983). The communication process in clinical settings. *Social Science and Medicine, 17,* 1371-1378.

McClure, M.L. (1984). Managing the professional nurse, Part 1: The organizational theories. *The Journal of Nursing Administration, 14,* 15-21.

McKay, P.S. (1983). Interdependent decisionmaking: Redefining professional autonomy. *Nursing Administration Quarterly, 7,* 21-30.

Monson, T. (1981). Mastering the art of planning by committee. *The Journal of Nursing Administration, 11,* 71-72.

Porter-O'Grady, T., & Finnigan, S. (1984). *Shared governance for nursing.* Rockville, Md.: Aspen Publishers, Inc.

Pranulis, M.F. (1980). Staff involvement in the problem-solving and decisionmaking processes. *Arizona Nurse, 33,* 1,12,14.

Strasen, L. (1983). Participative management: A contribution to professionalism. *Critical Care Nurse, 3,* 35-40.

**Part V**

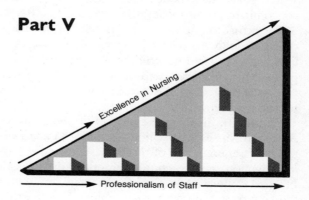

Excellence in Nursing

Professionalism of Staff

# Nurse Development and the Professional Climate

*Eleanore Kirsch*
Section Editor

149

The previous sections have described this book's conceptual framework from the groundwork laid in implementing and promoting unit-based quality assurance (UBQA), through the expansion of critical thinking utilizing the research process, to the acceptance of accountability and autonomy in the shared governance model. Part V examines the next step in the model, the concomitant professional growth of staff (see Book Model).

The actual timing of the events cited in this Part at times paralleled, preceded, or followed the progression of development in UBQA, research utilization, and shared governance. Professional development does not always proceed in an orderly, step-by-step process. However, all examples are intrinsically related to the overall conceptual framework and operation of professional growth.

Chapter 16 discusses the process of operationalizing the concepts of the American Nurses' Association *Social Policy Statement* and Chapter 17 outlines the staff's examination of theory-based practice. Both chapters describe the investigation of theoretical concepts at the direct request of the Nursing Practice Council (NPC). These chapters are examples of increased critical thinking by staff nurses as they struggle to define their practice in the context of shared governance.

Chapters 18 and 19 provide examples of the various roles a nurse can assume in gaining control over practice, through nurse-managed clinics, advanced practice roles, and participation in nurse-physician committees. These chapters exemplify expanded staff nurse decisionmaking supported and/or enhanced by the climate of shared governance.

Both nursing diagnosis and primary nursing, as discussed in Chapters 20 and 21, developmentally preceded UBQA at St. Michael Hospital. Thus, within this book's conceptual framework, they represent the earliest quests for autonomy, accountability, and decentralized decisionmaking. However, their developmental momentum accelerated with UBQA and shared governance.

For example, although the initial thrust in implementing nursing diagnosis came from the clinical nurse specialist (C.N.S.) group, subsequent development of nursing diagnosis was undertaken by unit quality assurance committees. These staff nurses frequently utilize the research process when developing nursing diagnosis documentation materials. Since these are a permanent part of the record, they are approved by the NPC. This is an excellent example of how shared governance gives staff control of nursing care delivery.

Primary nursing was practiced at St. Michael Hospital prior to UBQA and shared governance. However, it was not until the implementation of shared governance that the staff felt it necessary to integrate the primary nursing concept into the nursing department philosophy statement, the generic standards of care, the professional nurse evaluation system, and appropriate policies and procedures.

Chapter 22 on peer review is another example of the departure from centralized authority to more decentralized decisionmaking. It exemplifies the shared governance concepts of building trust, enhancing communication, and developing staff nurse autonomy and accountability. The chapter identifies factors that determine climate readiness for peer review, including support for professional growth, a primary nurse delivery system, UBQA, and objective, competency-based evaluations. Since that chapter was written, the NPC voted that peer review be implemented on all nursing units by all professional staff. Peer review is another link in the chain of professional growth described by the conceptual model of this book.

Chapter 23, on nursing grand rounds, demonstrates the integration of the theory-practice-research cycle through formal presentations by staff. These can be based on nursing theory, research findings, or specific unit practice issues as identified by the UBQA committee. The research framework is used in the presentation, and the outcomes can increase staff knowledge base, improve patient care, enhance staff-to-staff communication, and encourage the development of new standards of patient care. The process stimulates critical thinking and promotes staff nurse accountability for practice. Again, this is the same process as that promoted by the shared governance model.

As a part of peer review, competency-based evaluations as analyzed in Chapter 24 spur professional growth and development. These competencies include the same concepts cited previously: nursing diagnosis, primary nursing, quality assurance, the research process, and accountability for practice. In keeping with the philosophy of shared governance, it is the responsibility of each conference group to develop its own specific competencies and to assure that these standards are met.

Chapter 25 describes the development and implementation of an emergency department patient classification system. The need for this system was identified by the UBQA committee, which participated in its development, implementation, and analysis. This is another example of staff nurses' demonstrating their ability to grow professionally. The professional climate gave staff members the opportunity to question and challenge existing methods, use resources to study the problem systematically and seek change, and ultimately to become more accountable for their practice.

The final chapter in Part V addresses professional development beyond the organization. A professional climate such as that described in this book promotes the growth of nurses not only in their roles within the institution but also outside it. This conceptual framework describing the commitment to excellence and the professionalization of staff progressively builds upon UBQA, the research process, shared governance, and eventually professional growth.

However, it should not be construed as a linear process. In reality, it is an open system. The more an organization contributes to the professional growth of its staff members, the more they will have to give back.

Chapter 26 describes some of these behaviors: the sharing of ideas and the networking with other nurses outside the agency and with other organizations; the reporting of UBQA studies at research conferences; the participation in political, research, and specialty activities; and the quest for higher formal education. These behaviors can only benefit the organizations that employ these nurses.

Together, these chapters demonstrate the interrelationship of the various topics as they influence the overall professionalization of staff. Through increased critical thinking, enhanced communication, greater autonomy and accountability over practice, heightened awareness of practice expectations, and the sharing of ideas, nurses are provided the opportunity for continuing professional development and thus contribute to organizational enhancement. Professional excellence has come full circle.

**Chapter 16**

# The ANA Social Policy Statement: Implementing a Concept

*Eleanore Kirsch, Debbie Reitman-Judge, Janet Krejci, Tracy Dusenske, Sue Kasprzak, and Regina Maibusch*

*Operationalizing the concepts of a statement defining nursing practice can give direction and focus to nursing staff. The process of implementing such concepts can enhance the professional growth of nurses and reflect the nature of nursing practice in an organization.*

In 1980, the American Nurses' Association (ANA) published a statement titled *Nursing: A Social Policy Statement* (ANA, 1980). This document (the SPS) defined nursing and the nature, scope, and characteristics of nursing practice.

The SPS defines nursing as "the diagnosis and treatment of human responses to actual or potential health problem" (ANA, 1980, p. 9). It lists the four characteristics of nursing as:

1. Phenomena: Human responses that are the focus for nursing intervention (p. 9).
2. Theory: Concepts, principles, or process that serve as a basis for determining nursing actions to be taken (p. 11).
3. Actions: The performance of nursing practice (p. 12).
4. Effects: Outcomes evaluated by the process of nursing research (p. 12).

153

It gives as the four defining characteristics of the scope of nursing practice:

1. Boundary: The external limits of the nursing profession that can expand or reduce in response to change (p. 13).
2. Intersections: The nursing segment of health care that interacts intraprofessionally and interprofessionally (p. 16).
3. Core: The naming of phenomena through the process of nursing diagnosis as the basis of nursing practice (p. 16).
4. Dimensions: Characteristics that fall within and further describe the scope of nursing (p. 16).

By clarifying nurses' social responsibility, both society and the profession gain a perspective on the implications and significance of nursing practice. This chapter describes the process of adoption and implementation of the *Social Policy Statement* by the St. Michael Hospital Nursing Department, the model utilized for implementation, and the struggle to make the process meaningful. The value of the SPS to nurses and their profession also is addressed.

## NATIONAL IMPLEMENTATION OF SPS

In 1979, the ANA Congress for Nursing Practice and the ANA board of directors established a seven-member task force to develop a policy statement for the nursing profession and the public at large. This *Social Policy Statement* was published by the ANA in December 1980. Its implementation nationally is still in process.

According to Lang (personal communications, 1986), chairperson of the task force, the ANA has used the SPS in drafting testimony and in establishing standards, certification, and classification systems. ANA councils, such as the Council for Psychiatric and Mental Health Nursing, have begun extensive work on the identification of nursing phenomena, actions, and outcomes—all components of the SPS. Lang believes the measure of success in implementation will be reached when the SPS is used routinely for policy development—nationally, regionally, and locally.

Two reports in the literature describe at least small attempts at publicizing the SPS. Minnesota Nursing Association, District #3, printed a summary of the SPS on a bookmark and made 10,000 copies available to its constituents (Bookmark, 1985). The Oregon Nurses' Association presented a skit to its members depicting a patient care situation with and without the benefit of the SPS (Kerns, 1985). However, no specific model for implementation was found in the literature.

Although still in the neophyte stage of professional development, nursing has begun to make progress toward turning the SPS concepts into practice. One model of implementation was the one at St. Michael Hospital.

## A PHILOSOPHICAL BASE FOR PRACTICE

To promote the process of adopting and implementing the SPS, certain readiness factors are necessary. St. Michael Hospital identified a number of such factors:

- direct access to informational resources
- an effective communication network within the organization
- in-house leadership resources and skills
- motivational incentives for staff nurses
- organizational documents that guide practice.

These same factors could be beneficial to other institutions in implementing the SPS.

### Organizational Readiness Factors

Direct access to information about the SPS is essential and can be provided in a variety of ways. Initially, the nursing department provided each nursing unit with a copy of the SPS. The ANA film (ANA, 1981) on the SPS was presented, and a panel discussion was held. Because of its diverse membership (nurses, physicians, consumers), the panel was an effective means of providing exposure to the SPS from intraprofessional, interprofessional, and consumer points of view. At that time, the hospital orientation program introduced all newly hired registered nurses to the SPS.

Information on the SPS was disseminated before the department made its decision to integrate it into its operations. Nurses were not provided an in-depth opportunity to explore its concepts, but they generally were aware that an important document defining nursing had been written.

Implementation of such a major new philosophical position requires an effective communication network within the department that routes information, promotes discussion, and assists in decisionmaking. Nurses in all roles have to understand the relevance of the SPS in order to endorse its implementation fully. At St. Michael Hospital, the shared governance model (see Part IV) used to organize the nursing department provided such a network, channeling information and feedback in a consistent manner that helped to maintain momentum during the implementation process.

Leaders with the ability to articulate the conceptual components of the SPS effectively are an important part of successful implementation. They must be able to assist other nurses in understanding the concept, be attuned to the difficulties and resistance that might occur, and be able to apply group process skills to resolve problems. Leaders must take responsibility for co-ordinating and directing the implementation.

Motivational incentives are needed to encourage staff nurse participation. It is imperative that staff nurses understand the SPS in terms of their professional role behaviors. Their participation also is important politically to enhance departmentwide networking during the process. Motivational incentives include:

- a clinical career ladder that recognizes the staff nurses' involvement in department committee work
- nurse managers who support the staff nurses' need for additional time to attend meetings or work on related activities
- peer support as reflected by colleagues who demonstrate respect and esteem for other nurses' professional activities
- an organizational atmosphere that rewards professional growth.

Documents within the organization that collectively influence and guide the professional action of the nursing department are necessary (Cantor, 1973). The most influential document is the nursing department statement of philosophy; others include committee and department purposes and objectives, job descriptions, evaluation forms, standards of practice, and course or curriculum outlines. Endorsement of the SPS concepts in these documents is the most concrete indication that implementation is occurring.

## The Implementation Process

The organizational readiness factors noted earlier were already in place at St. Michael Hospital when the idea of adopting the SPS was presented at the Nursing Practice Council (NPC) in February 1983. (However, formal adoption of the statement did not occur until seven months later.) These supporting mechanisms and the level of professional development of the nursing staff stimulated the implementation process.

The inception of shared governance had changed the process of decision-making in the nursing department, requiring additional time to obtain feedback from all levels of professional nurses, conduct inservice workshops, negotiate organizational politics, and allow the Staff Nurse Conference Group (SNCG) to examine and discuss the SPS concepts.

At the outset, the staff nurses were hesitant to adopt a statement that they perceived implied requiring entry into practice at the baccalaureate level. The conceptual complexity of the document generated ambivalent reactions. Although not accepting on the basis of idealism, the SNCG eventually concurred with the belief of the staff nurse leaders, who promoted the concepts of professionalism as put forward in the SPS.

Next came the task of implementation. The NPC delegated this process to a task force whose membership consisted of volunteers from all conference groups except the head nurses.

At the first meeting, the following objectives were agreed upon:

1. to examine the nursing department statement of philosophy, identify how it reflects the SPS, and make recommendations for revision to the NPC, if necessary
2. to examine the purpose and objectives of all housewide nursing committees and conference groups, to identify how they reflect the SPS, and to make recommendations to the NPC, as necessary
3. to examine job descriptions and competency-based evaluations to identify how they reflect the SPS and make recommendations to the NPC, as necessary
4. to articulate operational guidelines for nursing practice as implied in the SPS
5. to identify evaluation materials to measure the success of implementation of the SPS.

Even though the task of the group was outlined clearly, the project seemed formidable and members needed mutual reassurance. It helped to keep in mind that the SPS was not a notion of what nursing was "supposed to be" but rather "what it is" and that there would be evidence from daily practice that would confirm this.

A model for implementation of the SPS was developed from the original objectives (Figure 16-1). The model demonstrated how integration of the SPS concepts affected all aspects of the nursing department.

The task force developed the model as a mechanism to communicate how these concepts could be measured in nurses' practice. The use of the model turned a grandiose statement of adoption of the SPS into concrete, observable terms.

The core of the model was a method developed to put the SPS concepts into practice. This was created drawing from the work of Paulen (1982) and Waltz, Strickland, and Lenz (1984). As the model demonstrates, it was utilized to document SPS implementation departmentwide. This model can be used by any organization to implement the SPS but it should be institutionally specific and incorporate its own role components.

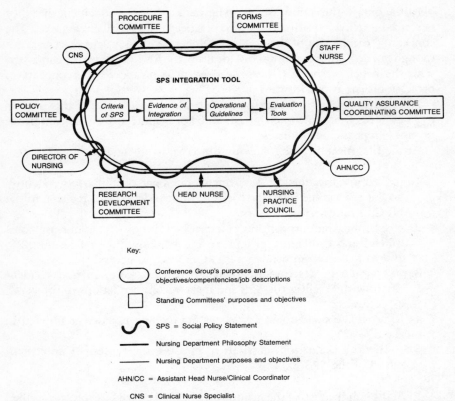

**Figure 16-1** St. Michael Hospital Model for SPS Implementation. *Source:* Courtesy of St. Michael Hospital, Milwaukee, Wisconsin © 1984.

The SPS integration format (Table 16-1) was initially used to address the nursing department philosophy statement. SPS criteria believed to be crucial for defining the statement and its implications for practice were pinpointed (see Criteria column in Table 16-1). The criteria were defined as the SPS concepts that defined the characteristics and scope of general and specialty practice (ANA, 1980).

Questions were developed that assisted the task force members in addressing each criterion and determined how the documents should be reviewed. They also increased mutual understanding of SPS terminology and developed the members' conceptual thinking abilities. The answers to these questions were listed under Column 2, Evidence of Integration.

The third column was used to document actual nurse behaviors. These Operational Guidelines were observable indicators that demonstrated how

**Table 16-1** Social Policy Statement Integration Format

**Entity:** (Example) Department of Nursing Statement of Philosophy

| Criteria | Evidence of Integration | Operational Guidelines (Nurse Behavior) | Potential Evaluation Elements |
|---|---|---|---|
| **General** | **(Example)** | **(Example)** | **(Example)** |
| 1. Definition of Nursing | 1.1 Definition of nursing not present; should be present and explicit. Evidence now in paragraph 2, sentence 2. | 1.1 Nurses articulate the definition of nursing. <br> 1.2 Nurses complete a nursing data base and derive appropriate nursing diagnosis. <br> 1.3 The definition of nursing is incorporated into registered nurse orientation. | 1.1 Nursing survey. <br><br> 1.2 Audit nursing care plans and data base. <br><br> 1.3 Audit orientation content. |
| 2. Phenomena | | | |
| 3. Theory | | | |
| 4. Actions | | | |
| 5. Effects | | | |
| 6. Boundaries | | | |
| 7. Intersections | | | |
| 8. Core | | | |
| 9. Dimensions | | | |
| **Specialty** | | | |
| 10. Functions | | | |
| 11. Activities | | | |

specific criteria were integrated into practice. They were not all-inclusive but were examples of nurse behaviors.

The criteria varied in degree of integration, depending on which document was being addressed. For example, the head nurse's job description might approach the concept of theory differently from that of the staff nurse's. The head nurse behavior may be to promote theory in practice by providing an environment for evaluation and research while staff nurses may implement the theory criterion by writing a patient care plan developed through a review of literature.

The fourth column, Potential Evaluation Elements, was developed as a mechanism for observing and measuring the existence of nurse behaviors (operational guidelines). Some of these mechanisms for monitoring practice already existed and others were recommendations for development.

Applying the integration format assisted the members in rewriting the nursing department philosophy statement. After several drafts and revisions incorporating feedback from the NPC, the council approved a philosophy truly reflective of the SPS.

## PROBLEMS/RESOLUTIONS

Implementation proceeded in a relatively smooth fashion for the first few months. Problems became apparent when the conference groups were asked to apply the integration format. In spite of the availability of task force members to assist with its application, conference groups felt overwhelmed. Organizational changes, shifting priorities, and repeated extremes in hospital census caused a variety of feelings among the staff members. Decentralization led to changes in job descriptions and eliminated or expanded certain roles and functions.

Several of the conference groups had yet to write purposes and objectives or competency-based evaluation forms for their job positions. With a time limit set by the task force for completion of implementation, staff members were feeling pressured. Some nurse managers voiced difficulty applying the practice-oriented SPS concepts to their role functions. The SPS language continued to be difficult to understand. There seemed, in general, less motivation than originally expressed for the implementation process.

Resolution of these problems and continued implementation of the SPS was still in process at St. Michael Hospital at this writing. It became apparent that there was a need to step back and allow conference groups more time to become comfortable with their evolving role in shared governance and other organizational changes. The passage of time decreased the initial anxiety and allowed completion of other tasks, i.e., writing of job descriptions and competency-based evaluation forms. Several standing committees and conference groups, including the SNCG, had addressed their purposes and objectives and job descriptions utilizing the SPS integration format.

The task force promoted a continued awareness of the SPS through interfacing with conference groups; poster presentations about the SPS at hospital, regional, and national conferences; participation at SPS-related conferences; and articles in the nursing department newsletter. The task force found the implementation of the SPS was a continuing process.

## VALUE TO NURSES/NURSING

The debate and discussion critiquing the SPS is continuing in nursing, as it should. The ANA has defined its perception of the characteristics and scope of professional nursing for the practicing nurse. In turn, by implementing this statement, practicing nurses can provide supportive or opposing evidence as to the value of the SPS.

Overall, the impact of implementing the SPS at St. Michael Hospital has been threefold:

1. Nursing staff members examined their professional role and function in a unified manner. This examination increased awareness of their accountability for practice.
2. Implementation helped nurses in conceptualizing their practice, using a common language. Abstract terms such as *theory* and *philosophy* were described in concrete behaviors that could be measured.
3. Implementation clarified the meaning of the SPS as it pertained to nurses' everyday practice. It promoted critical review of the document, assisted in interpreting its difficult terminology, and served as a directive to patient care.

For nursing in general, the SPS offers direction to define practice for both the profession and society. It gives nursing the opportunity to address its strengths and potential effectiveness. It unifies nursing's diversity in a common goal—quality patient care—while at the same time encouraging innovative and alternative delivery of care.

The SPS enhances nursing's distinctiveness of care by defining what humanistic situations nurses address. The end result is individualized patient care. At the very least, nurses owe the nursing profession a thoughtful review of the SPS.

## REFERENCES

American Nurses' Association. (1980). *Nursing: A Social Policy Statement* (ANA Publication Code: NP-63 35M 12/80). Kansas City, Mo.: Author.

American Nurses's Association. (1981). *Nursing: A social policy statement.* [Film]. Kansas City, Mo.: Author.

Bookmark lists key points of ANA statement. (1985). *The American Nurse, 17,* 21.

Cantor, M.M. (1973). Philosophy, purposes, objectives: Why do we have them? *The Journal of Nursing Administration, 3,* 21-25.

Kerns, W. (1985). Skit shows ANA statement helps R.N. improve care. *The American Nurse, 17,* 5.

Lang, N. (February 13, 1986). Personal communications.

Paulen, A. (October 1982), A philosophy of caring. Paper presented at the convention of the Wisconsin Nurses' Association, La Crosse, Wis.

Waltz, C.F., Strickland, O.L., & Lenz, E.R. (1984). *Measurement in nursing research.* Philadelphia: F.A. Davis.

# Chapter 17

# Theory and Practice of Nursing

*Mary T. Sinnen and Kathy Schmidt*

*Nurses want to be autonomous, to be able to work collaboratively with other professional disciplines, and to be both accountable and responsible for nursing care. To achieve these ends, nurses must explore the theoretical and applied knowledge necessary for the practice of nursing.*

Theory denotes a hypothesis describing a given set of phenomena backed by generally accepted evidence gathered through scientific methods. A second definition of the term *theory* also should be considered in defining nursing: Theory is a demonstrated explanation of something based on the system that makes it both "to be" and "to be what it is." In this definition, only one theory of "something" is possible. More simply, theory is the answer to the question, "What is it?"

If nursing is to be considered a profession it must be based on a practice and it must define its practice in terms of both theoretical and applied knowledge. Practice, in this sense, is a process performed on some matter for the sake of an end by an agent who possesses both the theoretical and applied knowledge of the process and therefore knows what is being done, as well as why, at every stage of the performance of the process (Hanlon, 1985, p. i).

This chapter briefly examines nursing's progress in its attempts to define itself as a profession. It discusses how its focus has changed over the years and reviews current literature in which nursing attempts to integrate theory into the practice setting. The staff experience of St. Michael Hospital is analyzed and the future of theory-integrated nursing practice is discussed.

## FROM A HISTORICAL PERSPECTIVE

Historically speaking, the nursing profession had its beginning with Florence Nightingale, who wrote in the 1800s about the basic foundations of nursing that still are practiced today. Nightingale's emphasis on the concepts of environment, health, person, and nursing set the stage for professional practice. Following her ideas, nurses were trained in the skills needed for their work.

It was not until the 1960s that the emphasis shifted toward the intellectual/scientific aspects of nursing, along with interpersonal communications. By the 1970s, the nursing profession was able to view itself "as a scientific discipline oriented toward a theoretical-based practice that focused on the client" (Griffith, 1982, p. 4). With this later emphasis came the development of various models, nursing diagnosis, and the nursing process. In the 1980s, nurses were using these modalities to identify, organize, understand, and guide their practice while researchers continued to define the profession in terms of theory.

Perry (1985, p. 34) summarizes the major shifts in theory development as evidenced by the literature since the mid-1960s. She describes these as a movement from Nightingale's four basic concepts to an emphasis on technical control derived from a mechanistic manner of thought. She also describes a movement toward the interpersonal skills of nursing, derived from a humanistic manner of thought. The emphasis has shifted to the process of theory development and the associated cognitive skills in nursing education and practice.

## RESEARCH ON THEORY INTO PRACTICE

The literature speaks of theory but actually refers to models or conceptual frameworks. It addresses the need to test and validate these models in the practice setting if theories are to be formulated. This testing for validation is a call for all nurses to become involved—not just those in education and research settings but those giving patient care as well (Mastal, Hammond, & Roberts, 1982, p. 9).

Research reports focus on the implementation of conceptual models into hospital-based nursing practice. Kinney (1984, pp. 5-6) points out that nurses' conceptualization of the profession is important in providing direction throughout the patient care process. The assessment data, the diagnosis or problems addressed, and the patient care outcomes all are determined by how nursing is viewed by the nurses. Adopting a nursing model could influence practice greatly. The approach to caring for patients would be more unified if nurses shared a common conceptualization.

In one example, Mastal, Hammond, and Roberts (1982) describe their efforts to implement Roy's Adaptation Model in a unit of a small community hospital. Their description includes:

- exploring the framework with Sr. Callista Roy
- planning the implementation with the hospital administration in terms of congruency with the institution's philosophy, standards of patient care, and cost effectiveness
- organizing the change structure on the unit; developing procedures and other elements such as a data base formulated from Roy's model
- educating the staff before implementation.

This project produced an improvement in patient care and patient satisfaction and a more professional nursing practice. It was noted that the care was less fragmented and the nurses were better directed and unified in providing quality care for the total patient. As a result of the study outcomes, the hospital administration adopted the Roy Adaptation Model as the structure for nursing practice throughout the hospital.

In another report, Schmieding (1984) speaks of using Orlando's theory (actually, model) in practice. Schmieding says that if every nurse in the same nursing service organization uses a different theory, chaos can result. She believes strongly that the use of one theory throughout a department produces a nursing team giving quality care. Orlando's theory was chosen based on the nature of both nursing care and nursing administration in the hospital and because of its easy language and application in practice as well as in administrative settings. The description of this experience emphasizes the need for a common starting point in terms of all nurses' understanding the theory and the process for applying it.

The assessment of what nurses believed to be their functions was a priority. The discovery that no common concept or function unique to nursing could be identified led to the preparation and utilization of Orlando's concepts and theory. Schmieding comments: "Without a framework, nurses were in an impossible position of being unable to say what tasks they should not perform."

After the theory was translated into practice, nurses were able to state why they could not perform nonnursing tasks and be understood by the other hospital personnel. The study results included their increased identity as nurses, relief in that nurses could identify clearly the functions for which they were accountable, and a more unified professional colleagueship.

## THE ST. MICHAEL EXPERIENCE

At St. Michael Hospital, the Nursing Practice Council (NPC) debated which framework should be used to develop a new nursing data base. The committee attempting to write a data base had researched various models and presented them to the NPC. The discussion questioned whether nurses should be limited to one framework in all aspects of practice. From this discussion, the NPC recommended the formation of a Theory Task Force. The task force was charged with formulating guide questions or providing information to nurses in the institution that would stimulate them to think in terms of theory and conceptual models regarding their practice.

As a separate committee, the nursing data base group later selected a conceptual framework based on Gordon's (1982) functional patterns around which to organize the admission assessment. The integration of theory assisted the group in developing a comprehensive format that reflected a holistic approach to clients and families.

The Theory Task Force began by researching the definitions of the terms theory, model, conceptual framework, and concept. After reviewing several frameworks already established in nursing, the task force had to decide how this information could best be disseminated to nurses in a nonthreatening and interesting manner, given the fact that the nurses had not demonstrated an interest in this information previously. The decision was to write a series of articles using the nursing newsletter as a vehicle for communication. This decision was based on the fact that the St. Michael Hospital newsletter was well established in the institution and was mailed every month to all nurses working there. The articles used nursing models in day-to-day practice situations.

Eight articles were published, each using a different conceptual framework or theory. Verbal responses from the staff and the Nursing Practice Council members were very positive. Many found that the descriptions of theories and models, and examples of how their use affected clinical practice, were enlightening. Some reported that because their basic nursing curriculum was developed according to a given theory, their practice always had reflected it.

Ultimately, the staff decided not to select a specific theory on which to base overall nursing practice. This decision was based on the sense that the staff was not ready to choose a separate theory, the loss of several committee members, and the lack of time to devote to the project. It was hoped that a new group could be formed and work continued on the subject.

## FUTURE OF THEORY-INTEGRATED PRACTICE

The critical task of defining nursing as a true practice based on a body of theoretical and applied knowledge has begun. However, this involves more than just model or conceptual framework construction. It involves a comprehensive look at theory, nursing practice, and the use of deductive as well as inductive research methods.

One example utilizing this focus is that of Sinnen (1981). She develops an outline of a theory and model of nursing based on the nurturance process. This work focuses on theory as defined earlier in this chapter and identifies disease/injury as partial or complete trauma to the patient's cybernetic system. Nursing intervention is based on the degree of the patient's loss of cybernetic control.

To introduce theory into the clinical setting and proceed with theory development is at best a difficult task. Many find the term *theory* new, abstract, and confusing, as seen in the example at St. Michael Hospital. This task could be made easier if the term *theory,* along with more theory-based practice, were learned in the academic setting. More colleges and schools of nursing should introduce students to theory and the state of this profession in terms of theory development so that, once into a clinical setting, theory and theory building could be enhanced. In this way, the work of theory development could enjoy the unified efforts of all those in nursing.

**REFERENCES**

Gordon, M. (1982). *Nursing diagnosis: Process and application.* New York: McGraw-Hill.

Griffith, J.W. (1982). Relevance of theoretical approaches in nursing practice. In J.W. Griffith and P.J. Christensen (Eds.), *Nursing process: Application of theories, frameworks, and models.* St. Louis: C.V. Mosby.

Hanlon, J.M. (1985). *The theory and practice of education and administration.* Unpublished manuscript.

Kinney, M. (1984). Nursing models. *Focus on Critical Care, 11,* 5-6.

Mastal, M.F., Hammond, H., & Roberts, M.P. (1982). Theory into hospital practice: A pilot implementation. *The Journal of Nursing Administration,* 9-15.

Perry, J. (1985). Has the discipline of nursing developed to the stage where nurses do 'think nursing'? *Journal of Advanced Nursing, 10,* 31-37.

Schmieding, N.J. (1984). Putting Orlando's theory into practice. *American Journal of Nursing, 84,* 759-761.

Sinnen, M.T. (1981). *A theory and a model of nursing based on the nurturance process.* Unpublished master's thesis. Marquette University, Milwaukee.

**BIBLIOGRAPHY**

Avant, K.C., & Walker, L.O. (1984). The practicing nurse and conceptual frameworks. *Maternal Child Nursing, 9,* 87-90.

Fawcett, J. (1985). Theory: Basis for the study and practice of nursing education. *Journal of Nursing Education, 24,* 226-229.

Hanlon, J.M. (1974). Theory and the practice of nursing. *The Journal of Continuing Education in Nursing, 5,* 12-18.

Long, Geraldine E. (1985). Professional advancement: Theory development through practice and research. *ANNA Journal, 12,* 35-38.

The Nursing Theories Conference Group. (1980). *Nursing theories: The base for professional nursing practice.* Englewood Cliffs, N.J.: Prentice-Hall.

Walton, J. (1985). An overview: Orem's self-care deficit theory of nursing. *Focus on Critical Care, 12,* 54-58.

**Chapter 18**

# Control over Practice

*Mary Beth McNichols and Jeffrey G. Miller*

*In the past century, nurses have made progress toward achieving autonomy, accountability, and control over practice. It is imperative that they continue this drive both within the profession as a whole and at the individual practitioner level.*

The quest for nurses to identify themselves as professionals and to gain control over their practice is both a historical and contemporary struggle. Levi (1980, p. 335) comments that nursing in a sociological context is considered a semiprofession characterized by three factors: (1) Nurses most often work in bureaucratic settings. (2) Nurses do not practice with a knowledge base rooted in specific nursing theory. (3) Nurses do not have control over the educational process.

This chapter examines these issues from a historical viewpoint and traces current and potential trends as nursing moves toward becoming a professional body of practitioners.

## HISTORICAL PERSPECTIVE

Historically, the greatest advances in the movement toward the professionalization of nursing involve upgrading its education and the establishment of standards of education and practice. Florence Nightingale, the founder of modern nursing, advocated education based on both theoretical and clinical training. The advancement of nursing education from traditionally hospital-based programs to those conducted in universities is considered the major achievement in obtaining professional status for nursing.

The formation of the National League for Nursing (NLN) and the American Nurses' Association (ANA) in the late 1800s helped nurses organize their energies toward the overall goals of reform in education and to establish a system of legalization of the profession by winning the passage of state nurse practice acts (Ashley, 1976; Levi, 1980). Many state statutes now are based on the ANA standards of nursing practice that advocate that performance be based on knowledge and application of principles of biological, physical, and social sciences and the use of specialized judgment and skill (Levi, 1980).

## ORGANIZATIONAL DESIGN FOR CONTROL

The battle has been long in seeking to determine the most effective organizational design to enhance nursing. This has occurred within, as well as outside of, nursing. Since the Industrial Revolution, the bureaucracy—the most widely used organizational model in most businesses—has included a hierarchical relationship between management and subordinates. In this model, all the control and accountability was held by a few people, with the majority having little input. It was this majority, however, that performed the behaviors needed to accomplish the organization's goals (Argyris, 1962; Drucker, 1974; McGregor, 1960; Peters & Waterman, 1982; Porter-O'Grady & Finnigan, 1984).

The bureaucratic model also has been used in the organization of nursing departments and of hospitals in general. Staff nurses make up the largest proportion of hospital employees, yet traditionally they have had little input in the organization's decisionmaking process. In many hospitals, staff nurses function in a hierarchical relationship with nursing management that culminates with the hospital administrator, who has ultimate control and accountability for nursing services.

In many hospitals, however, there now is a movement away from the bureaucratic model to one that dispenses power and accountability throughout the organization—that is, the concept of decentralization. In such a design, the traditional hierarchy becomes flattened. Hospital organizational design must undergo this type of change if nurses are to gain professionalization and control over practice.

One step in achieving this goal is that of decentralization. In this process, the organization is divided into interacting components. Thus, each nursing unit becomes accountable for its decisionmaking and problem solving, yet reports to the nursing department as a whole. In such a process, each nurse has an increased opportunity to participate in decisionmaking, which in turn enhances autonomy, accountability, and the ability to control individual practice with respect to patient care issues and nursing standards.

## EXAMPLES OF CONTROL OVER PRACTICE

The concept of organizational design in hospital nursing departments to enhance professional practice is gaining popularity and taking on a different format. Batey and Lewis (1982) describe the concepts of autonomy and accountability in an individual's practice as central to the focus and structure of a nursing department. The shared governance format (see Chapter 11) enhances the nurses' ability to make practice-related decisions and provides freedom for individuals to practice in a professional manner, exert greater control over clinical practice, and influence the overall quality of patient care (Moloney, 1986).

### Shared Governance

The shared governance model enhances nurses' professional practice only if they have a recognized and defined role in it. Staff nurses must utilize their opportunity to influence decisions on practice and at the same time nursing management must develop trust in the nurses' skill at effecting change. In other words, in a shared governance system, management gives the staff nurses the authority to act as professionals and expects them to be accountable for practice.

Much of the control over practice is returned to the staff level, giving the nurses a vested interest in making the system work. Moloney (1986) explains that shared governance, by dispersing authority and accountability for practice decisions down to the unit level where these decisions are carried out, allows individual nurses freedom to control their own practice and influence the quality of care.

### Advanced Practitioners

Until recently, nurses utilized their research, autonomy, and accountability in independent practice outside the hospital. The most notable accomplishments have been by nurse practitioners functioning in independent roles, often operating their own clinics. Nurse practitioners have had an impact on the health care system and have pioneered new approaches to patient care, especially in pediatrics, family-centered care, and primary care clinics. They have demonstrated the ability to deliver primary patient care, decrease health care costs, generate revenues, and, overall, lessen the frustration associated with dependent nursing practice.

In hospitals, clinical nurse specialists (C.N.S.s) also have demonstrated autonomy and accountability through their clinical expertise in a specialized area of nursing, their utilization of nursing research, and their collaboration with others on the health care team. Thus, both the C.N.S. and the nurse practitioner exemplify nurses' having control over their practice.

## Nurse-Managed Centers

Nurse-managed centers are another example of practitioners' having control over their work. These centers use the concepts of shared governance, autonomy, and the nursing process to evaluate the needs of the patient population as a whole, as opposed to those of individual patients. Thus, nursing can take control of practice of care based on identified population needs and develop and manage programs to meet such needs in the structure of an acute care setting.

An example is the development of a nurse-managed chronic pain control center at St. Michael Hospital. The nursing staff determined that the needs of chronic pain patients were not being met through traditional methods. This led to investigation and research as to alternative methods of aiding such patients, and the development of a center and of appropriate interventions. This included establishing a center philosophy, program goals, program components, physical plant needs, and staff requirements. Throughout this process, nursing and administration worked together on shared decision-making and planning.

The identified staffing requirements for the pain center provided nursing an opportunity to control practice. A multidisciplinary team approach was needed, with coordination provided by nursing. In the past, nursing often had not been identified with this role but had performed the function of coordinator informally without the benefit of formal autonomy and accountability.

Staff nurses traditionally have taken responsibility for coordinating multidisciplinary plans of care, assessing responses, and evaluating the need for changes. Nurse-managed centers and nurse-coordinated multidisciplinary teams have validated nurses' role in control of patient care and have placed accountability for such care in their hands.

Integral components of the multidisciplinary team obviously are the physician and collaborative care. The traditional physician-ordered approach is replaced with a team in which all disciplines have equal decisionmaking ability. It is imperative that this approach be negotiated with a physician with a similar philosophy from the outset of program development and with staff recruitment to facilitate coordinated patient care. Nurse-managed centers then will function in collaboration with the physician in settings that previously were solely under the doctor's control.

The coordinator role involves all aspects of the center. This includes financial management, assuring that program philosophy and goals are maintained, delivery of program components, and marketing the service to the target populations. Many of these roles are new to nursing in a formal context. To assure quality of patient care and excellence in practice, nursing must remain in the forefront in coordinating such endeavors.

The evaluation of such centers is based on the concepts of unit-based quality assurance. The nurse coordinator evaluates program effectiveness through monitoring of standards of care and determines whether such standards are met. Based on the results, the nurse coordinator, in conjunction with the multidisciplinary team and administration, can act to overcome program deficiencies and seek expansion and new target populations.

The process of program development, implementation, and evaluation is especially crucial in this time of transition in the health care industry. A major impetus for this transition has been the impact of changes in reimbursement such as diagnosis related groups (DRGs), health maintenance organizations (HMOs), preferred provider organizations (PPOs), and so on.

Health care is in a very cost-conscious climate yet is facing continued need to deliver quality service. Nurse-managed centers can have a major impact on cost containment. The centers provide services on an outpatient basis and focus on assisting patients in developing skills to maintain their independent functioning. The use of an outpatient format can reduce costs of inpatient stays and repeated hospitalizations. Specifically, nurse-managed outpatient centers eliminate the need for costly 24-hour staffing requirements, the cost of frequent physician visits because of collaboration in care planning, and the expense of a large physical plant. The combination of these factors leads to cost-effective quality care.

In addition to the pain center, nurses at St. Michael Hospital have the coordination role in the Ostomy Clinic, Foot and Ankle Center, the Spina Bifida Clinic, and a proposed Diabetes Center. This independent form of nursing practice provides nurses with a mechanism to achieve autonomy, excellence, and control.

## OBSTACLES TO CONTROLLING PRACTICE

As great as the advances in professionalization and control over practice in nursing have been, so too have been the obstacles in the health care industry and society at large. Society continues to have a hazy view of what nursing is and what individual practitioners do. What are the obstacles that continue to hinder nursing's progress toward professional autonomy and the ability to control what and how nurses practice?

Most nursing experts would agree that the failure to develop a theoretical basis for practice is a major obstacle. Levi (1980) and Moloney (1986) point to the fact that all other established professions have a framework soundly based in a "body of knowledge" to guide what they do.

Nursing has made steps in that direction with the definition of nursing as set forth in the American Nurses' Association *Social Policy Statement* and in the classification of nursing diagnosis. Defining what nursing is and what nurses do and how they do it is the best measure against functional redundancy or the ability of other disciplines to encroach upon nursing's self-described functions.

The individual nurse's ambiguity about nursing as a profession is a critical factor in the ability to resist external control over practice. Individual commitment to nursing as a career and not just a vocation has varied. Many practitioners leave nursing to pursue other careers or family responsibilities. This failure to develop a lifetime commitment is, in part, responsible for nursing's lack of credibility with other professions.

Perhaps the major obstacle affecting nursing's ability to control its own practice is the continuing issue of educational preparation for entry. The differing levels of nursing education further confuse the issue of what true professional nursing practice is and who is qualified to carry it out on the basis of their education. The drive toward professionalism must be accompanied by an upgrading of education to the baccalaureate degree for entry-level practice. The definition of professional versus technical nursing practice also must be further defined and clarified.

## FUTURE ISSUES

As nurses seek professional status in a changing health care economy, future issues need to be examined to determine their status as health care providers. The health care industry is expanding its focus toward community-oriented programs, and nursing needs to be in the forefront in developing and administering such activities. Nursing's orientation toward wellness, holistic care, and health promotion makes it the logical group to take the lead in moving away from the acute care setting and into the community.

This raises the issue of reimbursement for nursing care and the failure of many third party payers to endorse innovative and risk-taking practitioners by not paying for the services they offer. Similarly, in hospitals there is a need to recognize nursing's ability to have direct effect on the length of stay and, therefore, to reimburse directly for nursing care instead of burying its cost in the per diem rate.

The growth in medical technology and the subsequent increase in the level of sophistication needed to deliver patient care require that nursing direct its research and activities toward developing techniques that can keep pace with this burgeoning change. Nursing must continue to play a central role in health care and its research must demonstrate this to consumers. Its greatest challenge is to be able to synthesize technology with the humanistic ideals of nursing: care, comfort, and the promotion of health and wellness.

The historical continuum of nursing is one of a drive toward self-identity and professionalization. With that movement comes autonomy and control over practice. Nurses still are struggling with extrinsic control by other disciplines over what they do.

However, through research, self-definition, changing organizational attitudes about self-governance, and improvements in education, nursing is coming into its own as an independent and unique health care discipline. This process is not complete, but progress toward autonomy is the overall goal of nursing and will continue to be well into the next century.

---

## REFERENCES

Argyris, C. (1962). *Interpersonal competence and organization effectiveness*. Homewood, Ill.: Dorsey.

Ashley, J. (1976). *Hospitals, paternalism, and the role of the nurse*. New York: Columbia University, Teachers College Press.

Batey, M., & Lewis, F. (1982). Clarifying autonomy and accountability in nursing service (Part 1). *The Journal of Nursing Administration, 12*, 13-17.

Drucker, P.F. (1974). *Management: Tasks, responsibilities, practice*. New York: Harper & Row.

Levi, M. (1980). Functional redundancy and the process of professionalization: The case of registered nurses in the U.S. *Journal of Health Politics, Policy, and Law, 5*, 337-349.

McGregor, D. (1960). *The human side of enterprise*. New York: McGraw-Hill.

Moloney, M. (1986). *Professionalization of nursing: Current issues and trends*. Philadelphia: J.B. Lippincott.

Peters, T., & Waterman, R. (1982). *In search of excellence*. New York: Harper & Row.

Porter-O'Grady, T., & Finnigan, S. (1984). *Shared governance for nursing: A creative approach to professional accountability*. Rockville, Md.: Aspen Publishers, Inc.

---

## BIBLIOGRAPHY

Edelstein, R. (1979). Self-management in American nursing. *International Nursing Review, 26*, 78-83.

Jordan, C. (1982). Sharing decisionmaking with staff. *AORN Journal, 36*, 391-398.

Peterson, M., & Allen, D. (1986a). Shared governance: A strategy for transforming organizations (Part 1). *The Journal of Nursing Administration, 16*, 9-12.

Peterson, M., & Allen, D. (1986b). Shared governance: A strategy for transforming organizations (Part 2). *The Journal of Nursing Administration, 16,* 11-16.

Singleton, E., & Nail, F. (1984a). Role clarification: A prerequisite to autonomy. *The Journal of Nursing Administration, 14,* 17-22.

Singleton, E., & Nail, F. (1984b). Autonomy in nursing. *Nursing Forum, 21,* 123-130.

Sullivan, J., & Dachelet, C. (1979). Autonomy in practice. *Nursing Practitioner, 4,* 15-22.

## Chapter 19

# Physician-Nurse Committees: Expanded Decisionmaking for Staff Nurses

*SueEllen Pinkerton and Alvin Schachter*

*Relationships between nurses and physicians have long been the focus for discussion and writing. Establishment of physician-nurse committees is one approach to improved communications, better understanding of roles, healthier relationships, an additional opportunity for staff nurse decisionmaking, and ultimately an organizational climate that fosters better patient care.*

Prescott and Bowen (1985, p. 127) cite the fact that physician-nurse relationships were a focus in the literature 20 years earlier. Despite united efforts by the American Medical Association and the American Nurses' Association since then, there still is a continued call to improve relationships.

In the *Summary Report and Recommendations* of the National Commission on Nursing (1983), nurse-physician interaction was identified as a critical element in contributing to the highest possible quality patient care. Others also have supported the need to assess the organizational climate and to improve working relationships (Booth, 1983; Davis, 1983; Morgan & McCann, 1983).

The positive outcomes in addition to improved patient care also are related to nurses' job satisfaction, the focus of the study report *Magnet Hospitals,*

*Attraction and Retention of Professional Nurses* (ANA, 1983). Nurses who are satisfied with their work tend to stay on the same job longer, and physician-nurse relationships have been identified as important in job satisfaction (Pinkerton, 1983).

The basis for poor physician-nurse relationships is documented by Ashley (1976); her points are developed further in Chapter 9. The result has been a continuing pattern of physician dominance and nurse deference, linked to "sex roles; educational, economic, social status, and age differences; lack of understanding and sympathy for each other's perspective; overlapping and changing domains of practice that produce competition; and changing role relationships. . ." (Prescott & Bowen, 1985, p. 127). Continuation of adversary roles not only affects patient care and nurses' job satisfaction, it also jeopardizes marketing efforts of health care entities.

Luciano and Darling (1985) identify nursing's primary product as patient care, with direct service to the physician as a related product. If hospitals and nurses are to be successful in marketing to physicians, there must be a resolution to the dilemma of nurses' being able to practice autonomously while providing services to physicians as customers.

## PHYSICIAN-NURSE COMMITTEES

Brunner and Singer (1979) describe the formation and function of a joint practice council. These councils or committees focus on practice issues and the roles of the physicians and nurses. Most hospitals have but a single such committee, but at St. Michael, one committee has been organized for each medical specialty (internal medicine, surgery, emergency medicine, family practice, obstetrics/gynecology/pediatrics, and family practice residency).

Such a committee structure enables the membership to be homogeneous, promotes faster identification and resolution of issues, and provides greater participation of staff nurses. Committees generally meet on a monthly basis (some quarterly), depending on their business.

### Membership

Committee membership is composed equally of physicians and nurses, with numbers varying from four to seven from each profession. The chief of the medical department and the vice president for patient services are cochairpersons of the committees unless there is some time conflict; if so, a person from a different position would be cochair. Most nurse members are staff nurses appointed by the Staff Nurse Conference Group (SNCG) (described in Chapters 14 and 15).

A method has been established for requesting interested staff members to apply, for assuring that appropriate nursing units are represented, and for appointing members in a timely manner. A head nurse and/or director of nursing and/or assistant head nurse and/or a clinical nurse specialist also may be a member. However, only rarely is the committee composed of a majority from the administrative group.

The agendas are prepared and minutes are taken and written by a secretary from the medical staff office. Once minutes are distributed, a member of the SNCG summarizes them and reports to that group. Staff nurse members report to their own nursing units since they are members of a committee that primarily addresses issues of interest to their unit.

### Agenda

Any member of the committee may submit agenda items, or any physician or nurse may submit an item by way of a committee member. A wide range of items have been discussed, including preps for various X-rays, the nurse call system, daily patient weights, and decentralization of charts. In some instances, other physicians, nurses, or department members have been requested to attend meetings to help resolve problems. There has been no limit on agenda items, either number or content, since any issue that affects the environment in which patients exist is important as a topic.

## ISSUES AND APPROACHES

Mechanic and Aiken (1982) cite a lack of understanding of each other's problems as the basis for poor physician-nurse relationships. This in fact was a focus of the Family Practice Residency Physician/Nurse Committee at St. Michael Hospital. As a result, each profession presented a grand rounds for the other in an effort to create a better understanding.

In a similar effort, the chief of medicine and the vice president for patient services requested discussion of an agenda item titled "The role of the nurse in monitoring adequate medical care." This led to a discussion that was repeated later for the entire Department of Internal Medicine on the Wisconsin Nurse Practice Act as it relates to monitoring and reporting medical practices. Internal hospital policy for such reporting also was discussed.

Hundreds of agenda items have been discussed in the various committees. Some appear at intervals, some are resolved, and some are referred to committees, departments, administration, and the medical executive committee.

Some issues develop into extended studies. This was the case with patient weights, which came up repeatedly as an agenda item (inaccurate, not reported, not done). Eventually this became an evaluation study of the Nursing Department Quality Assurance Coordinating Committee and each nursing unit now monitors patient weights.

The important point is that much is accomplished through these committees, and the time and effort pays off. Strong relationships between physicians and nurses are developed as each has a better understanding of the other's concerns with each item. Support also extends beyond the formal committees to other problems. In several instances, doctors active in physician-nurse committees have been instrumental in promoting specific projects for nurses and in working with their physician peers to help promote implementation of change, such as decentralized charting and integrated progress notes.

Forums such as these have benefits for physicians, nurses, and patients. Physicians are faced with multiple expectations, the stresses of their role, and the requirement to remain technically expert. They coordinate their office work with hospital work and often cannot meet the requests of all patients and families (Mechanic & Aiken, 1982). Prescott and Bowen (1985) report the four elements of a positive nurse-physician relationship are: (1) having a practice in a hospital where there is mutual trust and respect, (2) open communication, (3) a willingness to cooperate and help each other, and (4) competence in performance of the role. Physician-nurse committees support and enhance these elements and provide a forum for discussion to improve each. In addition, once these elements are in place, the stress of the physicians is likely to be lessened.

Nurses also are faced with more complex technology, increased services to patients, and problems coordinating care (Mechanic & Aiken, 1982). Being able to extend practice decisionmaking to physician-nurse committees, supported by a shared governance model, leads to higher job satisfaction for nurses and ultimately to better patient care.

It also is possible to combine autonomous practice for nurses and their professional worth with a high level of customer service to physicians. Luciano and Darling (1985) identify nurses in their professional role as experts and in their organizational role as service providers, consultants, managers, or educators. Providing a service still allows them to be experts. Luciano and Darling report that the behavior of the chief nursing executive sets the example for good physician relationships, including the development of joint practice committees.

## PHYSICIAN-NURSE COLLABORATION

Just a word about collaborative practice, which would be the next element likely to follow successful physician-nurse committees. In this instance, this refers to collaboration regarding the practice roles of physicians and nurses to the extent that they may be redefined. This usually is accomplished initially through a demonstration project on a selected unit and is more intense and focused on daily patient care issues, with accountabilities for care sometimes being shifted from physicians to nurses (National Joint Practice Commission, 1981).

Coluccio and Maguire (1983), Ferguson-Johnston (1983), Gilliss (1983), and Koerner and Armstrong (1983) all address the implementation and varying successes of collaborative practice for those interested in the specific details. Makadon and Gibbons (1985) support a model of collaboration among faculty members so that young and inexperienced nurses and physicians can learn from them. They also endorse more independent practice for nurses so they can develop in parallel with the medical profession.

The goals of nurses and physicians are the same regarding patient care. Collaboration on care, in the spirit of professionalism, can lead to increased nurse and physician satisfaction.

## REFERENCES

American Nurses' Association. (1983). *Magnet hospitals: Attraction and retention of professional nurses* (Catalog No. G160 5M). Kansas City, Mo.: Author.

Ashley, J.A. (1976). *Hospitals, paternalism, and the role of the nurse.* New York: Columbia University, Teachers College Press.

Booth, R.Z. (1983). Power: A negative or positive force in relationships. *Nursing Administration Quarterly, 7,* 10-10.

Brunner, N.A., & Singer, L.E. (1979). A joint practice council in action. *The Journal of Nursing Administration, 9,* 16-20.

Coluccio, M., & Maguire, P. (1983). Collaborative practice: Becoming a reality through primary nursing. *Nursing Administration Quarterly, 7,* 59-63.

Davis, L.L. (1983). Professional collaboration in health care administration. *Nursing Administration Quarterly, 7,* 45-51.

Ferguson-Johnston, P. (1983). Why argue? Collaborative practice works. *Nursing Administration Quarterly, 7,* 64-71.

Gilliss, C.L. (1983). Collaborative practice in the hospital: What's in it for nursing? *Nursing Administration Quarterly, 7,* 37-44.

Koerner, B.L., & Armstrong, D.A. (1983). Collaborative practice at Hartford Hospital. *Nursing Administration Quarterly, 7,* 72-81.

Luciano, K., & Darling, L.A.W. (1985). The physician as a nursing service customer. *The Journal of Nursing Administration, 15,* 17-20.

Makadon, H.J., & Gibbons, M.P. (1985). Nurses and physicians: Prospects for collaboration. *Annals of Internal Medicine, 103,* 134-136.

Mechanic, D., & Aiken, L.H. (1982). A cooperative agenda for medicine and nursing. *The New England Journal of Medicine, 307,* 741-750.

Morgan, A.P., & McCann, J.M. (1983). Nurse-physician relationships: The ongoing conflict. *Nursing Administration Quarterly, 7,* 1-7.

National Commission on Nursing. (1983). *Summary report and recommendations* (Hospital Research and Educational Trust, Catalog No. 654200). Chicago: Author.

National Joint Practice Commission. (1981). *Guidelines for establishing joint or collaborative practice in hospitals.* Chicago: Author.

Pinkerton, S.E. (1983). *Staff nurses' job satisfaction as it relates to selected perceptions of power and employing organization.* Unpublished doctoral dissertation. Chicago: University of Illinois at Chicago Health Sciences Center.

Prescott, P.A., & Bowen, S.A. (1985). Physician-nurse relationships. *Annals of Internal Medicine, 103,* 127-133.

---

## BIBLIOGRAPHY

Blackwood, S. (1983). Now you have decided you want to, how do you do it? *Nursing Administration Quarterly, 7,* 55-58.

Crossen, C. (1986, January 7). Nurses, tired of answering to doctors, begin to treat patients on their own. *The Wall Street Journal,* p. 1.

Huntington, J.A., & Shores, L. (1983). From conflict to collaboration. *International Nursing Review, 30,* 167-169.

Sheedy, S.G. (1984). Vice president of medicine/vice president of nursing: Collaboration or conflict? *The Journal of Nursing Administration, 14,* 38-41.

Speedling, E.J. (1984). Nurse-physician collaboration: A review of some barriers to its fulfillment. *Bulletin of the New York Academy of Medicine, 60,* 811-819.

Tompkins, F.D. (1983). Seeing nurse-physician-administrator relationships as a circle. *Nursing Administration Quarterly, 7,* 52-55.

# Chapter 20

# Nursing Diagnosis

*Regina Maibusch*

*Nurses who engage in the diagnostic process contribute to the development of nursing theory. The diagnostic process is possible wherever nurses intervene, however briefly. Thus, using nursing diagnosis even in short-term hospital units can advance nursing science.*

Much has been written about nursing diagnosis, but most of the literature applies to inpatient or community health nursing. Literature on the application of nursing diagnosis in the short-term hospital unit is sparse. This chapter briefly discusses the impact of the North American Nursing Diagnosis Association (NANDA), some definitions of nursing diagnoses, and their relationship to theory development. The rest of the chapter deals with the implementation of nursing diagnosis–based practice in four short-term nursing units.

## BEGINNINGS OF NURSING DIAGNOSIS

The term *nursing diagnosis* began to appear in the nursing literature in the early 1950s. The earliest mention is by McManus (1951, p. 45), who defines it as "the identification of the nursing problem and the recognition of its interrelated aspects." Fry (1953, p. 301) calls it the creative approach to nursing. Abdellah (1957, p. 7) assumes that the term *diagnosis* is in the public domain so nurses were not excluded from appropriating its use for the problems they solved, despite resistance from physicians and other nurses over the use of the term.

## NANDA and Its Impact

NANDA has given the greatest impetus to the nursing diagnosis movement. In 1973 Gebbie and Lavin (1975, p. 1) recognized that many nurses must be experiencing similar dilemmas involving a lack of vocabulary and a classification system for the health problems they identify and treat. By calling together nurses from throughout the United States and a few other countries, NANDA focused the efforts, the struggles, the vision, and the goals of those interested in generating nursing diagnoses and sharing the process of its generation and refinement.

Considerations at the early conferences dealt with the empirical, experiential generation of nursing diagnoses and the process of diagnosing. Subsequent conferences considered the theoretical base of diagnosing and naming and the research questions of reliability and validity. At the 1986 conference, a taxonomic structure for the diagnostic labels generated up to that point was accepted tentatively. The nursing diagnosis movement now is firmly established among sufficient numbers of practitioners to ensure its continuing viability. How, then, has nursing diagnosis been defined?

## Definitions of Nursing Diagnosis

Gebbie and Lavin (1975, p. 1) speak simply of "the judgment or conclusion that occurs as a result of nursing assessment." Promoting wellness and nurturing healthful behaviors has been a constant of nurses' practice domain (Roy, 1982, p. 218). The definition by Gordon (1976, p. 1299) at first reading seems to be limited to problem health situations: "Nursing diagnoses . . . describe actual or potential health problems which nurses, by virtue of their education and experience, are capable and licensed to treat." However, the phrase "potential health problems" can be read to mean factors that, if not countered, could lead to a negative health state.

## Theory Development

Theory building, according to some authors, has four levels of progression (Dickoff, James, & Wiedenbach, 1968, p. 420; Jacox, 1974, pp. 5, 12):

Level I:  Naming the situations and conditions (phenomena) nurses see and treat. It is making a nursing diagnosis.

Level II:  Demonstrating relationships between individual conditions and situations.

Level III:  Demonstrating how clusters of related conditions and situations interact with other clusters of related conditions and situations.

Level IV:  Developing situation-producing theory, also called prescriptive theory, or being able to predict or produce a particular situation, given the right conditions.

Clinical practitioners of nursing can name the phenomena of concern to the profession competently and accurately because they deal with them every day. Both practitioners and theorists are essential for a service profession such as nursing. The doers and the thinkers complement each other. As Dickoff, James, and Wiedenbach (1968, p. 548) comment, "theory emerges initially from practice and the first movements are not self-consciously theoretical." So the expectation that staff nurses name the phenomena, i.e., make diagnoses, is reasonable.

## STRATEGIES FOR IMPLEMENTATION

As controversial as nursing diagnosis may be to some nurses, and as young as nursing diagnosis is in its own evolutionary process, it gained an early foothold at St. Michael Hospital in Milwaukee. Several factors contributed to that: (1) the expectation of the nursing leadership that nurses would define what it is that they were treating, (2) the expressed belief that patients came to a hospital for nursing care, and (3) the establishment of nursing care plans as a permanent part of the patient record.

Education of the total nursing staff was accomplished with repeated half-day mandatory workshops. Before the workshops began, selected reprints from the literature were made available to each nursing unit. At the workshops, nursing diagnosis was distinguished from medical diagnosis. Gordon's (1976, p. 1299) PES model:

$$P = \text{problem}, E = \text{etiology}, S = \text{signs and symptoms}$$

was presented as the format.

Practice sessions with actual patient vignettes, specific to the group at the inservice workshop, refined the nurses' diagnostic skills. The belief that patients come to the hospital for nursing care was reiterated. If patients did not need nursing care, nurses would cease to exist (ANA, 1980). The element of securing the position of nurses in the broad spectrum of health care providers was discussed, as were other motivators for implementing nursing diagnoses.

To continue the learning process after the workshops, the clinical nurse specialists (C.N.S.s) conducted nursing care plan rounds with staff. The expressed philosophy that every patient is expected to have a nursing diagnosis gave support during periods of stress and resistance such as at peak patient census.

To give continuing guidance to the nursing staff, the C.N.S.s developed a position paper that defined nursing diagnosis and explained the PES model. Examples of incorrect nursing diagnoses, such as those containing redundant wording in the etiology, were explained and corrected as proposed by Mundinger and Jauron (1975, p. 97). Reference also was made to the Wisconsin Board of Nursing Administrative Code, Chapter N-6, Standards of Practice for Registered Nurses and Licensed Trained Practical Nurses (1985), which states explicitly that nursing diagnosis is an integral part of the nursing process that must be used by every professional nurse in practice in the state.

Individual nursing units developed methods and forms for auditing the use of nursing diagnoses, asking such questions as:

- Does each patient have a written care plan with the components of nursing diagnosis, indicators, outcomes, and interventions?
- Is the diagnosis relevant and derived from appropriate indicators?
- Are the interventions relevant to the diagnosis?
- Do the nursing interventions address achievable outcomes?

Individual guidance then was provided. One unit chose to reward accomplishments rather than point out deficits. A commendation signed by the head nurse and assistant head nurse was sent to the individual. Over a period of a month at least one note was sent to each staff member, some receiving several.

The general nursing units progressed in diagnosis-based practice. The short-term speciality units such as obstetrics, postanesthesia recovery, operating room, and emergency department exempted themselves—for a while. But the philosophy that every patient cared for by a nurse is expected to have the nurse-patient relationship diagnosed could not be ignored. As nurses assumed more autonomy, professionalization demanded naming the phenomena for which nurses were intervening even when the nurse-patient encounter was brief.

## Nursing Diagnosis in Short-Term Units

The volume of published material on nursing diagnosis has increased more than tenfold since the start of the 1970s (Carpenito, 1984, p. 1418). But there is a paucity of literature on the use of nursing diagnosis by professionals in short-term units. Telephone surveys in the Milwaukee metropolitan area yielded equally little information. The short-term units at St. Michael Hospital therefore developed their own processes for identifying the nursing diagnoses used most frequently for their patient populations.

## Nursing Diagnosis in Obstetrics

Efforts to incorporate nursing diagnosis in practice began for obstetrical nurses when the housewide expectation became clear. Although the staff nurses from OB participated in the housewide inservice workshops in 1978, they were slow to arrive at a comfort level in the use of nursing diagnosis.

To assist them, the approved list from the Conference on Classification of Nursing Diagnosis was posted in various places in the nurses' station. Staff nurses hesitated to create their own nursing diagnosis when none on the list was applicable to mothers and infants. By 1982, the momentum toward the increased staff professionalization at St. Michael Hospital was beginning to build. Staff members were expected to be more accountable and were internalizing the concept of naming their phenomena of concern.

Largely through the leadership of the maternal/child health C.N.S. there was a desire to create positive nursing diagnoses that would be more germane to a healthy population undergoing a normal life process. Up to that time, alteration in comfort was the most frequently used nursing diagnosis. Through Kardex or nursing care plan rounds, the C.N.S. guided the staff nurses to recognize areas of responsibility where they intervened more independently and consequently had greater accountability. Diagnostic statements were developed around life-style changes for the mother and family and learning needs of the mother and/or family.

As markedly decreased lengths of stay became a reality, learning needs required reevaluation. This is an area where nurses have a fertile field for autonomous intervention. The problem: How to teach mothers all that nurses perceive that they ought to learn in two days where formerly they had four days. A research study queried 100 mothers two weeks after delivery about the impact of education by staff nurses during hospitalization. Based on these findings and the assumption that certain information is essential and cannot be omitted and other information may be known already, a new form for assessment and record of intervention was developed.

Another nursing care plan developed for new mothers is built around family dynamics and relationships. This form has the same possibilities as the previous one and for individualization of care in the areas of critical indicators, expected outcomes, and nursing orders.

## Nursing Diagnosis in ED, PARU, and OR

Building on the themes that patients are expected to have a nursing diagnosis and that nurses need to name what they contribute to patient care, the three units used similar processes. Literature on nursing diagnosis was made available to the professional staff. Concepts of nursing diagnosis were discussed at unit meetings or at inservice workshops specific to the unit. Quality assurance committees spearheaded the task under the leadership of the respective C.N.S.

The staff members on each unit were asked to study the NANDA-approved list of nursing diagnoses. A poll of the staff indicated which five nursing diagnoses they would use most frequently based on past experience. By prioritizing the choices, five or six were selected. This gave all staff members input and, subsequently, a beginning sense of ownership.

The Emergency Department QA committee took these diagnoses and developed printed forms. Each diagnosis form gave nurses the opportunity to select the appropriate etiology, indicators, interventions, and outcomes. Blanks were available for write-ins. This checkoff form met the objection citing time constraints as a problem in recording nursing diagnosis.

In the postanesthesia recovery room, the staff gradually accepted the philosophical stance regarding the essential nature of nursing diagnosis. The American Society of Post Anesthesia Nurses (ASPAN, 1984) developed standards that include the use of nursing diagnosis. After the PARU staff members adopted these standards at St. Michael Hospital, they began work on nursing diagnoses.

Generic references on nursing diagnosis were made available and the staff went through the same process of studying the NANDA list. Staff members also made lists of interventions that then were placed under appropriate diagnoses. The PARU placed five nursing diagnoses on one sheet (Exhibit 20-1) and provided a blank space for an additional diagnosis. One or more of the printed diagnosis forms can be used.

The OR QAC studied the issue of recording the nursing process. It soon realized that much of the care given to patients went unrecorded and consequently could not be viewed as provided by nurses. The study made it clear that many nursing interventions are implemented to protect an unconscious or sedated patient. The QAC decided to develop a form for the single nursing diagnosis of potential for injury, with space for other write-ins. The format includes checkoff possibilities for indicators, interventions, and outcomes. The entire nursing care given is recorded now.

The model of recording the nursing process under the heading of nursing diagnosis differs in these short-term units from that used for in-house patients. Recording is done at the time of the action or after the fact. Developing a plan of care is not possible when a patient in PARU or ED stays an average of only half an hour. Planning as an intellectual process of the experienced practitioner is more rapid than that of the novice. Identification of the diagnoses and interventions needed can be intuited in less time because of the information stored in the long-term memory (Tanner, 1984, pp. 78–81).

The profession of nursing may be in its prototype stage in the development of a taxonomy that describes its domain of practice. It is imperative that the nursing process in all settings be recorded so that as complete a picture as

**Exhibit 20-1** Nursing Diagnosis Form—PARU

---

**St MICHAEL HOSPITAL**

POST ANESTHESIA RECOVERY UNIT
NURSING DIAGNOSIS

PCC: _____     Date: _____

1. Potential for Injury r/t
   □ anesthesia □ _____
   Data:     □ see apgar □ restless
             □ on cart □ in bed
   Intervention:
             □ siderails up □ padded
             □ safety belt on
             □ EKG
             □ soft restraints
             □ wrists □ ankles
             □ skin intact □ ā □ p̄
             □ _____
   Evaluation:
             □ hazards identified
             □ safety maintained
             □ _____
   Time_____Signature_____

2. Alteration in Comfort Level r/t
   □ anes. □ surgery
   Data:     □ c/o nausea
             □ see graphic
             □ c/o pain _____
             □ _____
   Interventions:
             □ Analgesia given
             □ Repositioned to _____
             □ Supported with pillows
             □ Warm blankets
             □ Elevated extremities R_____ L_____
             □ Ice_____ □ PTR
             □ _____
   Evaluation:
             □ less discomfort
             □ _____
   Time_____Signature_____

3. □ Airway Clearance
   □ Breathing Pattern Ineffective
     r/t □ anes. □ _____
   Data:     □ airway
             □ ET tube □ see graphic/nursing notes
   Intervention:
             □ suction □ ET □ oral □ nasal
             □ airway removed
             □ ET tube removed □ criteria met
             □ assist ET tube insertion
             □ blood off art. line
             □ see graphic/nsg. notes
             □ PTR
             □ _____
   Evaluation:
             □ demonstrates effective coughing &
               air exchange
             □ effective respiratory rate, vent.
             □ _____
   Time_____Signature_____

4. Fluid Volume Deficit r/t
   □ abnormal fluid loss
   _____
   Data:     □ urine □ see graphic
             □ see lab results
             □ _____ □ _____
   Interventions:
             □ see graphic
             □ warm blankets
             □ check dressing; see box
             □ draw blood
             □ _____
             □ _____
   Evaluation:
             □ adequate fluid replacement
             □ _____
             □ _____
   Time_____ Signature_____

5. Anxiety r/t _____
   _____
   Data:     □ tachycardia
             □ see graphic
             □ restlessness
             □ _____
   Interventions:
             _____
             _____
             □ PTR
   Evaluation:
             _____
             _____
   Time_____Signature_____

6. Nursing Diagnosis: _____
   r/t: _____
   Data:     □ _____
             □ _____
             □ _____
   Interventions:
             □ _____ □ _____
             □ _____ □ _____
   Evaluation:
             _____
             _____
   Time_____ Signature_____

POST ANESTHESIA RECOVERY UNIT - NURSING DIAGNOSIS
*A Member of the Wheaton Franciscan System*
F24217MR 6/86                                   782/172

*Source:* Used with permission of St. Michael Hospital, Milwaukee, Wisconsin, © 1987.

---

possible can be developed. The efforts of the nurses in these four short-term units are contributing to that data base.

Recording of the nursing diagnoses and interventions is forming the data base for the development of a patient classification system and for the costing out of the nursing care given. This process, which began in the ED and was expanded to the PARU, can only be good for nurses and the profession.

# THE FUTURE OF NURSING DIAGNOSES

The future of nursing diagnoses requires the involvement of all professional nurses in identifying their areas of concern when caring for patients. As nursing departments become equipped with their own information systems, the data collection possibilities for staff nurses are infinite. Most baccalaureate and master's curricula include the concept of nursing diagnoses. For those who have not developed skill in nursing diagnoses in basic educational programs, the service agencies must provide opportunities to do so.

Continuing identification of nursing diagnoses is inevitable, but more imperative is the verification by research of their validity and of effective therapies. Margretta Styles (1982, p. 185) asks, "What will bring us to the proper realization that practice without verified knowledge must soon be considered unethical?" Recognition of the economic value of nursing care can be accomplished only if professional nurses continue to identify their diagnostic categories and respective interventions, and researchers validate these data.

## REFERENCES

Abdellah, F.G. (1957). Methods of identifying covert aspects of nursing problems. *Nursing Research, 6,* 4-23.

American Nurses' Association. (1980). *Nursing: A Social Policy Statement* (ANA Publication Code: NP-63 35M 12/80). Kansas City, Mo.: Author.

American Society of Post Anesthesia Nurses. (1984). *Guidelines for standards of care and management standards in the post anesthesia care unit.* Richmond, Va.: Author.

Carpenito, L.J. (1984). Is the problem a nursing diagnosis? *American Journal of Nursing, 84,* 1418-1419.

Dickoff, J., James, P., & Wiedenbach, E. (1968). Theory in a practice discipline, Part 1: Practice-oriented theory. *Nursing Research, 17,* 415-435.

Fry, V.S. (1953). The creative approach to nursing. *American Journal of Nursing, 53,* 301–302.

Gebbie, K.M., & Lavin, M.A. (Eds.). (1975). *Classifications of nursing diagnosis: Procedings of the first national conference.* St. Louis: C.V. Mosby.

Gordon, M. (1976). Nursing diagnosis and the diagnostic process. *American Journal of Nursing, 76,* 1298-1300.

Jacox, A. (1974). Theory construction in nursing: An overview. *Nursing Research, 23,* 4-13.

Kim, M.J., and Moritz, D.A. (1982). *Classification of nursing diagnosis: Proceedings of the third and fourth national conference,* pp. 281-282, 320, 321. New York: McGraw-Hill.

McManus, R.L. (1951). Appendix G: Assumptions of functions of nursing. *Proceedings of nursing education planning conference,* pp. 54-55. New York: Columbia University, Teachers College.

Mundinger, M.O., & Jauron, R.D. (1975). Developing a nursing diagnosis. *Nursing Outlook, 23,* 94-98.

North American Nursing Diagnosis Association (NANDA). (1985). Development/submission guidelines for proposed new nursing diagnosis. *Nursing Diagnosis Newsletter, 12,* 9-11.

Roy, S.C. (1982). Theoretical framework for the classification of nursing diagnosis. In M.J. Kim & D.A. Moritz (Eds.), *Classification of nursing diagnosis: Proceedings of the third and fourth national conference*. New York: McGraw-Hill.

Styles, M.M. (1982). *On nursing: Toward a new endowment*. St. Louis: C.V. Mosby.

Tanner, C.A. (1984). *Factors influencing the diagnostic process*. In D.L. Carnevali, P.H. Mitchell, N.F. Woods, & C.A. Tanner (Eds.), *Diagnostic reasoning in nursing*, 61-82. Philadelphia: J.B. Lippincott.

Wisconsin Board of Nursing. (1985). Chapter N-6, Standards of practice for registered nurses and licensed trained practical nurses. *Wisconsin Administrative Code, Rules of the Board of Nursing*. Madison, Wis.: Author.

## BIBLIOGRAPHY

Carnevali, D.L. (1984). Nursing diagnosis: An evolutionary view. *Topics in Clinical Nursing, 5*, 10-20.

Gebbie, K.M. (1976). *Summary of the second national conference*. St. Louis: Clearinghouse-National Group for Classification of Nursing Diagnosis. 1310 South Grand Blvd., St. Louis, Mo 63104.

Hurley, M.E. (Ed.). (1986). *Classification of nursing diagnosis: Proceedings of the sixth national conference*. St. Louis: C.V. Mosby.

Henderson, B. (1978). Nursing diagnosis: Theory and practice. *Advances in Nursing Science, 1*, 75-83.

Kim, M.J., McFarland, G.K., & McLane, A.M. (Eds.). (1984). *Classification of nursing diagnosis: Proceedings of the fifth national conference*. St. Louis: C.V. Mosby.

McLane, A.M. (1987). *Classification of nursing diagnosis: Proceedings of the seventh conference*. St. Louis: C.V. Mosby.

Komorita, N.I. (1963). Nursing diagnosis. *American Journal of Nursing, 63*, p. 83-86.

Kritek, P.B. (1978). The generation and classification of nursing diagnosis: Toward a theory of nursing. *Image: The Journal of Nursing Scholarship, 10*, 33-40.

Kritek, P.B. (1979). Commentary: The development of nursing diagnosis and theory. *Advances in Nursing Science, 2*, 73-79.

McLane, A.M. (1979). A taxonomy of nursing diagnosis: Toward a science of nursing. *Milwaukee Professional Nurse, 20*, 33-35.

Roy, S.C. (1975). A diagnostic classification system for nursing. *Nursing Outlook, 23*, 90-94.

Shamansky, S.L., & Yannie, C.R. (1983). In opposition to nursing diagnosis: A minority opinion. *Image: The Journal of Nursing Scholarship, 15*, 49.

Shoemaker, J. (1984). Essential features of nursing diagnoses. In M.J. Kim, G.K. McFarland, & A.M. McLane (Eds.), *Classification of nursing diagnosis: Proceedings of the fifth national conference*. St. Louis: C.V. Mosby.

# Chapter 21

# Primary Nursing

*Nancy Wilde*

*Primary nursing is a critical factor in the development of a professional nursing practice model. The essence of primary nursing rests in the nurse-patient relationship and in accountability for patient outcomes.*

Primary nursing was implemented at the Minnesota Hospital and Clinics in 1969. The values, beliefs, and practices central to primary nursing evolved from a dissatisfaction with the bureaucratic principles around which delivery of nursing care was organized, and from a concern about the negation of professional ideals.

The practice of primary nursing most closely meets the criteria of a profession as applied to the delivery of nursing care (Hegyvary, 1982). This chapter discusses the concepts of primary nursing, research findings, and organizational issues affecting its implementation. Advantages, disadvantages, resolutions, and future implications also are addressed.

## CONCEPTS OF PRIMARY NURSING

There are several definitions of the concepts and practice of primary nursing. Manthey, Ciske, Robertson, and Harris (1970, p. 65) describe it as "a one-to-one nurse-patient relationship in a highly complex care context." The major components consist of that one-to-one relationship, decentralized decisionmaking, responsibility and accountability for nursing decisions, 24-hour care planning, direct communication by nurses with other disciplines, and inclusion of the patient in the planning of care.

The term "primary" emphasizes the primacy of the nurse-patient relationship and the fact that this relationship transcends shifts. Manthey (1986) makes it clear that primary nursing is not merely a staffing pattern or an assignment but rather a state of mind, something a person becomes inside.

The patient-centered focus on primary nursing as opposed to the task-centered focus of team or functional nursing is highlighted by Marram, Barrett, and Bevis (1979): Primary nursing as a philosophy of care supported by a unique assignment or delivery system facilitates continuous, comprehensive, coordinated, individualized, and patient-centered care. The concept of autonomy is emphasized.

Accountability is clarified further by Zander (1985), who differentiates task responsibility from outcome accountability. Patient care outcomes are specified in terms of end products or observable, measurable results of nursing care that are the consequences of nursing interventions generated from assessment and nursing diagnosis. A primary nurse is answerable for these outcomes even though other staff members participate in the delivery of care.

## RESEARCH FINDINGS

Primary nursing is both a philosophy of care predicated on a set of beliefs about the nurse's role and the nurse-patient relationship and a delivery system or assignment pattern that implements those beliefs. Misinterpretation in either of these areas can lead to confusion and frustration and a potential negation of the benefits to be derived from this modality.

Many studies have investigated primary nursing's impact on patient satisfaction, nurse satisfaction, quality of care, and cost, including a survey of 29 empirical studies published from 1970 to 1984 (Giovannetti, 1986). A variety of approaches have been used to evaluate the implementation of primary nursing in meeting predetermined objectives, to compare process and outcome criteria before and after implementation, and to compare primary nursing with other delivery systems. The literature reflects mixed findings.

Results of evaluation and research are difficult to compare because of the many variations in definition and adaptations of the primary nursing system. In addition, questionable methodology as to the variables, confusing definitions of concepts, poorly developed forms, a lack of use of sophisticated statistical treatments, and insufficient sample size make it risky to draw conclusions about the findings.

While some generalizations can be made about the effectiveness of primary nursing over other types, it probably is premature at this point to assert that these outcomes are derived from exactly the same methods (Van Servellen & Joiner, 1984). Finally, because primary nursing is based on a philosophy of care, Giovannetti (1986) concludes that philosophic inquiry into its nature must be conducted, in addition to scientific investigation.

## ISSUES IN IMPLEMENTATION

It is vitally important to consider the organizational context and supports necessary for successful implementation of primary nursing. Anderson and Choi (1980) consider it a partnership between nurses and the organization, particularly in regard to autonomous, decentralized decisionmaking. Careful planning to assure organizational readiness is essential because the adoption of primary nursing will have an impact throughout the health care facility.

Hale (1984) lists the following components as necessary for successful implementation of primary nursing:

1. administrative support
2. staff involvement in the decisionmaking process
3. decentralized organizational structure
4. adequate professional staff
5. clear objectives to be achieved
6. a systematic evaluation plan

In addition, to facilitate primary nurses' actually spending more time in direct care, it is important that adequate communication, documentation, unit management, and supply distribution systems be in place (Skula, 1982). Indicators of staff readiness include competencies in clinical and interpersonal skills, commitment to professional goals and behaviors, interest in increased responsibility and accountability, trust in peers, self-confidence to facilitate openness to suggestions, and ego strength (Ciske, 1979).

The change to primary nursing at St. Michael Hospital was facilitated by the vice president for nursing. She derived support from the nursing leadership group and also collaborated closely with the other hospital administrative staff members to obtain their understanding and endorsement. A steering committee met in January 1975 and developed objectives and plans to implement primary nursing on a single, 34-bed medical-surgical unit in September 1975. Three critical care units were converted from team to primary nursing in January 1976 and the remaining medical-surgical, psychiatric, obstetric, pediatric, and dialysis units followed by June 1976.

Once commitment to and implementation of primary nursing has been achieved, it is necessary to establish a maintenance or support system. At St.

Michael Hospital, the Primary Nursing Coordinating Committee met regularly to discuss such issues as barriers and facilitators to primary nursing, care planning, orientation needs, assignment planning, and unit communication. A clinical nurse specialist functioned as resource for practice and problem solving for each unit.

The values and beliefs of primary nursing must be supported constantly throughout the organization to reinforce and reward its practice. The nursing department philosophy must value interpersonal relationships, patient involvement in care, and the advocacy role of the nurse. In addition to inclusion in the philosophy statement, primary nursing has been incorporated into generic standards of care, the professional nurse evaluation system, and various policies and procedures at St. Michael Hospital.

## ROLES IN A PRIMARY NURSING SYSTEM

Primary nursing requires a redefinition of the roles of the professional nurse, the licensed practical nurse and nursing assistant (if utilized), and the head nurse. The work of nursing includes intellectual, interpersonal, and physical functions (Halloran, 1983), and the primary nurse therefore should possess sound clinical, critical thinking, and communication skills. It is not possible to hide deficiencies in assessment or functional competencies by delegating these to other team members. Because the primary nurse also functions as a case manager, management and coordination skills are essential (Zander, 1985).

The focus of the role of the nursing assistant shifts from aiding the patient to helping the nurse in the completion of various tasks. The role of unit clerks also changed at St. Michael Hospital, taking on increased importance as communication among staff members, physicians, and other departments required significant coordination.

The head nurse retains a key management position. That individual's leadership effectiveness is the most crucial factor in implementing professional nursing practice standards. The head nurse thus must understand, accept, and—most importantly—internalize the concepts of primary nursing.

## ADVANTAGES

Primary nursing supports the nursing process and also facilitates growth of individual nurses toward professional goals through the nurse-patient relationship. In addition to increased patient and nurse satisfaction, improved quality of care, and cost-effectiveness, two additional benefits can be achieved: (1) more effective recruitment and retention of nurses and (2) closer physician-nurse collaboration.

Forty-one hospitals across the nation, including St. Michael Hospital, were designated as "magnet hospitals" by a task force of the American Academy of Nursing (1983). The success of the magnet hospitals in attracting and retaining professional staff, together with the creation of hospital and practice environments that facilitate the fulfillment of professional and personal needs, was accomplished through primary nursing. Coordination, interdisciplinary planning, and nursing's control over practice issues also were promoted, resulting in further success at these hospitals.

Improved physician-nurse communication and collaboration is a substantial benefit of primary nursing. Physicians are directed to the primary nurse for their patient when they make their daily rounds. This gives the physician and nurse the opportunity to exchange information and plan care, resulting in a more collaborative relationship. While difficulties may be experienced during the initial phases of this major change, primary nursing is an essential factor in achieving true physician-nurse collaboration where power bases are equal and mutual trust and respect exist (Devereux, 1981). In the past, the physician-nurse relationship was dominated by the doctor. Primary nursing increases the demands on physicians for information and coordination as nurses advocate and plan care throughout a patient's hospitalization.

## DISADVANTAGES

Primary nursing is not without disadvantages. Isolation, guilt, and unsatisfactory peer relationships have been experienced. Exclusiveness, expressed in terms of "my patient," has resulted in territoriality, ineffective delegation, and the withholding of information. Tunnel vision develops and the esprit de corps, partnership, and team morale that were satisfiers in team nursing may erode, thus leading to isolation of the individual nurse.

Anxiety about fear of failure and guilt over potentially not being able to do everything for a patient cause feelings of inadequacy. Nurses become more aware of their competencies and their deficiencies and how they compare with others. Self-doubt and unhealthy competition also may develop.

Peer relationships can be quite complicated in primary nursing and do not develop automatically (Ciske, Verhey, & Egan, 1983). Nevertheless, improvement in this area is necessary to enhance the effectiveness of primary nursing. The power and authority structure is disrupted. In the team system, each member is treated democratically and all persons feel valued; in primary nursing, the status of each individual is different, even among the registered nurses. Professional maturity must be fostered so that objective feedback can be given and received in a collegial manner. Details of achieving this maturity through peer review is an indicator of excellence in primary nursing (described in detail in Chapter 22).

## RESOLUTIONS

One very effective resolution for isolation of the practitioner is the development of a formal associate nurse system. Twenty-four-hour accountability can be enhanced through collaboration with a complementary associate nurse for days off and other shifts. Frequent patient care conferences can increase the quality and quantity of information and communication to enhance more comprehensive planning and evaluation of care.

Head nurses need to be sensitive to signs and symptoms of stress in their staff and thus must know their nurses as persons. Since a major goal of primary nursing is to deliver patient-centered, individualized care, it is imperative that this same philosophy be demonstrated in supervisory and peer relationships. A nucleus of caring combined with anticipatory guidance and support must be provided by the head nurse so that, while all stress cannot be eliminated, coping skills of staff members can be improved.

The use of a psychosocial clinical nurse specialist to facilitate individual expression of feelings, group problem solving, and team building was an important element of the initial implementation, and remains a valued component, in primary nursing at St. Michael Hospital.

## THE FUTURE

Since its inception, primary nursing has been adapting to changes in the economy, patient acuity, political climate, and the developing nursing profession. It must be remembered that the product of nursing is the physical, emotional, activity, and knowledge outcomes for which the primary nurse is accountable (Zander, 1985). Because the cost of health care is a major factor in decisionmaking at the national and local hospital level, research is needed to document the correlation of achievement of these patient outcomes to increased revenues and/or decreased cost.

Some view primary nursing as too expensive, but prior staffing may not have been adequate to meet patient needs, and since increased staffing requirements followed, primary nursing was seen as the cause.

Total R.N. staffing is not required for primary nursing, but careful assessment of the staff-to-patient ratio and efficient utilization of resources always reflect sound management and thus are necessary regardless of the care modality. Examination and possible revision of the assignment pattern and other factors having an impact on a hospital's delivery system may be needed while the major concepts of primary nursing are maintained.

Alternatives to primary nursing do exist. If acuity and/or census is too high, a primary nurse may not be able to provide 24-hour continuity, and it may be more realistic to implement eight-hour accountability. The primary team, which involves concepts from both primary and team nursing (Marram, Barrett, & Bevis, 1979), perhaps combined with elements of modular nursing without 24-hour accountability, is another alternative.

Primary nursing should not be considered an end but rather a beginning in a continuum of changes resulting in the development of a professional practice model (Deiman, Noble, & Russell, 1984). Primary nursing takes a long time to implement fully and must have total commitment from practitioners and managers. Focusing on the patient's achievement of outcomes rather than task completion is one major change in orientation that must be valued, internalized, and then operationalized for primary nursing to succeed.

No one can predict the future in health care except to say that change is inevitable and the results are unclear. The practice of primary nursing presents a challenge to redefine and invigorate nurses and nursing. The question to be asked is whether nurses are willing to accept this challenge.

## REFERENCES

American Nurses' Association. (1983). *Magnet hospitals: Attraction & retention of professional nurses* (catalog No. G160 5M). Kansas City, Mo.: Author.

Anderson, M., & Choi, T. (1980). Primary nursing in an organizational context. *The Journal of Nursing Administration, 10,* 3, 26-31.

Ciske, K.L. (1979). Accountability: The essence of primary nursing. *American Journal of Nursing, 79,* 891-94.

Ciske, K.L., Verhey, C.A., & Egan, E.C. (1983). Improving peer relationships through contracting in primary nursing. *The Journal of Nursing Administration, 13,* 2, 5-9.

Deiman, P.A., Noble, E., & Russell, M.E. (1984). Achieving a professional practice model: How primary nursing can help. *The Journal of Nursing Administration, 14,* 7, 16-21.

Devereux, P.M. (1981). Essential element of nurse-physician collaboration. *The Journal of Nursing Administration, 11,* 5, 19-23.

Giovannetti, P. (1986). Evaluation of primary nursing. In H.H. Werley, J.J. Fitzpatrick, & R.L. Taunton (Eds.), *Annual review of nursing research.* Vol. 4., pp. 127-151. New York: Springer.

Hale, J.F. (1984). Factors affecting the implementation, success, and failure of primary nursing as a delivery system in U.S. hospitals. *Hospital Topics, 62,* 30-31.

Halloran, E.J. (1983). Staffing assignment: By task or by patient. *Nursing Management, 14,* 8, 16-18.

Hegyvary, S.T. (1982). *The change to primary nursing: A cross-cultural view of professional nursing practice.* St. Louis: C.V. Mosby.

Manthey, M. (1986, October 22). *Primary nursing: State of the art 1986.* Seminar held in Evanston, Ill.

Manthey, M., Ciske, K., Robertson, P., & Harris, I. (1970). Primary nursing. *Nursing Forum, 9,* 65-83.

Marram, G., Barrett, M.W., & Bevis, E.O. (1979). *Primary nursing: A model for individualized use.* St. Louis: C.V. Mosby.

Skula, R.K. (1982). Primary or team nursing? Two conditions determine the choice. *The Journal of Nursing Administration, 12,* 11, 12-15.

Van Servellen, G., & Joiner, C. (1984). Congruence among primary nurses in their perception of their nursing functions. *Nursing and Health Care, 5,* 213-217.

Zander, K. (1985). Second-generation primary nursing: A new agenda. *The Journal of Nursing Administration, 15,* 3, 18-24.

**Chapter 22**

# Peer Review

*Mary Gerstner, Lillie McAllister, Peggy L. Wagner, and Connie Kraus*

*Peer review is a method of quality control and consumer protection that exemplifies the autonomy and accountability of a nursing group. A process model that is implemented in stages can provide staff nurses with the necessary time and skills to incorporate peer review into their professional practice.*

Key elements common in any definition of peer review include: (1) the evaluation of work performance, (2) by a peer or colleagues of equal rank, (3) against existing criteria or competencies. The American Nurses' Association (ANA) promotes peer review as "the process by which R.N.s, actively engaged in the practice of nursing, systematically assess, monitor, and make judgments about the quality of nursing care provided to patients or clients by other peers as measured against established standards of practice" (ANA, 1983, p. 2).

This chapter presents a process model for implementation at the staff nurse level, identifies obstacles and solutions, and discusses factors that enhance a nursing system's readiness for peer review.

The concept of peer review in nursing originated with the development of quality assurance standards in the early 1970s. Since then, the primary objective has shifted away from the evaluation of group practice through the quality assurance audit to the assessment of the professional competence of individuals.

## THEORETICAL FOUNDATIONS

The overall purpose of peer review is to evaluate and improve the quality of nursing care through peer input (ANA, 1983, p. 2). Its conceptual foundation is grounded on the principles of professional autonomy, accountability, and collegiality. Establishing a system of peer review provides greater assurance that control over practice remains within the realm of nursing rather than with nonnursing professionals. If nurses value professional autonomy and establishing their own standards of practice, they must accept their responsibility for evaluating their performance against standards.

Peer review also demonstrates a commitment toward greater accountability to the recipients of nursing care. Passos (1973) states: "Evaluation of one's practice by peers is a hallmark of professionalism, and it is through this mechanism that the profession is held accountable to society " (p. 18). Accountability to the public can be achieved, however, only if nurses are willing to assume accountability for their own practice and that of their peers.

Curtin, in addressing collegiality (1980, p. 7), contends that one of the greatest injustices self-imposed on the nursing profession is the tolerance of mediocrity, because nurses often lack the courage and honesty needed to work together with colleagues to improve practice. She notes that professional collegiality carries with it the obligation to promote excellence in practice—not only one's own but one's peers.

## CONCEPTUAL MODEL

The conceptual model for peer review is a flexible continuum consisting of four basic components: (1) group process, (2) case presentations, (3) role review, and (4) peer evaluation. The constructs of the model build on each other in terms of complexity and expertise and, once achieved, form a collective whole (see Table 22-1).

### Group Process

Skills in group process provide the basis for successful peer review. Objectives of group process meetings center on the development of professional communication skills both to promote staff cohesiveness and trust and to give individuals a picture of how they relate to and affect others in the group.

It is important that managers and other nonpeers not participate as the staff struggles to learn communication skills so the goal of peer-to-peer accountability is not complicated by others. Emphasis in this phase is on the process of working through staff problems rather than on outcomes.

**Table 22-1** Conceptual Model for Peer Review

| Group Process | Case Presentations | Role Review | Peer Evaluation |
|---|---|---|---|
| **Objectives** | | | |
| Enhance communication among group members | Information communicated regarding presenter's role | Critique of role components | Monitoring of practice |
| Cohesiveness | | Growth of individual (education) | Basis for reimbursement |
| Give feedback to individuals regarding role within the group | Individuals taught to become accustomed to "exposing their practice" | Role modeling | Accountability to the hospital or institution |
| **Criteria** | | | |
| Peers only | Peers (may include other team members, patient/family) | Peers (may include those outside the hospital) | Peers plus management |
| Cost-effective | Cost-effectiveness | Cost-effectiveness | Cost-effectiveness |
| Process, not outcomes | Educational objectives Evaluating nursing process | Educational | Educational |
| | | Evaluation of process and outcome against standards, criteria, and norms | Evaluation of process and outcomes against standards, criteria, and norms |
| | | Not associated with monetary reimbursement | Associated with monetary reimbursement (salary) |

*Source:* Courtesy of St. Michael Hospital, Milwaukee, Wisconsin.

## Case Presentations

Case presentations can be defined as an organized view of a patient's care, either retrospective or concurrent, in which relevant participants in that care are present. Group process skills can be utilized to discuss alternate interventions and/or to critique those used. These presentations evaluate nursing process against new knowledge, policies and procedures, standardized nursing care plans, or other professional or institutionalized standards.

## Role Review

Role review is a further step toward peer evaluation. Nurses work daily with each other, as associates in patient care, and on committees. Although a peer may not have a total picture of another's practice, these interactions yield valuable information for professional evaluation. Information may be obtained in narrative form, or the peer reviewers (who have gone through the phases of group process and case presentations) may rate competencies related to an area of practice.

In either case, reviewers must have objective criteria on which to base their comments and concrete examples to illustrate behavior to keep the evaluation focused on practice rather than on personalities. The nurse's feedback then is shared with the reviewer. This draws on communication skills and introduces an additional element of peer accountability.

## Peer Evaluation

Peer evaluation is the pinnacle of the continuum in which nurses conduct performance evaluations of their peers. Although managers may be responsible for evaluations, peers collate data from various sources, complete the evaluation form(s) with comments and recommendations, and conduct the evaluation interview.

The panel is a small (three to five) group of peers to whom the responsibility of evaluation has been delegated. Panel memberships should rotate among all nurses and may include such variations as: one nurse from each level on the clinical ladder, three nurses chosen randomly, or one from each shift. A competency-based evaluation method and/or form is essential to the success of the system. Well-structured requirements that are known to the nurses introduce objective criteria that minimize the potential for self-protection and defensiveness of the reviewee.

Although the continuum (Table 22-1) progresses naturally from left to right, it can be entered from any point. For example, nurses on a unit may be involved already in patient care conferences (case presentations) and plan to expand peer review through developing group process skills. New daily unit activities encompass all points on the continuum.

This conceptual model is being used by the clinical nurse specialists (C.N.S.s) at St. Michael Hospital after they floundered with a variety of approaches. Beginning with a facilitator to develop group process skills, the C.N.S. group progressed through a series of case reviews and role reviews before implementing peer evaluation two years later. The peer evaluation system finally adopted is predicated on a competency-based method.

Using these criteria as a guide, the C.N.S.:

1. obtains written feedback from peers, head nurses, assistant head nurses, directors of nursing, staff nurses, and colleagues from other departments on performance of a competency or a group of competencies

2. gathers evidence of achievement of competencies (studies, meeting minutes, memos, proposals, etc.)
3. incorporates these elements into a portfolio.

The portfolio is reviewed by a peer committee of three clinical nurse specialists chosen randomly, who rate the competencies and give comments and suggestions for improvement. The evaluation conference also is attended by the clinical specialist coordinator and the vice president for patient services, the direct supervisor who uses the completed evaluation to determine merit increases.

## INTERPERSONAL COMMUNICATION SKILLS

Since effective communication skills are the vehicle through which peer review is implemented, a model delineating specific interpersonal skills can be useful in guiding nurses through their collegial responsibilities and bringing the process to a more pragmatic level.

The communication model (Figure 22-1) underscores the interdependence between the reviewee and the reviewers by emphasizing that each must as-

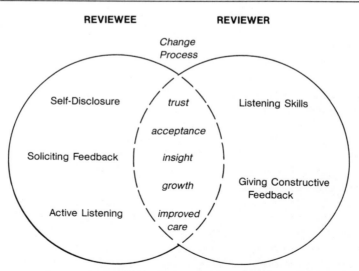

**Figure 22-1** Model of Interpersonal Communication Skills for Peer Review. *Source:* Courtesy of St. Michael Hospital, Milwaukee, Wisconsin.

sume reciprocal responsibilities if the ultimate goals of peer review are to be achieved. Building trust and cohesiveness through small-group process and case presentations is the first objective of the change process.

As trust builds, emphasis is placed on creating an atmosphere of peer acceptance. Within this framework, acceptance is viewed as: (1) the respect of each individual as unique in professional assets and limitations and (2) a necessary element in laying the groundwork for developing insight, professional growth, and improved quality of care.

Reviewees' first major interpersonal responsibility is to become comfortable with disclosing aspects of their practice with peers via small-group process meetings and case presentations. The reviewers' first major interpersonal responsibility is to facilitate self-disclosure by listening to peers without interrupting, judging, or discounting. Good listening skills, often overlooked and minimized in nursing practice, can be a powerful tool for fostering an atmosphere of acceptance.

The reviewees' second and third interpersonal responsibilities include soliciting feedback from peers and being receptive to feedback once given. When the reviewees convey a readiness to receive feedback and accept it without defensiveness and resentment, the reviewers' reciprocal role in giving feedback is made easier.

To ensure that these skills are incorporated into peer review, a consultant with expertise in group process and communication skills is needed to assist nurses in practicing these skills as well as to facilitate open group discussions of the anxieties that inevitably surface in the implementation phases (Morrison, 1983).

## WORKSHOP

The stimulus for introducing peer review at the staff nurse level arose from a small number of units that saw it as a potential for professional growth and listed it among their yearly unit objectives. With head nurse and clinical nurse specialist collaboration, a plan was proposed to the entire nursing staff to conduct a one-day workshop for any unit wishing to initiate peer review.

The primary objective of the morning session of the workshop was to provide theoretical foundations for peer review. Lecture subjects included: (1) elements of professionalism, (2) a process model for peer review, (3) colleagueship and interpersonal skills to facilitate peer review, and (4) assessment of the nurses' readiness for peer review. The afternoon session was devoted entirely to small-group work in which each core group developed its own implementation plan. This approach maximized each unit's control over its own process and encouraged a greater degree of ownership and accountability for outcomes.

Each plan was to include: (1) objectives, (2) participants, (3) a model for implementation, (4) a method of evaluation, and (5) costs. Models for peer review were creative and varied (Table 22-2).

**Table 22-2** Initial Implementation Models for Peer Review

|  | Model A | Model B | Model C | Model D | Model E |
|---|---|---|---|---|---|
| Objectives | Develop group process/communication skills | | | | |
| Participants | Staff R.N.s | Staff R.N.s AHN/clinical coordinators, HN | Staff R.N.s | Unit quality assurance staff R.N.s, later expanding to entire R.N. staff | Staff R.N.s, AHN/clinical coordinator, HN |
| Implementation Plans | Nurses evaluate one another on a mutually agreed-upon clinical procedure. Feedback given on 3 × 5 cards and collated by peer review core committee. | Communication skills workshop, with psychosocial C.N.S. | Communication skills/group process workshop with psychosocial C.N.S. | Communication skills workshop with QA committee and psychosocial C.N.S. | Intrashift communication skills and assertiveness training sessions (exchanging positive feedback, then constructive/objective feedback) |
|  |  | Skit presentation at unit meeting on principles of good communication. | Small-group (4-6) meetings every three weeks to practice communication skills | Communication skills sessions with entire staff (QA members as group leaders) | Cycle repeated with intershift staff groupings |
|  |  | Explicit staff commitment to support direct/objective feedback as opposed to "backstabbing." | | | Group process meetings to discuss feelings on giving feedback. |
|  |  | Unit posters designed on constructive communication and group process skills | | | Peer contract signed to assume accountability for utilizing constructive and direct communication skills |

*continues*

**Table 22-2** continued

|  | Model A | Model B | Model C | Model D | Model E |
|---|---|---|---|---|---|
| Evaluation Plan | Nurses' feelings on critique of their practice by peers measured along a defensiveness continuum | Survey of staff feelings on peer review | Periodic group discussion of process | Development of questionnaire assessing levels of trust and interpersonal communication skills | Self-assessment form to evaluate comfort with communication |
|  |  | Repeat of a previously completed study examining nurse stressors | Decision to proceed by group consensus |  |  |

*Source:* Courtesy of St. Michael Hospital, Milwaukee, Wisconsin.

Objectives for all groups centered on the development of group process. The major cost projections included staff salary for the core group planning time, peer review meetings, and any overtime to cover patient care during these activities. During the implementation phase, all core groups were responsible for monitoring their plan and maintaining communication with the head nurse. A report and evaluation of each plan was due at a joint meeting of all core groups after each six months.

The units progressed at varying rates. The unit starting with quality assurance members made consistent and steady progress. Another unit initiated role review in which each nurse is reviewed annually by two randomly selected peers, using a competency-based model as the basis of evaluation. The reviewee is responsible for collecting the peer input along with optional input from additional sources, which then is used in the annual review with the assistant head nurse/clinical coordinator and head nurse.

## OBSTACLES AND SOLUTIONS

Obstacles from such diverse forces as time and monetary constraints, anxiety and resistance, inconsistency in core group leadership, and lack of head nurse support have challenged the implementation process. Units with a higher ratio of part-time to full-time personnel found it difficult to arrange group process meetings without exceeding budgeted limitations. Solutions therefore must fit the individual needs of the unit. Scheduling group process sessions before and after unit meetings helped maximize time together. Subdividing the staff into smaller groupings (three to five) can minimize staffing disruptions and foster an atmosphere conducive to active participation and trust building.

Several aspects of implementation led to staff anxiety and resistance. Smaller units with low staff turnover initially viewed peer review as a threat to the existing stability and staff cohesiveness, while larger units with higher turn-over rates found that the process created feelings of turmoil and frustration as nurses adjusted to accommodate new members. The risks involved in introspective examination and exposure of liabilities to peers were threatening, as was giving and receiving positive feedback. Not unexpectedly, giving constructive criticism produced the greatest anxiety, with many avoidance behaviors evidenced.

Staff anxiety and resistance can best be dismantled if acknowledged openly. An off-unit consultant can be useful in diffusing resistance by encouraging discussion of concerns in group process meetings. Movement along the continuum may not always reflect steady progress. Instead, each step in the progression requires frequent reassessment and refinement by the core group.

Inconsistency in the core group leadership can be another hurdle. Units whose core group members did not remain constant suffered from interruptions in the process and varying degrees of commitment. To increase the validity of peer review and chances for success, a core group should consist of motivated and competent nurses who are respected by peers for delivering a high standard of care (Morrison, 1983; Spencer-Legler, 1983). Members must be able to depersonalize staff criticism and demonstrate persistence by allowing the staff a strong voice in determining when and how the process is established while providing the leadership necessary to progress along the continuum.

## ASSESSING SYSTEM READINESS

A system's readiness for peer review should be considered from various vantage points before implementation. Readiness is determined by assessment of nursing administration support, head nurse readiness to establish the climate for peer review, and identification of unit level factors that can facilitate the process.

There must be explicit and implicit management support for peer review at all levels of nursing administration, with leaders committed to participative decisionmaking and fostering a spirit of professionalism among staff members. Management support is essential since the monetary investment of time and effort can be high, with considerable cost being incurred before a unit reaches the role review or peer evaluation phases.

Factors that assist in determining head nurse readiness to establish the climate for peer review include (1) a participative leadership style with staff involvement in unit decisionmaking and (2) the ability to role model effective communication skills, including the expectation of staff assertiveness in peer problem resolution.

Once the unit has decided to initiate peer review, the head nurse supports the process by budgeting for necessary inservice training and arranging coverage for patient care during scheduled meetings. The head nurse then must be able to let go and allow the process to evolve while holding the staff accountable for progress toward defined goals.

Factors that enhance a unit's readiness to proceed include (1) a relatively confident and mature staff that demonstrates support for individual and unit professional growth and (2) a relatively stable environment in which major systemwide and/or unit changes are not occurring simultaneously. Other mechanisms that can facilitate peer review by fostering a climate of professional accountability include a primary nursing delivery system, a unit-based quality assurance program, and an objective competency-based performance system reflecting a clinical ladder progression.

## VALUE TO NURSING

The overall value of peer review to staff nurses may not be fully realized until progress through the phases has been accomplished and both the individual's and unit's professional growth examined retrospectively. The potential benefits include (1) the ability to communicate more effectively with peers and develop stronger collegial relationships; (2) increased personal and peer accountability for evaluation, reducing the passivity inherent in the traditional supervisory evaluation process; and (3) challenging nurses toward more critical thinking about their own and their peers' practice.

When individual groups of nurses assume greater accountability for monitoring their own practice, the profession benefits as a whole through a heightened autonomy and control from within. Peer review conveys a commitment to the public that nursing is willing to challenge incompetency and mediocrity and to strive toward excellence in practice.

### REFERENCES

American Nurses' Association. (1983). *Peer review in nursing practice.* Kansas City, Mo.: Author.

Curtin, K.L. (1980). Professional collegiality. *Supervisor Nurse, 11,* 7.

Morrison, S. (1983). Application of group dynamics to effective nursing review. *Quality Review Bulletin, 9,* 371-373.

Passos, J.Y. (1973). Accountability: Myth or mandate? *The Journal of Nursing Administration, 3,* 17-22.

Spencer-Legler, M.A. (1983). Peer review in nursing: Specifics for implementation. *Ohio Nurses Review, 58,* 8-10.

### BIBLIOGRAPHY

Allbritten, D., Boland, M., Hubert, P., & Kiernan, B. (1982). Peer review: A practical guide. *Pediatric Nursing, 8,* 31-32.

Brown, L. (1982). Developing a peer review process to facilitate skill acquisition for clinical performance and advancement. *Nursing Administration Quarterly, 6,* 20-24.

Dickson, B. (1979). Maintaining anonymity in peer evaluation. *Supervisor Nurse, 10,* 21-29.

Gold, H., Jackson, M., Sachs, B., & Van Meter, M. (1973). Peer review: A working experiment. *Nursing Outlook, 21,* 634-636.

Gorecki, Y. (1977). Faculty peer review. *Nursing Outlook, 25,* 439-442.

Hauser, M.A. (1975). Initiation into peer review. *American Journal of Nursing, 75,* 2204-2208.

Lamberton, M., Keen, M., & Adomanis, A. (1977). Peer review in a family practitioner program. *Nursing Outlook, 25,* 47-53.

Liebold, S. (1983). Peer review. In A.B. Hamric & J. Spross (Eds.), *The clinical nurse specialist in theory and practice* (pp. 219-233). Orlando, Fla: Grune.

Mio, J.S., Speros, D.G., & Mayfield, A.M. (1985). The effect of peer review evaluations upon critical care nurses. *Nursing Management, 16,* 42A-42H.

Mullins, A.C., Colavecchio, R.E., & Tescher, B.E. (1979). Peer review: A model for professional accountability. *The Journal of Nursing Administration, 9,* 25-30.

O'Loughlin, E.L., & Kaulbach, D. (1981). Peer review: A perspective for performance appraisal. *The Journal of Nursing Administration, 11,* 22-27.

Page, S., & Loeper, J. (1978). Peer review of the nurse educator: A process and development of a format. *The Journal of Nursing Education, 17,* 21-29.

Plourde, C. (1976). The evolution of OR peer review. *AORN Journal, 24,* 754-762.

Ramphal, M. (1974). Peer review. *American Journal of Nursing, 74,* 63-67.

Richardson, K., & Sebilia, A.J. (1982). Motivating critical care nurses through peer evaluation. *Critical Care Nurse, 2,* 54-57.

Vengroski, S.M., & Saarmann, L. (1978). Peer review in quality assurance. *American Journal of Nursing, 78,* 2094-2096.

# Chapter 23

# Nursing Grand Rounds

*Margie Smerlinski and Sue Straub*

*Clinically focused continuing education is central to the professional development of staff nurses. Nursing grand rounds is one method that can be used to promote this development.*

Nursing grand rounds (NGR) are formal presentations that focus on nursing practice, theory, and research. For those interested in utilizing this method of staff development, the definition and purpose of NGR and a model that portrays its objectives and outcomes are described. Implementation of NGR as well as ideas on content, problems that commonly arise, problem resolution, and evaluation also are discussed.

## DEFINITION AND PURPOSE

Cooper (1982) discusses some essential differences in the use of nursing rounds, bedside clinics, and NGR:

- Nursing rounds are actual visits to the bedside of a number of patients. They may be used, for example, to acquaint nursing staff members with various pieces of equipment, e.g., traction and IV setups.
- Bedside clinics are conducted with fewer patients than are nursing rounds, usually are focused on a specific problem, and are used chiefly to demonstrate some aspect of physical assessment such as lung or heart sounds.

210

• Nursing grand rounds generally are not thought of as rounds specifically but rather as a formal presentation of a specific case. The patient may or may not be present.

At St. Michael Hospital (1982), NGR are defined as clinical presentations that focus on various aspects of nursing practice, integrating practice, theory, and research. The purpose is to provide continuing education through collegial sharing of knowledge about current practice by articulating and describing nursing situations.

The sharing of knowledge with peers helps create a positive image of nursing and build self-esteem of individual practitioners (Shaneberger, 1984). The objectives of NGR are focused on the development of nurses as caregivers, their growth as contributing professionals, and the enhancement of nursing as a profession.

The profession is working toward the development of a taxonomy for nursing practice (see Chapter 20 on Nursing Diagnosis). This will provide a common language as well as a scientific base for identifying and evaluating nursing events and situations that improve the health status of clients. For growth in understanding and explaining such situations, nurses need an opportunity to discuss and share them with their colleagues. Nursing grand rounds provides this opportunity to communicate the struggles, successes, trials, and innovations that nurses experience in their daily practice.

As the profession's advance improves practice and confidence, and as experience is gained in presenting nursing grand rounds, the focus sharpens. This has been evident from evaluations by participants and presenters. Evaluations consistently include remarks that indicate increasing confidence in the ability to identify what nurses do that has an impact on an individual's level of wellness (Krejci, 1984).

## MODEL OF NGR

A model developed at St. Michael Hospital (Exhibit 23-1) illustrates the basic components of the objectives for NGR and the outcomes. Each NGR presentation provides an opportunity for staff members to integrate their knowledge of theory, practice, and research and to share this knowledge with peers.

The use of the nursing process as the basis of the presentation may result in the development of new ideas for patient care and/or new standards of care by both presenters and participants. Potential research questions may be stimulated in the preparation of material for NGR or in the presentation. NGR can lead to nurses' growth through development of presentation skills. The development of nurses as caregivers advances the profession and ultimately improves the quality of patient care.

**Exhibit 23-1** Model of Nursing Grand Rounds

Professional Articulation of the Topic

↓

New Ideas for Patient Care

↓

Continued Development of Nursing Standards

↓

Stimulation of Research Questions

↓

Growth of Profession through Integration of Theory-Practice-Research

↓

Better Patient Care

*Source:* Courtesy of St. Michael Hospital, Milwaukee, Wisconsin, © 1986.

## IMPLEMENTATION

Nursing grand rounds may be implemented in a variety of ways, depending on an organization's resources. However, involvement of staff members in preparing and presenting the rounds is key to achieving their growth as caregivers.

One approach is to develop an NGR handbook describing the overall program objectives, guidelines for presentations, and specific responsibilities of those involved in coordinating and conducting the rounds. Staff members on different nursing units then can be accountable for preparing and presenting NGR. A clinical nurse specialist (C.N.S.) can serve as the coordinator of each NGR. Each unit can decide the topic, research and develop the content, prepare handouts, and present the rounds. The C.N.S acts as facilitator in assisting the staff in this process; this role also can be carried out by a member of the nursing staff development department.

Another approach is to ask for staff volunteers from various nursing subspecialties to act as a planning and development group. Additional staff members then could be solicited to participate in specific presentations related to their interests. Staff development personnel also could be asked to coordinate the planning group. Whatever approach is used, it requires a collaborative effort and a commitment to achieving specific outcomes for staff development.

The hospital education department can offer its expertise in developing an attractive flyer and posters to increase awareness and attendance at nursing grand rounds. Distribution of the NGR announcements can be expanded to all hospital departments to promote interdisciplinary sharing.

## Content

Topics for NGR should focus on nursing and be consistent with the program's objectives. Examples might include any of the following:

- a particular nursing diagnosis
- a concept (e.g., pain management, loss and grief, sleep deprivation)
- a discussion or review of recent research findings on management of a specific nursing diagnosis
- a specific patient/family case study emphasizing the use of the nursing process in overall management of the case
- the application of a specific nursing theory to the care of a patient or group of patients

Experience at St. Michael Hospital indicates that topics that are applicable to the most nursing settings have the best attendance; topics focused on a specialty unit have somewhat variable attendance, depending on the interest of other staff members. Whatever the topic, the staff members must be involved in the process of selecting the subject to promote professional development consistent with their interests and needs.

Presentations can be innovative in both content and presentation style. Content can focus on creative and less traditional nursing elements. Examples include (1) approaches to relaxation, (2) play therapy as a priority, (3) working with and teaching unique clients (adolescent mothers, illiterate patients), and (4) cancer as a family disease. Modes of presentation can include such teaching aids as role playing, videotapes, patient interviews, and exhibits.

## Problems and Solutions

Implementation of NGR on a regular basis in a department of nursing will not be without some problems, most of which can be anticipated. Problems, and strategies for solving them, include:

1. *Problem:* Scheduling—that is, determining the frequency and appropriate timing of the rounds to promote staff attendance.
   *Solution:*
   a. ask staff members for suggestions as to the best days/times
   b. videotape the presentation so it may be viewed by those unable to attend
   c. limit presentation to one hour or less
   d. schedule during the lunch break (arrange for sale of box lunches)
   e. schedule just prior to the beginning of another shift to facilitate attendance by nurses on more than one shift.

2. *Problem:* Arranging for time for the staff to prepare and present rounds while still providing adequate unit coverage.

> *Solution:*
>     a. utilize change-of-shift time for preparation time
>     b. utilize overlap time if the hospital uses 10- or 12-hour shifts
>     c. provide coverage from a following shift or exchange coverage with another unit.

3. *Problem:* Assuring that each presentation meets the overall program objectives and outcomes.

> *Solution:*
>     a. use a C.N.S facilitator
>     b. use a central coordinator (such as staff development personnel) to assist all units in achieving NGR objectives.

4. *Problem:* Enhancing staff skills for presenting the topics.

> *Solution:*
>     a. use a C.N.S facilitator to review each presentation and make suggestions for change, if necessary
>     b. conduct individual practice sessions
>     c. hold group practice sessions
>     d. schedule seminars by staff development personnel on "How to Make a Professional Presentation."

Strategies for solving problems will vary, depending on each organization's specific mode of implementation of NGR, its organizational structure, and its specific program objectives.

## EVALUATION

NGR can be evaluated with each individual presentation and collectively at the end of the year. Each presentation can be evaluated by all participants on the achievement of the objectives and on individual presentation skills and appropriateness of content. Attendance and topics should be evaluated yearly. These assessments can be used for problem identification and resolution, such as finding an evaluation process that provides better and more accurate feedback to individual presenters.

The implementation of NGR provides benefits to patients, nurses, and the profession. Patients benefit indirectly through the growth of the nurse as a caregiver. New standards of care and the increased knowledge that nurses gain from preparing, presenting, and/or participating in NGR result in improved care delivery. NGR has proved to be an effective vehicle for staff members to provide continuing education for each other.

Finally, the profession benefits from the NGR contributions to the potential setting and refinement of patient care standards, initiating nursing research, and its possible dissemination to the larger professional community.

## REFERENCES

Cooper, S.S. (1982). Methods of teaching revisited: Nursing rounds and bedside clinics. *The Journal of Continuing Education in Nursing, 13,* 19-21.

Krejci, J.W. (1984). *Nursing grand rounds annual report*. Milwaukee: St. Michael Hospital.

Shaneberger, K.E. (1984). Opinion: Nursing grand rounds is one way to improve nursing's image. *AORN Journal, 40,* 462-463.

St. Michael Hospital. (1982). *Handbook on nursing grand rounds*. Unpublished.

## BIBLIOGRAPHY

Batty, K., Cook, P.D., Kreutzer, L., Peckous, B., Post, B., & Rees, E. (1983). NGR: A project. *Nursing Management, 14* (12), 56-59.

Martin, M.T., Miller-Church, A., & Sadowski, D. (1984). Nursing rounds: Discharge planning. *Journal of Burn Care and Rehabilitation, 5,* 244-246.

McNeil, S., Paradis, A., Wig, P., Edwards, E., & Link, H. (1983). Nursing grand rounds: Toxic shock syndrome. *Canadian Nurse, 79* (4), 38-41.

Tobin, H.M., Yoder, P.S., Hull, P.K., & Scott, B.C. (1979). *The process of staff development: Components for change* (2nd ed.). St. Louis: C.V. Mosby.

# Chapter 24

# Competency-Based Evaluation

*Peggy L. Wagner, Mary Beth A. Kenney, and Jeff Martz*

*Competency-based evaluations have applicability to all professional job classifications in a department of nursing. Competency criteria are the cornerstones for appraisal activities such as peer review and self-education and for testing of clinical skills in staff development.*

Performance appraisal is a part of the self-monitoring process by which nurses strive for quality care and professional stature. According to DelBueno (1977, p. 21) the evaluation process should be a positive experience that "provides the opportunity to set goals, reinforces positive behavior, corrects unacceptable behavior, and provides the basis for advancement, reward, and recognition." This often is not the reality of the yearly evaluation. Whether or not the experience is, indeed, growth producing depends on several factors that are manifest in a competency-based evaluation (CBE) system.

This chapter reviews the history and rationale for competency-based evaluation and describes competency criteria and their applications. It also includes models for development and implementation of CBE by staff nurses, nurse managers, and clinical nurse specialists.

## BEGINNINGS IN THE 1960s

Competency-based evaluations developed from the theory of competency-based learning that originated in education in the early 1960s (Scott, 1982). These concepts have been adapted by health professionals to create a con-

216

ceptual model for measuring performance. Competency-based evaluation derives from principles of criterion-referenced measure, a comparison of performance against preexisting criteria, as opposed to norm-referenced measure, which is based on a comparison of performance of one individual against another or against an ideal model (Bell, Miller, & Bell, 1984; Krumme, 1975).

Competency-based evaluations measure behavioral criteria based on standards of practice. The standards may be of any level, such as organizational, professional (American Nurses' Association), or specialty (American Association of Critical Care Nurses), depending on the philosophy and scope of practice of the nursing department. Gale and Pol describe competencies in relationship to roles as "the abilities, skills, judgment, attitude, and values required for successful functioning in that position" (1977, p. 25).

Competency criteria reflect these dimensions in the work-related role of the professional nurse. The emphasis in competency-based evaluations is on the professionals' "ability to demonstrate proficiencies that are of central importance to a given task, activity, or career " (Alspach, 1984, p. 655). The focus shifts from the traditional norms of what professionals should know to what they must do or perform in everyday practice.

Competency-based evaluations are one way to assure that nurses are delivering quality patient care. State licensing exams test only cognitive ability. A nurse may be well versed in theory and knowledge base and not have the ability to apply this knowledge to practice. Establishment of competency criteria for performance, based on standards, provides an objective means to measure the ability of an individual registered nurse to deliver quality patient care.

The concept of CBE supports excellence in the nursing profession; CBE is in concert with recommendations from the Joint Commission on Accreditation of Hospitals (JCAH) standards for performance appraisals. When high standards of performance are implemented and enforced consistently in the nursing community, consumers can be assured of a minimal level of care from any professional nurse. The JCAH supports competency-based evaluations because they measure performance in relationship to standards of practice. CBE offers benefits to individual nurses, the organization, the profession, and to consumers in search of good care.


## RESEARCH AND THEORY

Competencies have been an area of interest to nurses in administration and education for some years. Information is readily available to guide their development.

## Characteristics of Competencies

There are several rules guiding the writing of competency criteria. Competencies should be written as single behaviors that are measurable and objective, i.e., that can be documented with evidence of performance. A competency statement should be (1) a description of a general category of behavior integrating cognitive, affective, and psychomotor capabilities; (2) learner (or evaluatee) oriented; (3) free of conditions; (4) validated by experts and staff (Alspach, 1984, p. 658). Competencies can measure either process or outcomes. They are based on minimum standards consistent with the job description and supervisors' expectations (Lachman, 1984, p. 9).

When the criteria are put together in an evaluation format, competencies generally are grouped according to broad categories or standards statements. The number of competencies should be limited to key behaviors so that the length of the form does not become unwieldy and overwhelming. The two major dimensions that should be addressed are doing the thing right by (1) technical competence, and (2) the accurate use of diagnostic process in clinical decisionmaking (DelBueno, 1977, p. 21).

The competency-based form should provide information that will identify: (1) technical competency; (2) how patient care outcomes are affected by that competency; (3) the unique contribution of the professional (or primary) nurse; (4) outstanding work; and (5) areas for growth and development (O'Louhglin & Kaulbach, 1981, pp. 22-23).

Criteria have been developed in nursing to evaluate many job classes in several settings (Bray, 1982; Budd & Doulen, 1984; Burns, Chubinski, & Freiburger, 1983; Davis, Greig, Burckholder, & Keating, 1984; Deckert, Oldenburg, Pattison, Swartz, 1984; Lunde & Durbin-Lafferty, 1986; McCall, Bair, & Gaspar, 1983; Miller, 1984; O'Louhglin & Kaulbach, 1981; Richardson & Sebilia, 1982).

## Application of Competencies

Competencies rooted in professional and organizational standards are the fulcrum of many appraisal activities. Competencies are grouped by clinical ladders into levels designed to stimulate professional development and advancement. Competency-based evaluation can be the basis for peer review, supervisory appraisal, or self-evaluation. Continuing monitoring of performance and interim evaluation sessions can be more objective when based on specific and known criteria.

Competencies for evaluation can be incorporated with various other formats. For example: management by objectives (MBO) is a method of performance appraisal based on principles of motivation (Drucker, 1954; Brucks,

1985). Phases of MBO include: (1) setting goals and objectives with managers; (2) action planning; (3) periodic review; and (4) performance appraisal (Cain & Luchsinger, 1978). Both CBE and MBO have strengths, and the optimum method of performance appraisal is a marriage of the two—that is, competency-based evaluation incorporating a goal-setting mechanism to stimulate and monitor growth of individuals between evaluation periods.

Competencies can be used for staff development in professional settings, for example in measuring the impact of continuing education (Greaves & Loquist, 1983, p. 82) and defining behaviors to be accomplished in orientation programs (Alspach, 1984; DelBueno, 1977; DelBueno, Barker, & Christmyer 1981; Selfridge, 1984). Criteria can be developed for testing routine clinical skills, such as competency in interpreting electrocardiogram (ECG) rhythm. Some existing competencies, such as cardiopulmonary resuscitation (CPR) certification, which has been developed by the American Heart Association and the Red Cross, are well established and can be incorporated into programs.

Although many well-constructed competency-based measures have been identified for nurses, reliability (the consistency of measurement) and validity (measures what it is supposed to measure) testing have been inconsistent, which is unfortunate since the entire system relies on strong measurement forms. One system, behavior anchored rating scales (BARS), is a simple competency-type measure based on critical incidents (Sheridan, Fairchild, & Kaas, 1983). Reliability and validity measures have been established that facilitate development and implementation of the system.

## COMPETENCY-BASED EVALUATION MODELS

Competency-based evaluation is appropriate at all levels of professional practice. Development of the criteria is a growth experience for individuals and groups of nurses taking on the challenge.

### For Staff Nurses

Performance evaluations can be stressful. Since promotions and raises hang in the balance, anxiety is inevitable. However, unnecessary concern may be introduced if performance standards are subjective or unclear. In addition, if the nurse feels powerless, there can be resentment toward the evaluator rather than professional growth. One way to minimize these difficulties is by using CBE, which clearly delineates objective standards of performance, removes questions of personality style from consideration, and can open the door for the staff nurse to be involved actively.

The process of developing the competencies is almost as important to success as the final product. Probably the key factor contributing to a positive development experience is that nurses in staff positions need to be closely involved (Bray, 1982, p. 36; Davis et al., 1984, p. 44). Pilot testing of the model will disclose otherwise overlooked problems. Content validity can be established by distribution of the form to experts such as staff nurses and first-line managers.

These steps are necessary to gain a consensus as to expected performance and to eliminate interpretive discrepancies. Once the competencies are developed, periodic evaluation should be planned to keep them current. The method by which staff nurses are prepared for implementation of the competency-based evaluation system is also important.

Although representative staff members should be involved in the development and testing of the system, all of them eventually will be evaluated, and individuals need to be prepared properly. Inservice training should be given by persons who know the system well. All instructions should be succinct and in writing to avoid misinterpretations that can lead to disaster at appraisal time.

Competencies for staff nurses can be grouped under various categories based on the philosophy of the nursing department (Exhibit 24-1). Special considerations may be made for new, on-call, or specialty area nurses. One way of dealing with special needs is to develop competency addendums addressing specific behaviors or skills under the existing headings. This method maintains cohesiveness yet allows for individuality and inevitable variation.

Once the criteria are spelled out objectively and agreed upon by staff and managers, the appraisal process can be developed further. Options include self-evaluation, peer evaluation, and supervisory appraisal. In any case, the staff has an opportunity to begin to assume the burden of proof for performance and to collect materials validating criteria achievement such as care plans or thank-you notes from patients. This is a method of delegating some control over the appraisal to the evaluatees and increasing their sense of professionalism.

## For Managers

Management competencies can be developed into different categories, including roles such as : (1) leader; (2) manager; and (3) member of a profession. One approach in a system with several levels of managers is to begin with generic management competencies as a framework. From this model all job classes in management can develop their own specific competencies in a way that complements the roles of others. Specific responsibilities are developed to match general accountability within a framework created jointly

**Exhibit 24-1** Categories of Competency Criteria for Staff Nurses

**Sheridan, Fairchild, & Kaas,** 1983

Nurses need:

1. Job knowledge and judgment
2. Observational skills
3. Organizational skills
4. Leadership skills
5. Communication skills

**Davis, Greig, Burkholder, & Keating,** 1984

The nurse:

1. Provides direct care to patients and families
2. Teaches patients and families
3. Documents practice
4. Consults and collaborates with other professionals
5. Teaches nursing staff and other professionals
6. Exercises leadership within the hospital or community
7. Participates in or implements research
8. Participates in activities for professional development

**Bray,** 1982

Nursing elements:

1. Nursing process
2. Leadership skills
3. Interpersonal relationship/communication skills
4. Professional development
5. Personal qualities

**St. Michael Hospital,** 1986

The nurse is a:

1. Provider of care
2. Teacher
3. Communicator
4. Manager/leader
5. Researcher
6. Member of a profession

and satisfactory to all groups. The result is a unified whole without duplication of tasks.

An example of diversification of a generic competency to specific roles is the responsibility for performance appraisals (Exhibit 24-2).

Another option is to develop separate competencies for each level of management. However, some system for assuring compatibility and integration of roles, lack of overlap, and parallel structure would be needed at some point in the process.

In keeping with shared governance, the responsibility for developing the competencies should remain within each practice and/or management group. In looking toward peer review and self-evaluation, the focus of responsibility should shift from evaluator to the professional being evaluated.

## Clinical Nurse Specialists

The clinical nurse specialist (C.N.S.) performance appraisal is a blend of competency evaluation and negotiation of role objectives. Although com-

**Exhibit 24-2** Generic Competency to Role Responsibility: Performance Appraisals

Generic Competency for Manager:

- Facilitates proper utilization of staff
- Provides staff members with timely feedback and evaluation

Assistant Head Nurse/Clinical Coordinator Competency:

- Writes performance appraisals
- Conducts evaluation conferences

Head Nurse Competency:

- Provides input into evaluation

Director of Nursing Competency:

- Oversees timeliness and content of the evaluation

petencies serve as an anchor for peer review, one difficulty in pinpointing them for the C.N.S. has been that job functions vary between specialists in an organization, depending on the specialty and institutional demands. One way to solve this problem is to develop competencies that span the possible criteria in categories of role responsibility (Exhibit 24-3). Each C.N.S. can negotiate which competencies are to be included in yearly objectives and then be evaluated in those categories.

**Exhibit 24-3** Categories of C.N.S. Competencies

1. Speciality Practice
   a. clinical knowledge and skills
   b. program development
2. Consultation
   a. patient/family centered
   b. nursing unit centered
   c. organizationwide
   d. Professional Nursing Development and Clinical Research Consortium
3. Education
   a. nursing staff development
   b. patient/family education
   c. student education
4. Evaluation and Research
   a. quality assurance
   b. research
5. Personal and Professional Development
   a. communication
   b. organizational role
   c. professional role

Because of the smaller C.N.S. peer group, it should be possible to include each member in the development, validity testing, and testing of individual criteria. C.N.S.s not only would be committed to the success of the competency-based evaluation but also would be familiar with the criteria. This familiarity makes the model easier to use and gives individuals security in knowing their role expectation.

Objective testing procedures assist in gaining group consensus and facilitating progress when nurses become bogged down in group debate during the development phase. In fact, procedures such as the Delphi Technique— a methodology in which several rounds of questionnaires are given to a panel of experts with the results of previous questionnaires included (Polit & Hungler, 1978)—may save time and money.

One problem during implementation that seems continuous (and may be related to the nature of the C.N.S.) is the difficulty in limiting competencies and in negotiating role priorities. The C.N.S.s need to limit the extent of their influence to specific categories if they are (1) to be able to complete tasks within a reasonable time and (2) to increase job satisfaction.

The C.N.S. competency-based evaluation should be reviewed periodically for change and updating. Additional suggestions to add to its readability and validity include: (1) testing content validity against literature and (2) inter-rater reliability.

## FUTURE AND VALUE

Competency-based evaluation can be valuable for the profession of nursing. A good model defines exactly what it is that nurses do. Comparing competencies among departments and institutions helps nursing and its specialty areas to update standards of practice and in quality assurance evaluations.

For individual nurses, competency-based evaluation has value in defining standards of practice and performance expectations in the work setting, outlining accountability for that practice, and structuring continuing self-evaluation and performance appraisal. Patients can only benefit from a cost-effective system that improves quality of care by nurses.

### REFERENCES

Alspach, J. (1984). Designing a competency-based orientation for critical care nurses. *Heart and Lung, 13,* 655-662.

Bell, D., Miller, R., & Bell, D. (1984). Faculty evaluation: Teaching, scholarship, and services. *Nurse Educator, 9,* 18-27.

Bray, K. (1982). Performance appraisal of staff nurses, Part 3: Developing perfect standards and an evaluation tool for staff nurses. *Critical Care Nurse, 2,* 36-40.

Brucks, A. (1985). Performance appraisal: Evaluating the evaluation. *The Health Care Supervisor, 3,* 17-30.

Budd, R., & Doulen, J. (1984). Clinical evaluation of the neonatal transport team. *Critical Care Nurse, 4,* 24-26.

Burns, C., Chubinski, S., & Freiburger, O. (1983). A criteria-based performance appraisal for the critical care nurse. *Nursing Administration Quarterly, 7,* 46-58.

Cain, C., & Luchsinger, V. (1978). Management by objective: Applications in nursing. *The Journal of Nursing Administration, 8,* 35-38.

Davis, D., Greig, A., Burkholder, J., & Keating, T. (1984). Evaluating advanced practice nurses. *Nursing Management, 15,* 44-47.

Deckert, B., Oldenburg, C., Pattison, K., & Swartz, S. (1984). Clinical ladders. *Nursing Management, 15,* 54-62.

DelBueno, D. (1977). Performance evaluation: When all is said and done, more is said than done. *The Journal of Nursing Administration, 8,* 21-23.

DelBueno, D., Barker, F., & Christmyer, C. (1981). Implementing a competency-based orientation program. *The Journal of Nursing Administration,* 24-29.

Drucker, P.F. (1954). *The practice of management.* New York: Harper & Row.

Gale, L., & Pol, G. (1977). Determining required competence: A needs assessment methodology and computer program. *Education Technology, 17,* 24-27.

Greaves, P., & Loquist, R. (1983). Impact evaluation: A competency-based approach. *Nursing Administration Quarterly, 7,* 81-86.

Krumme, U.S. (1975). The case for criterion-referenced measurement. *Nursing Outlook, 23,* 764-770.

Lachman, V. (1984). Increasing productivity through performance evaluation. *The Journal of Nursing Administration, 14,* 7-14.

Lunde, K., & Durbin-Lafferty, E. (1986). Evaluating clinical competency in nursing. *Nursing Management, 17,* 47-50.

McCall, J., Bair, J., & Gaspar, A. (1983). A performance evaluation system for a pharmacy-based IV therapy team. *NITA; Journal of the National Intravenous Therapy Association, 6,* 79-83.

Miller, M. (1984). Staff performance evaluation: What? Why? How? *Journal of Emergency Nursing, 10,* 74-81.

O'Louhglin, E., & Kaulbach, D. (1981). Peer review: A perspective for performance appraisal. *The Journal of Nursing Administration, 11,* 22-27.

Polit, D., & Hungler, B. (1978). *Nursing research: Principles and methods.* Philadelphia: J.B. Lippincott.

Richardson, K., & Sebilia, A. (1982). Motivating critical care nurses through peer evaluation. *Critical Care Nurse, 2,* 54-57.

Scott, B. (1982). Competency-based learning: A literature review. *International Journal of Nursing Studies, 19,* 119-124.

Selfridge, J. (1984). A competency-based orientation program for the emergency department. *Journal of Emergency Nursing, 10,* 246-253.

Sheridan, J., Fairchild, T., & Kaas, M. (1983). Assessing the job performance of nursing home staff. *Nursing Research, 32,* 102-107.

# Chapter 25

# Emergency Department Patient Classification System

*Eleanore Kirsch and Gregory A. Smith*

*An important facet of professional development is realizing one's po-
tential and worth, monetarily as well as conceptually. Concretely demonstrating this worth can be the first step in actively promoting the
value of nursing care as it relates to the financial viability of the total
hospital organization.*

Nursing generates revenue for hospitals. Although this fact is not always
recognized by patients, hospital administrators, or even nurses, it is a reality.
As nurses develop professionally, they must realize they do not function in
isolation but as an integral part of the business of health care.

It is nursing's responsibility to demonstrate its financial contributions and
its ability to monitor productivity and the subsequent allocation of personnel.
Accountability includes defining the parameters of nursing care delivered, as
well as monitoring the accuracy of patient charges.

Outcomes of nursing care must be measured not only by quality of care
but also by the satisfaction of consumers, repeat utilization of services, and
the contributions of nursing to the financial health of the hospital.

This chapter describes one example of how this can be accomplished through
the process of developing and implementing an emergency department (ED)

patient classification system (PCS). Specific emphasis is placed on developing attributes that will assure acceptance by the four major audiences in the institution: hospital administration, finance, nursing, and ED physicians. The value of such a system to nursing, patients, and the organization also is addressed.

## REASONS FOR DEVELOPMENT

Traditionally, EDs have been perceived as expensive by consumers and other health care purchasers. The belief was that prices were inequitable when related to the actual services received. It was not uncommon for hospital administrators to believe that EDs operated at a financial loss, although they were perceived as an important referral source for other hospital services and inpatient admissions.

Hospital charges for services and measures of patient acuity were subjective and limited and were not related to staff productivity. Patient acuity often was determined by medical diagnosis. In recent years, the cost of supplying the services increased. Patient care became more sophisticated and time consuming for ED staff and thus more expensive for the hospital. Economic changes caused patients to wait longer or hesitate before seeking health care, thus intensifying their illness.

The staff's perception was that patient acuity was increasing. It was felt that patient activity no longer could be estimated on the number of ED visits alone. A better understanding was needed as to acuity and the resulting hours of nursing time that went into patient care so staffing issues could be addressed with data to support recommendations for changes.

Because of the past glut of patients, EDs were not forced to be competitive with other health care delivery systems. Then came distinct changes in the health care market. ED census and revenue decreased. Competing health care systems expanded their services. With the increase in urgent care centers and walk-in clinics, hospital-based EDs experienced a significant loss of market share of lower acuity patients. The increase in health maintenance organizations (HMOs) limited the number of patients who could be treated in the ED.

Market research demonstrated that consumers were becoming increasingly price sensitive. This resulted in a change in their behavior as they began to consider alternatives to the traditional hospital ED.

In order to maintain quality care, provide data for proper distribution of resources, better correlate cost and price, and attain and maintain profitability in the ED, hospitals (sometimes at the prodding of third party payers) decided to develop and implement a patient classification system (PCS). The intent was to categorize patients according to the amount of nursing care received for the purpose of determining both the allocation of nursing personnel and the basis for the hospital charge.

## DEVELOPMENT AND IMPLEMENTATION PROCESS

Although the impetus to implement the system came from two separate directions—the nursing need to provide evidence of increased patient acuity and the marketing need to develop a competitive pricing system—the final goal was accomplished in a collaborative effort.

In nursing, the unit-based quality assurance committee had identified the need to measure patient acuity. This committee, composed mainly of staff nurses and with management representation, was chaired by the ED clinical nurse specialist (C.N.S.). Both professional and nonprofessional nursing staff members were closely involved in the process and the overall success of the project. Staff participation was critical in designing the initial study, developing the model, testing it, and implementing the system. The C.N.S. acted as the liaison between the nursing staff and the marketing director, vice president of patient services, and the medical director of the ED.

The director of marketing served primarily as the interface between the team and members of senior administration, including the president, executive vice president, and vice president of finance. In retrospect, a stronger relationship between nursing and finance could have been developed if a nursing representative had participated in these meetings. Additional team members included the management engineer and a contracted statistician who conducted time studies and assisted in collecting, coding, computerizing, and interpreting data.

The process began through meetings between the C.N.S. and the director of marketing. Strategies, tactics, responsible parties, and specific deadlines were outlined. After development, review by other team members, and approval of the initial plan, the following strategies were implemented to accomplish the overall goal.

### Review of Literature

There was a plethora of information in the literature on inpatient classification systems. However, only since the 1970s had there been an attempt to develop PCSs for outpatients. When this project began in December 1984, only two references to ED PCSs were found in the literature (Kromash, 1984; Schulmerich, 1984). A site visit was made to a hospital that had implemented a PCS. Since EDs vary in resources and structure, it was decided it would be necessary to develop a PCS specific to the needs of this department.

## Additional Data Collection

To determine the specific needs of this ED, numerous data were necessary. The existing hospital pricing system was examined, including evaluation of the criteria for charges and the categorization of patients.

There were three levels of patient charges: minimum, moderate, and maximum. However, the criteria to determine them were subjective (i.e., not based on concrete data but frequently left to the discretion of the nurse). They also were not based on actual nursing time.

Additional pricing data examined included existing ED revenue and expenses, percent of ancillary service utilized, the criteria for charges, who was responsible for determining charges and who could change the process, and the ability to negotiate with other departments. Data on monthly census, percent of admissions, average number of patients seen per shift, and number of patients in each charge level were collected and analyzed.

To determine how to set charges to meet those of the competition, it was necessary to identify and evaluate those rivals. The competition included other hospital EDs and ambulatory care clinics, this hospital's (nonemergency) ambulatory care services, free-standing convenience care centers, and industrial clinics. The information collected included pricing data, accessibility, convenience, quality of services, patient demographics, and promotional activities.

Third party reimbursement for ED services was examined and defined: how ED prices were screened, how carriers were billed, and what percent of the total ED business could be allocated to each payer. Any marketing strategy to make prices competitive had to include all charges. This involved examining the physician charges: criteria for charges, collection policies, interface with third party reimbursement, and interface with the hospital billing system.

All of this information was analyzed in relation to the overall marketing needs. The intent was to develop a system that would best meet these needs. Costs that could be cut because they were not related to acuity, extra services that could be provided for lower level acuity consumers at no charge, and charges that could be increased because they were related to greater use of nursing staff time all were studied.

## A System to Assign Acuity Values

The next strategy involved the most commitment of staff time. Since the nursing staff bore the majority of responsibility for implementing this system, it was imperative to keep that group involved throughout the development process. Staff members participated actively in providing input, collecting and collating data, and instructing other staff nurses.

The first step in developing the acuity system was to define all staff functions related to patient care, both direct and indirect. Details were pinpointed by the various persons who carried out the functions. These were further refined in terms of which functions directly involved every patient. This constituted the baseline for patient care activities.

Next, it was necessary to time, or estimate the time, for performing each function. The management engineer was helpful in completing this task. Direct and indirect activities were categorized separately. Direct activities were nursing functions for which the patient would be charged and would constitute the PCS model. To utilize this information for staff purposes, it was necessary to know what percent of staff time was spent in direct versus indirect activities. The staff conducted a separate timing study to collect these data.

In developing the patient acuity model, all direct functions were categorized under major headings. These categories were given number values based on average times to complete each function or group of functions. The minimum amount of nursing time every patient required was considered baseline and constituted the lowest of the acuity values.

The range for each final acuity rating was determined on the basis of a one-week pilot study utilizing the new model. All direct nursing time for each patient was calculated and totaled. Using predetermined guidelines, a final category was selected for each patient. These data were collated and average minutes for each final acuity rating were determined. The guidelines for utilization of the model then were reviewed and revised by the staff and explained at another inservice workshop.

## Pricing Each Acuity Level

An audit of past charts was conducted to determine how each level should be priced. Tentative monetary values for each new level were set and compared with 100 charts. This audit and information from the pilot study guided the determination of the final charges and percents for each acuity level needed for the hospital to remain solvent. The new system then was implemented after revision of billing forms, minor changes in the model, and completion of staff inservice instruction.

## Continuing Evaluation

A monthly analysis of both pricing and staffing data was implemented to evaluate the model. To evaluate pricing, a simultaneous billing study comparing the new system with the old was generated. This examined the expected dollars (from the old system) less the actual dollars generated from the new system, then calculated the percent of change. In one year the new system produced a 35 percent increase in revenue on the charge for nursing care alone.

In using the PCS information to determine staffing productivity, a computer program was designed that could evaluate certain data per a 24-hour period (Exhibit 25-1). Information analyzed included number of patients in each category per shift, total patient care time required, total available direct nursing time, and the difference between the latter two totals.

The average minutes of nursing time required for each category were determined from the initial pilot study. For each 24-hour period, the total minutes are calculated, then divided by 60, with the total constituting the hours of patient care time needed for that day (A in Exhibit 25-1).

The total staffing hours available are documented by multiplying the hours available by the percent of time each role is involved in direct patient care. This percent was determined in a previous time study that showed that staff members spent approximately 50 percent of their time in direct patient care. B in Exhibit 25-1 is the total nursing hours available that day. The difference between A and B indicates the need for more or fewer staff nurses that day. This information assists in planning staffing allocations.

When evaluating this information, it is important to keep in mind the following:

1. EDs have certain standards of care not related to acuity or census. For example, on the night shift, staffing will remain constant regardless of a decrease in census. Although the productivity evaluation demonstrates a need for less staff, the number should remain constant to be able to provide the quality of care needed at any given time.
2. The data can be used only for trending staffing needs since ED patient utilization is unpredictable. For example, although the productivity demonstrates a need for fewer staff members, five high-acuity patients may enter the ED at the same time and need everyone available.
3. Acuity and pricing data should be evaluated separately. Occasionally, for marketing purposes, the patient charge may not reflect the nursing time associated with that category. For example, patients returning for suture removal are not charged. Although this is allocated the baseline in nursing time—14 minutes—the nurse may spend additional time in education but not charge the patient more because this is a promotional activity.

In addition to pricing and productivity evaluation, it is necessary, especially at the beginning of such a project, to evaluate the reliability of the model.

**Exhibit 25-1** Staffing Productivity Evaluation

| Date: | | | | Day of Week: | | Census: |
|---|---|---|---|---|---|---|

**Number of Patients in Each Category/Shift**

| Category | Shift | | | Total | Average Minutes/Category | Total Minutes/Category |
|---|---|---|---|---|---|---|
| | 1 | 2 | 3 | | | |
| No Charge | | | | | X 14 | |
| I | | | | | X 14 | |
| II | | | | | X 25 | |
| III | | | | | X 50 | |
| IV | | | | | X 100 | |
| V | | | | | X 170 | |
| Voided | | | | | | |
| Missing | | | | | X 14 | |

Total A

$$\text{Total A} = \frac{\text{Total minutes/category}}{60} = \text{Total direct patient care hours required}$$

**Staffing in Hours/Shift**

| Role | Shift | | | Subtotal | % Time in Direct Patient Care | TOTAL |
|---|---|---|---|---|---|---|
| | 1 | 2 | 3 | | | |
| Assistant Head Nurse | | | | | X .50 | |
| Registered Nurses | | | | | X .50 | |
| Nursing Assistants | | | | | X .50 | |

Total B

Total B = Total nursing hours available for direct patient care
A − B = C: If C is +, more staff is needed; if C is −, less staff is required.

This is accomplished by random audits of patient records and the associated PCS model. The purpose of the audit is to ensure that all activities circled on the PCS model are documented in the patient record. This assures consistent and reliable utilization of the model by the nursing staff and enhances its value.

## VALUE TO PATIENTS

If a pricing system is to be truly consumer driven, the price patients pay has to be based on the actual resources they utilize while in the ED. The PCS promotes sensitivity to the needs of consumers and local industry for equitable pricing. The ED does not overcharge or undercharge while maintaining the quality and health care backup (emergency surgery) rarely available in free-standing urgent care centers.

This model reduces subjective patient charges stemming from staff bias because the criteria for charges are based on actual care received. Frequent audits of the model tend to diminish attempts to manipulate the system; they also identify inadequacies.

## VALUE TO PHYSICIANS

Although ED physicians charge separately for their services, the PCS promoted collaborative hospital and doctor charges for the lower acuity patients. To remain competitive with urgent care centers, the hospital's return visit or no-charge and level I categories were consistent with the physician charge. The use of pricing as a promotional plus encourages patients to return to use the services. Since ED physicians often depend on patient census for their livelihood, they also benefit from the PCS.

## VALUE TO HOSPITAL

To manage a business effectively, the costs of manufacturing a product or providing a service must be understood. For decades, health care had no motivation to understand this cost or to manage it efficiently. The PCS provided a significant aid in understanding the cost of the service and how it could be adjusted to changes in market conditions. This made the hospital sensitive to the elasticity of demand based on price.

A great deal of flexibility was built into the pricing system to allow the hospital to evaluate other costing strategies. For example, if the hospital were to discount the lowest level of acuity to obtain an HMO contract, it could make minor adjustments in pricing at the higher levels of acuity to assure that overall profitability was maintained. This flexibility also allowed the hospital to make revenue projections at the beginning of the year based on volume and patient acuity and then to adjust the criteria used to assign patients to levels of acuity to assure that overall financial goals were met.

Once the ED was profitable and generating a significantly larger revenue stream, other marketing activities could be considered, developed, and adopted. The least of these was the development of advertising to create a greater community awareness of the availability of the hospital's emergency services. More importantly, top administration approved additional enhancements to emergency services such as better patient and community education, the establishment of professional educational and certification standards for physicians and nurses, and improved amenities for patients and their families.

## VALUE TO NURSING

Both the process and the outcomes of developing and implementing the PCS have been of value to nursing. The process itself has enhanced the staff's professional development. In the unit-based quality assurance committee, staff nurses identified the need for a PCS. With management support and the use of appropriate resources and research, they developed and implemented the system and participate in its continuing evaluation.

During the process of developing the model, direct and indirect patient care activities and the length of time spent on each type of function were identified. These data plus historical specifics on ED utilization make possible the prediction of future staffing needs based on patient acuity rather than on census. This model also can measure how efficiently nurse managers match workload to staffing. It bases acuity on the existing practice of nursing; as new and different patient care interventions are developed, the model must be adapted.

This system has made nursing accountable to patients by defining the care delivered, then charging appropriately for the services. However, the acuity ratings describe not the care patients should receive but rather the care they did receive. Patient care should be addressed according to predetermined standards and, in conjunction with a quality assurance program, priorities should be established for attainment and improvement of care.

Through the implementation process, nursing demonstrated its ability to be revenue producing, to participate in marketing activities, to collaborate with other hospital departments, to be responsible for nursing productivity, and to remain accountable to the consumers. The contributions nursing care makes in nontraditional roles received increased recognition.

In addition, the overall success of the pricing system attracted the attention of the president of the parent holding corporation, who requested that the PCS be considered for implementation at other hospitals in the system. This type of process can only benefit nursing as it enhances its reputation in the health care business.

---

## REFERENCES

Kromash, J.E. (1984). Patient classification and required nursing time in a pediatric emergency department. *Journal of Emergency Nursing, 10,* 69-73.

Schulmerich, S.C. (1984). Developing a patient classification system for the emergency department. *Journal of Emergency Nursing, 10,* 298-305.

---

## BIBLIOGRAPHY

Buschiazzo, L. (1985). Adapting PCS to emergency services. *Nursing Management* [Critical Care Management Ed.], *16,* 34B-34H.

Giovannetti, P. (February 1979). Understanding patient classification systems. *The Journal of Nursing Administration,* 4-9.

Ranseen, T.A. (December 1982). A holistic approach: Recognizing emergency department price components. *Hospital Financial Management,* 12-29.

Schulmerich, S.C. (1986). Converting patient classification data into staffing requirements for the emergency department. *Journal of Emergency Nursing, 12,* 286-290.

**Chapter 26**

# Professional Development beyond the Organization

*SueEllen Pinkerton and Ross J. Workman*

*As staff nurses gain professional maturity through the successes they achieve within the organization, they begin to respond to experiences beyond it. Numerous opportunities are available for involvement in professional activities, which lead to more growth in the individuals, their professional organizations, and the institution.*

Several opportunities for staff growth present themselves daily. This chapter describes some of these opportunities and the results of staff participation. One of the most obvious is in the legislative arena.

## AWARENESS OF LEGISLATIVE ISSUES

If nurses are to fulfill their role as advocates for quality health care, they must realize that caring for and about people is not enough. Nurses must act politically (Archer, 1985). Eunice Cole reinforces nursing's professional responsibility when she states that "only by being willing to enter the political arena can we ensure that our elected representatives legislate in the interests of health needs of their constituents" (1985, p. xxix).

The first step toward effective political involvement is to become aware of the legislative process and current issues. Many avenues are available to nurses who on their own strive to stay politically informed and active (Exhibit 26-1).

235

**Exhibit 26-1** Opportunities for Political Information/Involvement

- The media: television, radio, newspapers, news/political magazines
- Community forums: issue-specific meetings with legislators, etc.
- Local hearings: legislative, regulatory agencies, etc.
- Professional groups: legislative updates via publications, seminars, and meetings of the American Nurses' Association, National League for Nursing, and many specialty organizations
- Political action committees: inclusion of financial contributors to any of the numerous nursing or special interest PACs on a political information mailing list
- Political campaigns: involvement in races from city council to President of the United States, from stamp-licker to campaign manager
- Membership in political party or club: real grass-roots politics
- Communication with elected officials: newsletters, correspondence, legislative hot line, phone calls, personal meetings

One of the long-term objectives of the Department of Nursing at St. Michael Hospital is to "develop a climate of awareness regarding political and legislative activity." Pinkerton, Schuler, and Glass (1984) analyze the results of research on political activity and political knowledge of registered nurses. Their recommendations include encouraging participation in political activities and professional organizations that are engaged in such work.

Many nurses did not take full advantage of the opportunities listed in Exhibit 26-1. It thus was clear that another vehicle to disseminate legislative information was necessary. This has taken the form of a political column in the hospital's monthly nursing newsletter that is distributed to all nursing staff members and department directors.

The articles are written by a nurse whose avocation is politics. The subjects have included:

- motivational pitches for political involvement by nurses
- brief descriptions of legislative processes
- basic synopses of local, state, and national issues affecting nursing/health care
- election updates
- political directories (local, state, national)
- suggested political references.

In addition to the options in Exhibit 26-1, ideas come from other nurses and hospital administrators (many hospital associations and medical societies also distribute legislative updates). The columnist takes great pains to present issues in a nonpartisan and factual manner (this is assured by having it checked by several reviewers before printing).

The columns have been well received by the nursing staff and copies are sent to selected legislators. Other plans to enhance the staff's political knowledge base include purchase of political reference materials for the nursing department, political inservice sessions (videotapes, nonpartisan speakers), and issue-specific forums.

The professional climate at St. Michael Hospital has facilitated this open discussion of a broad range of legislative issues. The recognition of the importance of this information to nurses both personally and professionally has led to its acceptance and endorsement.

## BOARD OF NURSING ACTIVITIES

Issues and topics on the agenda of the Board of Nursing may have a direct effect on the governance of nursing practice. As opportunities arose to provide input on agenda items, a staff member was asked to attend the meetings. A clinical nurse specialist attended for the first year, both for her input and to accustom the Board of Nursing and the Department of Nursing to her presence. Since then, nurses have attended on a rotating basis. The hospital receives the agenda and minutes of the meetings, copies of which are provided to the attendee.

The nurse attending is required to write a summary report in the newsletter, which the staff then comes to expect. In this manner, all nurses are kept current on actual and pending changes. In addition, requests are made of staff members for responses to certain Board of Nursing issues in which individuals have expertise. This activity demonstrates the obligation of professional involvement since it extends beyond the employing institution to the administrative agency that implements statutes governing the practice of nursing (Pinkerton, 1985) through licensure.

## PROFESSIONAL ORGANIZATIONS, NURSING SCHOOLS

Partridge (1985) lists 23 specialty nursing organizations, not including subdivisions of such groups as the American Nurses' Association. There thus is ample opportunity for nurses to become involved in an organization of their choice and interest.

Nurses are encouraged to join professional organizations in the interest of learning more about their specialty area, meeting other nurses practicing in the same specialty, and sharing some of the creative and innovative things they may have accomplished.

One successful strategy has been to encourage nurses to submit research posters or abstracts that report quality assurance studies completed under their unit-based QA system. The hospital offers as many resources as it has available, such as secretarial time, consultation from the Education Department for creating the poster, and encouragement to complete the project. Recognition is also important; in addition to individual responses, acknowledgment is given in the newsletter.

In the event occasions arise in which staff members may have a special interest or personal objective, information is circulated to them. Examples are participation in the Midwest Alliance In Nursing (MAIN), committees of district organizations (legislative, cost containment), and committees at schools of nursing (curriculum, continuing education). Once the community and region are aware of interest, availability, and competence, numerous opportunities arise.

## ROLE IN A MULTIHOSPITAL SYSTEM

St. Michael Hospital is part of a multihospital entity, the Wheaton Franciscan System, Inc., Milwaukee, and as such is involved in the integration and combination of services. As new areas for collaboration appear, staff members are requested to participate, usually based on expertise or interest.

Examples include specialty areas such as rehabilitation, women's health, and oncology. Staff members represent the system on committees, task forces, advisory boards, or product teams. This familiarizes them with other hospitals, provides opportunities to extend their professional growth, and gives them the experience of observing the complexities of a multihospital system.

Some specialty groups, such as the clinical nurse specialists and the quality assurance coordinators, have organized to share information. This collaboration extends the availability of resources and networks.

## ADVANCED EDUCATION

Given the debate and activity regarding entry into professional practice, many nurses are pursuing formal education. Many also are interested in graduate education. In whatever ways are possible, the hospital supports such individual efforts.

The most obvious moves are to try to arrange work schedules to accommodate class time. Others are assisting with projects by making data available, opening use of the library, executives' consenting to be interviewed, making suggestions for topics for projects and research, and providing time for consultation in such areas as thesis proposals and special projects. The investment in these activities is multiplied in return by the enhanced expertise of the practitioners and their increased professional maturity, both of which improve patient care.

In summary, professional development beyond the organization has been achieved as a natural outgrowth of the internal growth. A goal will have been reached when individuals begin to carry the concepts and skills to other organizations and stimulate the same growth.

---

## REFERENCES

Archer, S.E. (1985). Politics and the community. In D.J. Mason & S.W. Talbott (Eds.), *Political action handbook for nurses* (pp. 67-77). Menlo Park, Calif.: Addison-Wesley.

Cole, E. (1985). Introduction. In D.J. Mason & S.W. Talbott (Eds.), *Political action handbook for nurses* (pp. xxix-xxxi). Menlo Park, Calif.: Addison-Wesley.

Partridge, R. (1985). Should there be one nursing organization? In J.C. McCloskey & H.K. Grace (Eds.), *Current issues in nursing* (2nd ed.), (pp. 877-890). Boston: Blackwell Scientific Publications.

Pinkerton, S.E. (1985). Legislative issues in licensure of registered nurses. In J.C. McCloskey & H.K. Grace (Eds.), *Current issues in nursing* (2nd ed.), (pp. 469-479). Boston: Blackwell Scientific Publications.

Pinkerton, S.E., Schuler, S., & Glass, L. (1984). *Political activity and knowledge: How do nurses measure up?* Unpublished Research Report. Milwaukee: St. Michael Hospital.

**Part VI**

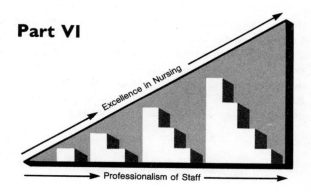

# The Growth of Excellence in Nursing

*Shelly Malin*
Section Editor

Professional development in a nursing department may lead to an opportunity to formalize a method to interface with the larger nursing community—a way to market nursing.

At St. Michael Hospital, this led to the Professional Nursing Development and Clinical Research Consortium. The Consortium and its components are described in enough depth here to provide important information on how to plan and market nursing education, consultation, research, and products.

Chapter 27 focuses on the process of developing the Consortium as a natural outgrowth of professionalism in a nursing department. Marketing concepts are explored, as well as strategies to introduce the Consortium to the nursing community. Chapter 28 analyzes marketing strategies as they pertain to product testing and product development. Chapter 29 focuses on development and marketing of consultation, seminars, workshops, and conferences. Specific strategies for networking are included, with the goal of a quality product as well as financial success.

# Chapter 27

# Formation of the Consortium

*Gregory A. Smith and SueEllen Pinkerton*

*Publication of the book* Nursing Quality Assurance: A Unit-Based Approach (*Schroeder & Maibusch, 1984*), *with contributions by nine other St. Michael Hospital nurses, meant national recognition of the professional level and achievements of the hospital's Nursing Department. The unique qualities of nursing practice at St. Michael Hospital designated it as a magnet hospital: shared governance, primary nursing, unit-based quality assurance, high academic and professional qualifications and standards, career ladder, national recognition, innovative programs, and continuing research. The hospital established the Professional Nursing Development and Clinical Research Consortium (the Consortium), designed to focus and build on these aspects of the Nursing Department (Professional, 1984).*

The Consortium was formed as a marketing vehicle to accomplish a number of functions, including:

- gaining recognition of the revenue being generated by new services developed by the nursing staff
- contributing to the financial performance of the hospital
- providing nurses an opportunity to grow professionally through consulting work outside the hospital
- improving the overall quality of care provided patients

- researching and developing products and services for the larger health care community
- assisting in providing a referral source for the medical staff.

To appreciate the formation and growth of the Consortium, it is necessary first to understand what marketing is, the market pressures that dramatically changed the health care delivery environment and nursing, and the parallels between nursing and marketing philosophies and practices.

## MARKETING DEFINED

There are many formal definitions of marketing. Dr. Phillip Kotler, recognized for his major contributions to marketing for more than three decades, defines it as "the analysis, planning, implementation, and control of carefully formulated programs designed to bring about voluntary exchanges of values with target markets for the purpose of achieving organizational objectives" (1982, p. 6). He describes marketing as the discipline that analyzes and manages exchange relations with groups inside the hospital (employees, medical staff, and nurses) and groups outside (consumers, agencies, and group medical practices). Marketers research the needs of other groups and how to satisfy them through mutually beneficial exchange processes (Kotler, 1985).

These definitions rest on five core concepts of marketing: (1) The consumers have needs, wants, and demands. (2) These manifest themselves in products and services. (3) These products and services have value and satisfy the needs, wants, and demands of consumers. (4) This results in a transaction in which elements of value are exchanged. (5) Finally, markets (managed by marketers) are developed to make this process as efficient as possible.

Kotler emphasizes the requirement to concentrate on the needs of the consumers. Health care consumers include patients, their families, visitors, physicians, other hospital departments, insurance companies, and industry. Traditionally, health care has been self-driven or inwardly driven as opposed to consumer driven. This is evidenced by the fact that hospitals and other health care providers decided what services they would like to offer, and since there was sufficient demand for these services, the providers were successful more often than not.

There are many misconceptions about marketing in health care. Most professionals in the field view marketing as promotion, including advertising, public relations, and personal selling. In the true definition, promotion represents 5 percent of the activities of a marketer and is the final step in the marketing process. The four basic variables a marketer can manage—the so-called four Ps—are the product, price, place (distribution channel), and promotion.

It is essential that the product or service meet the needs of the consumer, that it be priced profitably and competitively, and that it be located in a place where it is easily accessible to consumers, either in the hospital or at an outside setting. Only after these three key variables have been addressed does the promotional side of marketing come into play. Unfortunately, in health care, many promote a service without taking the first three steps and are then usually disappointed with the results.

In 1975, Kotler first addressed the issue of marketing health care in *Marketing for Nonprofit Organizations*. He describes how the marketing process and the marketing philosophy can be brought to bear on the problems facing the health care industry. Kotler recognizes and accounts for the complex organizational structure of health care and the multiple markets represented by patients, physicians, industry, and insurance companies. He outlines the need to look at the demands of these various groups and to structure alternative delivery systems and financing mechanisms based on those demands. Only since 1980 have many in health care organizations responded to these environmental changes and begun to look at competitive responses to the marketplace.

## MARKET PRESSURE AND THE ENVIRONMENT

Since 1980, hospitals and physicians have been under increasing pressure from insurance companies, local industry, the federal government, and consumers to contain the growth of health care costs. This has resulted in decreasing admissions and shorter lengths of stay. Health care systems are competing openly for shrinking and sometimes limited markets.

Their responses have been varied. Some have banded together, created systems, and integrated them with financing mechanisms such as health maintenance organizations (HMOs). Others have sought alternative revenue sources through for-profit ventures and increasing the range of services offered.

Hospitals are marketing and positioning themselves with physicians, in-house staff, insurance carriers, and industry. By so doing, they are attempting to gain recognition of the fact that they are an integral and indispensible part of the overall health care delivery mechanisms of their community.

Increasingly, nursing has had to recognize the need to market itself to administration and to broader communities. These communities, as noted earlier, include physicians, patients, their families, visitors, other departments in the hospital, insurance companies, local industry, and other nurses. They are responding to the same threats as the hospital and are developing strategies to demonstrate their value to their various markets.

A review of the reasons for the formation of the Consortium shows the strategy was to demonstrate to administration that nursing can affect the bottom line, expand services being offered, and improve the overall quality of care. These are three key elements in the survival of the hospital and in the growth of the professional practice of nursing.

Nurses are capable of identifying market opportunities and capitalizing on them. An example is nursing's major role in the growth of the home health care market, an activity that began well before the growth of HMOs and shrinking utilization of hospitals accentuated the need for home health. Of the $400 billion spent in health care, home health costs represent only 3 percent of that market.

The rapid changes in health care created opportunities for nurses to become independent of hospitals and to become consultants to patients, physicians, hospitals, and other providers (Felton, Kelly, Renehan, & Alley, 1985). This is another example of how nursing has recognized the changing environment and has responded by developing new products and services that are meeting the needs of specific customer groups.

## NURSING AND MARKETING PARALLELS

Marketing is so basic a philosophy that it must permeate the organization for its effect to be maximized. The philosophy of serving the customer is inherent in the philosophy of nursing. In many health care delivery settings, nursing is the basis of the service provided. The nursing and marketing philosophies both recognize the needs of the consumers (patients) and the responsibility to serve them in such a way that all of their requirements are met.

In comparing those philosophies and processes, it becomes evident that the basic approach and elements of marketing have long been part of nursing. Although little has been written about the history of the marketing of nursing, it is evident that nursing was active in its basic constructs long before Kotler first defined marketing (Kotler & Levy, 1969).

The steps of the nursing process parallel those of marketing: assessment, diagnosis, planning, evaluation, and revision. Adaptation of the process from a nursing to a marketing focus is accomplished easily.

## FORMATION OF THE CONSORTIUM

Ideas for the Consortium were generated in a way similar to those identified by Trofino (1985) and Armstrong et al. (1985). Assessment of the market indicated needs for (1) professional nursing development and (2) clinical agencies that could provide systematic testing and development of products.

These needs matched several of the strengths of the Department of Nursing at St. Michael Hospital:

- recognition of and requests for unit-based quality assurance, workshops, and consultation with either a clinical focus (orthopedic foot and ankle clinic, mother-baby care) or an administrative and organizational focus (emergency department patient classification system, shared governance, social policy statement implementation)
- product research and evaluation based on the incorporation of research standards into the quality assurance program, and hence an understanding by the nursing staff of the need for rigor in clinical research.

In designing the Consortium, three areas were developed: professional nursing development program, community outreach program, and the product research and evaluation program. These met the needs identified in the market and matched the expertise of the nursing staff. (These three programs are discussed in detail in Chapters 28 and 29.)

At its inception, the Consortium was identified as a separate cost center, which provided a clear mechanism for tracking costs and revenues. Designated individuals were assigned responsibility for the Consortium. The concept is similar to that of the research facilitator (described in Chapter 8) who coordinates research and the researchers' research. For the Consortium, the coordinator assesses, diagnoses, plans, and implements, using other resources in the nursing department, then evaluates and revises.

## REACTIONS TO THE CONSORTIUM

The concept of the Consortium was presented to the nursing staff (unit by unit), hospital department heads, physicians, the boards of directors of the hospital and the Wheaton Franciscan System, Inc., the multihospital health network with which St. Michael Hospital is affiliated. The response was positive and supportive. The real bonus, however, was the individuals who already had ideas that helped the Consortium move ahead swiftly (quality assurance workshops and Pediatric Crash Cart Kardex).

The physicians also were supportive since one of the objectives is based on contacts with consumers and other agencies that can lead to referrals to the medical staff, thus enhancing the hospital's relationship with the physicians as customers.

Beck (1985) and Luciano and Darling (1985) discuss the difficult issue for nurses of treating physicians as valued customers of the hospital while maintaining their own values and beliefs about professional behavior. Based on the historical relationship of physicians and nurses, the latter too often are viewed as the doctors' handmaidens when in fact they are striving for autonomy in practice.

Physicians can expect superior service, amenities, and attention, yet these elements still can be combined with the professional autonomy of the nurse. Luciano and Darling (1985) suggest viewing:

1. doctors' orders as prescriptions for patients, not as commands
2. helping a doctor as a skill based on professional competencies, not as subservience
3. physicians' complaints as customers' reactions to what they perceive as inadequate service rather than judgments on nurses' personal competence.

Incorporating such conceptualization of practice requires changing the culture of the nursing department. This is necessary, however, in defining the market to include physicians as customers of nursing service.

Other persons and groups informed of the development of the Consortium were deans and faculties at the schools of nursing in the community and other groups of professionals. Some individuals resented the competition, believing that hospitals did not belong in the professional development market. Others objected to the name and the logo, despite a search by the marketing director to avoid similarities and several earlier revisions in the name to avoid duplicating existing programs.

Probably the most discouraging reaction was that of the marketing firm hired to develop the logo and design, write, and print the brochures. After nurses spent hours with its executives explaining why the Consortium was being developed, how nursing was growing and changing as a profession, and why nurses felt they were leaders in the profession, the marketers went off to develop the logo. They came back with a design that was sexist and reflected nursing in the 1950s: a nurse with a white cap, holding a needle and syringe. From the nurses' reactions, they realized their conceptualization was off target and changed the logo, but it was unclear even then whether they knew why they were asked to redesign it.

## THE FUTURE OF THE CONSORTIUM

The Consortium, by the late 1980s, had met all of its goals in varying degrees. Chapters 28 and 29 detail the strengths and weaknesses of the individual programs, which vary from encouraging staff to participate, to great success in marketing products. The effort that brought the greatest satisfaction was the improved quality of care. This was evidenced through the development of products such as the Pediatric Crash Cart Kardex, a resource available at a critical time in some children's lives. The Kardex lists drugs used in emergency situations and has dosages calculated by age and weight, so critical moments aren't lost computing these calculations and, more importantly, errors are avoided. This is helpful to nursing care not only at St. Michael Hospital but also at more than 500 other hospitals in the United States and Canada. The Kardex has been promoted at national pediatric conferences, which has resulted in these sales. Some promotion was also accomplished by mail order, but to a lesser degree.

Improvement in patient care also developed from (1) the sharing of expertise via clinical nurse specialists who consult in hospitals unable to afford such experts and (2) nurses who learn foot care and treatment in the Orthopedic Foot and Ankle Clinic.

The impact of the Consortium on the nursing profession by the late 1980s still was small, but the potential was great. Nursing and marketing obviously share a great deal. The challenge of nursing as described by Porter-O'Grady (1986) is to create organizations, such as the Consortium, through which nurses can meet the needs of the markets and receive recognition for having done so in a profitable, cost-effective manner that improves the quality of care provided in the hospitals and the communities.

## REFERENCES

Armstrong, D.M., Amo, E., Duer, A.L., Hanson, M., Hijeck, T., Karwoski, P., & Young, S. (1985). Marketing opportunities for a nursing department in a changing economic environment. *Nursing Administration Quarterly, 10,* 1-10.

Beck, C. (1985). Nursing administrator establishes marketing strategies. *Nursing Success Today, 2,* 26-29.

Felton, G., Kelly, H.D., Renehan, K., & Alley, J. (1985). Nursing entrepreneurs: A success story. *Nursing Outlook, 33,* 276-280.

Kotler, P. (1975). *Marketing for nonprofit organizations.* Englewood Cliffs, N.J.: Prentice-Hall.

Kotler, P. (1982). *Marketing for nonprofit organizations* (2nd ed.). Englewood Cliffs, N.J.: Prentice-Hall.

Kotler, P. (1985). The role and development of marketing in today's health care institution. *Health Care Strategic Management, 3,* 21-24.

Kotler, P., & Levy, S.J. (1969). Broadening the concept of marketing. *Journal of Marketing, 33,* 10-15.

Luciano, K., & Darling, L.A.W. (1985). The physician as a nursing service customer. *The Journal of Nursing Administration, 15,* 17-20.

Porter-O'Grady, T. (1986). *Creative nursing administration* (Chapter 8). Rockville, Md.: Aspen Publishers, Inc.

*Professional nursing development and clinical research consortium.* (1984). (Brochure). Milwaukee: St. Michael Hospital.

Schroeder, P.A., & Maibusch, R. (1984). *Nursing quality assurance: A unit-based approach.* Rockville, Md.: Aspen Publishers, Inc.

250    Commitment to Excellence

Trofino, J. (1985). Marketing nursing: A community medical center perspective. *Nursing Administration Quarterly, 10,* 58-61.

---

## BIBLIOGRAPHY

Anderson, R.A. (1985). Products and product-line management in nursing. *Nursing Administration Quarterly, 10,* 65-72.

Beckham, J.D. (1984). A strategic alternative for community hospitals: The principle of peripheral penetration. *Journal of Health Care Marketing, 4,* 37-40.

Eliopoulos, C. (1986). Customer relations in the health care setting. *The Health Care Supervisor, 4,* 19-31.

Fine, R.B. (1985). Exchange behavior in administrative nursing marketing interactions. *Nursing Administration Quarterly, 10,* 53-55.

Gamm, K.R. (1985). Nursing's impact on a business venture. *Nursing Administration Quarterly, 10,* 90-96.

Hybben, L.B., & Hansen, A.N. (1985). Patient care administration: Marketing leadership. *Nursing Administration Quarterly, 10,* 11-17.

Klann, I.S. (1984). Good news and bad news in the marketing age. *AORN Journal, 40,* 790-791.

Krampitz, S.D., & Coleman, J.R. (1985). Marketing: A must in a competitive health care system. *Nursing Economics, 3,* 286-289.

Kuhn, R. (1985). Marketing critical care nursing: The time is right. *Heart and Lung, 14,* 19-23.

Norbett, B. (1985). The role of nursing in marketing health care. *Nursing Administration Quarterly, 10,* 85-89.

Smith, B.A. (1984). Toward a more profitable nursing image. *Nursing Success Today, 1,* 18-23.

## Chapter 28

# The Product Process: Research, Evaluation, Development, Marketing

*Karen Rauen and Christine Sperry*

*Unprecedented opportunities to become involved with the product process await nurses in many health care settings. The product process is the interplay of four basic components—research, development, evaluation, and marketing—that results in a product that provides quality care and generates profit.*

The product process is a new arena for nurses, requiring them to expand their knowledge base to include business concepts and marketing strategies. By combining this knowledge with their clinical expertise and creativity, nurses have unlimited possibilities for generating new products and product lines and maintaining a competitive edge in the health care marketplace.

This chapter discusses the product process and its individual components (Figure 28-1). Two specific products, a pediatric crash cart Kardex and an age-appropriate play Kardex, illustrate the process. Considerations involving prevention, reduction, and resolution of problems and risks are addressed. The chapter concludes with a discussion of the inherent value of the product process and how it affects the consumer (the patient), the health care entity, and the nursing profession.

251

**Figure 28-1** The Product Process Model. *Source:* K. Rauen and C. Sperry, © 1986.

## THE PRODUCT PROCESS

The product process, as noted, is the interplay of four basic components: research, development, evaluation, and marketing. Its desired outcome is a product or product line that provides quality care for consumers and generates additional profits for the health care entity.

Typically, a hospital's product line is its clinical services and the health care it delivers. These products are traditional in the sense that they are strictly patient/service oriented. Nontraditional product lines benefit nurses by providing job satisfaction, a secure positioning in the marketplace, and professional esteem. These product lines can include the development of clinical methods and products and the marketing of specialized services such as health programs, consultation services, and continuing education workshops.

The four components of the product process are cyclical in nature in that they evolve from one stage to another. Depending on the type of project, entry into the process can occur through any of the components and may focus on one, several, or all of them. For example, manufacturers contact St. Michael Hospital to evaluate various health care products they are offering. The focus is on the evaluation component. The hospital determines whether a product is acceptable for use (quality care) and a fee for service is received (profit). However, in the event that an individual wishes to develop a new product, the entire process would be needed.

## Research

Research is the disciplined analysis of the needs, wants, perceptions, and preferences of target markets. It is the basis for effective product design, pricing, communication, and distribution.

Before a product can be developed, ideas must be generated, analyzed, and structured. Ideas for a product may come from a variety of sources: the user of an existing product, intuitive observations on perceived or real needs, a competitor's products, members of a targeted market segment (focus group), and/or product evaluation committees.

However the idea emerges, its perceived value must be assessed and validated by a focus group. In essence, this means: "Ask the consumer." This is done by a market survey (needs assessment). The survey's importance cannot be overemphasized. It can be done formally or informally. In either case, it is necessary to ask well-structured questions that will elicit useful information without inducing biased responses.

### Formal Surveys

This type of needs assessment can be accomplished by following the five steps recommended by Keckley (1985, p. 32):

1. identify the information needed and how it will be used
2. identify the survey techniques to be used
3. develop and test specific survey data collection methods and procedures
4. conduct the survey
5. evaluate the data and formulate a marketing plan.

Keckley notes that common techniques include: statistically valid surveys, patient satisfaction surveys, focus group surveys, face-to-face interviews, and primary and secondary (qualitative and quantitative) data analysis. Since primary data measure opinions, attitudes, behaviors, and intentions and secondary data measure factual characteristics, Keckley recommends that blending and analyzing both can lead to better assumptions and plans about a product.

The type of survey will depend on the group being targeted. Keckley feels that physicians respond better in face-to-face interviews while employees react better to sealed-ballot questionnaires.

## Informal Surveys

In this type of survey, the originator of the idea seeks to validate the need for the product by communicating with experts in the field, colleagues, or potential users in a particular setting. Once the need is validated, a feasibility study should be conducted to determine the entity's ability to develop the product.

## Fundamental Issues

For either survey approach, several basic questions need to be addressed:

- Who would use the product?
- What are its advantages/disadvantages?
- Are similar products available on the market?
- Is the product likely to fulfill its intended purpose and function?
- What design would meet the needs of consumers?
- What options for manufacturing are available?
- What are the anticipated costs of production and labor?
- What benefit would be derived from the product?
- Are resources available to develop and market the product?
- Does the product reflect the institution's mission?

At different times, informal surveys were conducted at St. Michael Hospital to determine whether there was a need for the development of a crash cart Kardex and/or a play Kardex (which is a ready reference for age-appropriate play and behaviors) for use with pediatric patients. The ideas for both originated from the observations and perceptions of the parent/child clinical nurse specialist. These ideas were submitted to the Unit-Based Quality Assurance Committee and the hospital's Cardiopulmonary Resuscitation Committee for review and recommendations, which approved both. The development of the pediatric crash cart Kardex became the unit's main quality assurance project for the year.

Keckley (1985, p. 31), in discussing the use and misuse of marketing (product) research in the health care industry, identifies four key mistakes that can invalidate the usefulness of the research:

1. the lack of appropriate, market-oriented analysis
2. the belief that the research product is an end in itself rather than a means to a greater end

3. the belief that market research should validate a preconceived idea rather than provide information to be used in the decisionmaking process
4. the belief that a market research project report, complete with recommendations and an implementation guide, has served its purpose by filling space on a bookshelf—the "shelf syndrome."

Keckley concludes that market research without action is meaningless. At this point, a structured proposal detailing the idea, results of the surveys and feasibility study, and the answers to the following questions should be submitted to administration for approval:

- Who will be involved with the project?
- What are the costs and resources needed?
- Why is the project being undertaken (who will benefit)?
- When will it be accomplished?
- Where will it be marketed and how?
- What is the profit potential?

Not all ideas will pass from the research component into the development stage. It may be discovered that similar products are available on the market at a lesser price to consumers or that the perceived need for it does not exist.

Following completion of the research component, one of three decisions must be made, whether to (1) discontinue pursuing the product, (2) investigate and evaluate similar products that are available, or (3) enter the development or marketing component of the process. Through the Professional Nursing Development and Clinical Research Consortium at St. Michael Hospital, ideas for new products that pass through the research component are sold to product manufacturers under royalty agreements.

## Development

At this stage, the product has been designed and manufactured. One individual should be assigned as a product manager, responsible for following through with the rest of the product process.

The product manager must have a comprehensive knowledge of the process and a high level of interest in the product. This manager must make things happen. As the process evolves, the manager continually evaluates its progress, establishes and reinforces time frames for each component, and reports the status to administration. The manager reviews inventory levels, turnover rates, expenses, revenue, and trends in the market, and changes the process accordingly. Beckham (1985, p. 61) emphasizes that those who have breathed life into a product should have the opportunity to participate in its success.

Nurses make excellent product managers. Their management skills and clinical judgment abilities can be adapted easily to the product process. Product management provides them with a new opportunity to influence patient care in a positive manner. The product manager assigned to implement the process for the pediatric Kardexes was the parent/child clinical nurse specialist.

Components of a new product include its function, design, and costs. All three need to be defined in detail each time a new item is to be developed. Refinement is a continuing process as the product evolves.

Design of a new product obviously is important. It should be durable, require only low maintenance, contain essential content, be assembled easily, and packaged attractively. Colors and graphics should be chosen carefully. Safety and accuracy must be assured.

Costs include expenses for supplies, equipment, overhead, labor, and marketing. Careful calculation of all costs is necessary to determine the production expense of the item and the cost to the consumer. At this point, it will become apparent whether the product can be profitable and whether the process should continue.

Products will be manufactured either by the health care organization or presented to outside firms for competitive bids. A caution: The lowest cost estimates do not always produce the best results.

Problems can occur in any area of product development. Beckham (1985, pp. 59-60) identifies the most common reasons why hospitals have product failures:

- inadequate allotment of human and financial resources
- lack of commitment to new product; therefore involvement of as many people as possible to support the development of the product
- inordinately high expectations for the new product
- lack of understanding that a relatively low percentage of new products in any industry succeed
- committee and consensus decisionmaking rather than a single-minded determination so essential to bringing a competitive product to market; therefore a carefully chosen product manager is essential.

Another area of concern is product liability. The product manager is responsible for making sure that the manufacturer addresses safe product design.

The development of the pediatric Kardexes took well over a year. The crash cart Kardex provides immediate lifesaving information for physicians and nurses on children age 10 and under. It contains information about resuscitation equipment, protocol, and drug doses based on age and weight. The age-appropriate play Kardex is a reference for appropriate behaviors of groups up to age 18. It contains information on growth and development tasks, behaviors and responses, appropriate play, and safety alerts.

Specialists from various disciplines (physicians, nurses, pharmacists, etc.) took part in the design and evaluation stages of the Kardexes. A concerted effort was made to gather all available information and compile it into a workable format. The participation of a multispecialty group in the development assured that each Kardex contained information that was accurate and safe.

Setbacks occurred at various stages: lack of sufficient clerical support, inconsistency in language usage in reference material, and unexpected timeframe modifications. Communication problems with the marketing firm that designed the styles and label of the Kardexes were frustrating. A special project typist solved the clerical problems. Language in the Kardexes was refined through tedious attention to each card. Problems with the marketing firm were resolved by more frequent communication. Each major problem had been resolved by the time the Kardexes were finalized (Figure 28-2).

## Evaluation

In this component, the decision is made whether a product or product line can meet the needs of consumers and establish itself in the marketplace.

**Figure 28-2** Examples of two Kardex Projects

Evaluation is the trial period when consumers use (test) the product. Causier (1982, p. 237) reports that nurses and supply officers now put more emphasis on product appraisal by users. Any product under consideration should qualify for testing in broad terms:

- There already is a need for the item, or its introduction will enhance nursing.
- The design or method of use is compatible with the clinical procedures for which it is to be used.
- The price is reasonable.
- No obvious design faults are discernible.

Nurses have always been involved in the evaluation of patient care products (Smith, 1985, p. 51). In their day-to-day tasks, they determine whether the supplies and equipment they use meet patients' needs. Many institutions have product evaluation or standardization committees that serve a variety of purposes. They receive complaints from nurses that supplies are ineffective and research the marketplace for replacements; or they introduce new items (to replace existing stocks) for quality assurance, standardization, or cost reduction.

Entry into the product process can occur at the evaluation stage when institutions are seeking replacements for existing products or equipment. Exhibit 28-1 is an example of a product information form designed by St. Michael Hospital that is used by its Evaluation Committee. The nursing staff uses this form to request: (1) information on supplies, (2) the price of new or competitive manufacturers' products, (3) samples of these products, and/ or (4) evaluation of new or replacement products.

Products have a greater chance of being successful if they are field tested, revised, then finalized. Health care employees who are likely to use a product serve as an excellent focus group for testing.

The evaluation process for new products being developed must be structured so that it is evident to the product manager that the items meet their intended objectives. Formal or informal surveys must be completed by the focus group and should address areas such as:

| | | |
|---|---|---|
| • frequency of use | • packaging | • content |
| • ease in handling | • functions | • advantages |
| • disadvantages | | |

The results of the survey will indicate whether modifications (major or minor) must be made and whether the product is suitable for distribution.

Upon completion of the crash cart Kardex, its contents were copied and distributed to every member of the Pharmacy and Therapeutics Committee

**Exhibit 28-1**  Example of a Product Information Form

```
St
MICHAEL              PRODUCT   INFORMATION   REQUEST
HOSPITAL
Milwaukee, Wisconsin


ORIGINATOR:  Please complete the sections below to the best of your ability.  What you
cannot complete will be completed by Purchasing.


Product Name: _____
This is a request for:  (please check appropriate box and date request)

[ ] Information ____   [ ] Price _____   [ ] Samples _____   [ ] Evaluation _____
Product Manufacturer:_____  Distributor: _____
How is the item packaged? _____
What is the cost of the item? _____  Estimated Usage _____
Why is there a need for this product? _____

What are its specific functions? _____


What units will use this product? _____
Does it replace another item? _____  Which one? _____
Where was that item obtained from:  Storeroom___  Central Distribution___  Direct order___
What is that item's cost? _____Annual Usage: _____
ADDITIONAL COMMENTS: _____


Originator's Name: _____  Extension: _____

Unit Management Rep: _____ _____ Purchasing: _____ _____
                                              Date                           Date


              STANDARDIZATION AND EVALUATION COMMITTEE
Should this product be evaluated? _____  Why: _____


If so, Where? _____  When? _____
Assigned to: _____  Date:_____
Where will item be stocked:  Storeroom _____  Central Distribution _____  Unit _____


Form 23304   6/83
```

*Source:* Used with permission of St. Michael Hospital, Milwaukee, Wisconson. © 1983

and Emergency Department and Pediatric Department physicians for review and approval. Nursing staff members from pediatrics, surgery, postanesthesia recovery unit, intensive care, and emergency then had inservice workshops on how to use the Kardex and an evaluation period began. After eight months, an informal survey found the crash cart Kardex satisfied the users' needs in lifesaving situations. Modifications were made and the product entered its final stage of development.

## Marketing

Marketing has become a major factor in successful business ventures (Gannon, 1985, p. 90). It is one of the most vital components of the process. It begins in the initial phase of research when consumer needs are being addressed.

Drucker (1979, p. 60) declares that the aim of marketing is to know and understand the consumers so well that the product or service fits them and sells itself. One way to approach marketing in an organization is to identify those responsible for the product's approval and use, develop a plan, and promote the project.

A marketing committee should be developed in the research phase. Its purpose is to provide input to the nursing department on planning, evaluation, and marketing activities. This committee usually includes the project manager, a purchasing agent, a financial representative, and the marketing director. The committee develops a written plan that should include the philosophy and objectives and any long- or short-term goals of the process (Gannon, 1985, p. 91).

The committee objectives could be as basic as: (1) learn the techniques and concepts of marketing, (2) generate ideas for promotion, (3) assist with and evaluate the marketing process, and (4) modify the plan as necessary. This plan should detail all the marketing strategies that are to be used. The committee must agree with these strategies and be willing to make modifications as the plan is put into effect. Time frames must be established and adhered to as closely as possible.

## PROMOTION

Promotion is one of the four Ps of marketing and an extremely important principle. Even if a product meets consumers' needs and, as Drucker (1979, p. 64) says, can "sell itself," the process cannot continue unless potential users are aware of the item's availability. The public relations equation is:

$$Exposure = Awareness = Sales$$

Assuming a quality service, one key to hospital marketing success is the ability to generate a continuity of exposure sufficiently strong to create awareness in the proper demographic audience (Cushman, 1983, p. 11).

Before selecting various methods for promotion, it is important to define the target population (or consumers) that will benefit most from the product. The first population targeted for the pediatric Kardex was defined as external agencies involved with the care of pediatric clients within the continental

United States. Once this population was established, it was easier to select the method(s) of promotion.

Certain promotional methods are more appropriate than others, depending on the product and the consumer. Some methods are:

- advertisements
- brochures
- employee awareness programs

- direct mail distribution
- promotional events
- direct sales

Regardless of which methods are adopted, it is important to let the consumers know why the product is more suitable than a competitor's.

Direct mail distribution is an excellent way to reach a widespread group of consumers. Displays or booths (direct sales) at conferences and workshops for groups or associations that would utilize the product also offer good exposure. In this setting, the consumer can view the product and ask questions concerning it. Person-to-person communication is important.

In May 1985, the pediatric Kardexes were introduced at the Association for the Care of Children's Health (ACCH) convention in Boston. Fifty Kardexes were sold in two days. Five hundred more have been sold and they are still selling; 30 percent of the sales were a direct result of the exposure at the ACCH conference. The rest were from direct mail distribution of Kardex brochures to head nurses of pediatric departments and emergency departments in several targeted states.

## IMPACT AND RESULTS

Personnel budgets generally do not reflect the time needed for product development and marketing. A lack of financial commitment from administration can leave programs hanging. A good marketing plan should project, in detail, the income and expenses for three years of the product process—a profit cannot always be realized in the first year. If the product manager has other responsibilities outside of the process, a shifting of responsibilities or a temporary one-year budget increase is essential.

Marketing techniques from the business sector are being used by health care entities. The successful application of these techniques in a hospital requires a proper understanding of the concept of marketing both in the boardroom and in the administrative offices (Peters, 1985, p. 20). Administrators must realize that to make money, they must spend some.

Some nurses are comfortable as health care providers and are afraid of any role change in the marketplace. However, they must step out of their traditional roles into that of entrepreneur. Who is more appropriate to sell nursing products than a nurse? Nurses must take the initiative in identifying and promoting their unique services to compete effectively in the health care marketplace. Only then can nursing protect its professional identity and succeed in a competitive environment (Krampitz & Coleman, 1985, p. 289).

"Quality care with human touch provides a superior competitive edge. Winners provide a product of superior value rather than one that simply costs less" (Strange, 1984). The involvement of nurses as key contributors to the product process of research, development, evaluation, and marketing is an important example of the professionalization of nursing. Through this process, nurses have new opportunities to influence patient care outcomes.

Several values are inherent in the product process. Consumers receive quality care through quality products. They are assured of a wide range of services and products that will meet their needs. Health care entities have increased sources of revenues. They utilize the resources and skills available in their own institutions to design and develop new services and products. They retain their professional staff and maintain acceptable productivity levels. Often, they become known as leaders in their fields.

Nursing influences trends in patient care. Nurses develop and establish skills outside their traditional clinical roles. They maintain a high degree of job satisfaction and they emerge as image emissaries to promote the professionalization of nursing.

---

## REFERENCES

Beckham, J.D. (1985). New product development. *Hospital Forum, 28*, 59-61.

Causier, P.M. (1982). The equipment resource. *Nursing (Oxford), 2*, 237-238.

Cushman, A.D. (1983). Hospital marketing in the eighties. *Hospital Topics,* 11-12.

Drucker, P.F. (1979). *Management: Tasks, responsibilities, practices.* New York: Harper & Row.

Gannon, K.R. (1985). Nursing's impact on a business venture. *Nursing Administration Quarterly, 10,* 90-96.

Keckley, P.H. (1985). Using and misusing marketing research in the health care industry. *Healthcare Financial Management, 39,* 31-35.

Krampitz, S.D., & Coleman, J.R. (1985). Marketing: A must in a competitive health care system. *Nursing Economics, 3,* 286-289.

Peters, J.B. (1985). Using marketing to size up employer needs and sell hospital services. *Trustee, 38,* 20-21.

Smith, T.C. (1985). Materials management: A model for product review. *Nursing Management, 16,* 52-54.

Strange, D. (October 1984). Service to product: A transition of focus. Paper presented to the American Society of Nursing Administrators, Chicago.

---

## BIBLIOGRAPHY

Anderson, R. (1985). Products and product-line management in nursing. *Nursing Administration Quarterly, 10,* 65-72.

Strong, V. (1985). Nursing products: Primary components of health care. *Nursing Economics, 3,* 60-61.

Chapter 29

# Nursing Development and Community Outreach

*Shelly Malin, Janet Krejci, and Mike Bleich*

*The Professional Nursing Development and Clinical Research Consortium has been described in general in Chapter 27. This chapter focuses on two programs of the Consortium: nursing development and community outreach. Strategies for providing consultation and offering continuing education through seminars, workshops, or conferences are presented, with emphasis on practical information. A model for consultation is reviewed in depth and an administrator's view as a consumer on how to use consultants is included.*

Continuing education (CE) and providing consultation are services that help nursing grow in a dynamic profession in which members must keep current in their knowledge. Legislative, social, scientific, and technological trends all have impact on the profession. New roles, new responsibilities, and changing work patterns all create learning needs.

## HISTORY OF CONTINUING EDUCATION

Cooper (1983) traces the history of continuing education in nursing. Briefly, interest in gaining recognition for CE was evident in the late 1960s. State nurses' associations responded by establishing a voluntary recognition program. In 1971 the first mandatory CE act was passed in California. A proliferation of similar legislation followed. The American Nurses' Association established its Council on Continuing Education in 1972. Many key documents have come from this Council as well as cosponsorship of an annual conference on CE and a mechanism for its accreditation.

CE also is influenced by the increasing professionalization of nursing. One of the hallmarks of a profession is that commitment to life-long learning be incorporated as a value. Nursing has a societal mandate, as the Social Policy Statement (ANA, 1980) states clearly, to be responsive to changes if it is to fulfill its contract.

Continuing education has a much clearer, more developed history than does consultation in nursing. The term consultation in nursing usually brings to mind fairly traditional images that center on patient consultation (e.g., staff nurse to staff nurse or clinical nurse specialist to staff nurse). Outside consultation may be found most often in the mental health literature. Caplan (1970) defines consultation as communication or interactional process between a professional (a specialist) and a consultee who seeks assistance with a problem. He believes this process can be taught, applied, and analyzed systematically. Caplan outlines four types of consultation: client-centered, consultee-centered, program-centered, and administrative consultee–centered.

Until the early 1980s, it was rare, outside of mental health, to see nurses in service entities marketing their skills to other users. When services were shared, it often was as a courtesy rather than on a fee-for-service basis. With the advent of health care changes in the 1980s and the growth in the nursing profession, fees are beginning to be included in many transactions.

For many nurses these changes create a quandary. There are advantages for those who have worked hard to develop innovations to be able to share through formal consultation. There are potential dangers as well. As nurses turn toward entrepreneurial activities, there is a risk that the profits might become more important than the product.

Many nurses also are being encouraged to pursue degrees in business. There are clear advantages to having them understand the financial aspect of providing quality care. The risk is that the socialization process they experience in a business program may result in self-serving attitudes that focus priorities on revenues rather than on quality care.

## SEMINARS, WORKSHOPS, CONFERENCES

The prototype for continuing education in the United States is an outreach service offered through an extension of a university or college. Service agencies have provided education for their own employees for many years. In the 1980s CE became a marketing product for many others—private companies, individual entrepreneurs, and hospital nursing divisions. Although this creates an atmosphere of competition, all of nursing will benefit if it is done well.

The effort of the Professional Nursing Development and Clinical Research Consortium (Professional, 1984) in putting on seminars, workshops, and conferences stems from requests for such services following publication of a book on quality assurance (Schroeder & Maibusch, 1984). Clinical nurse specialists (C.N.S.s) in the institution had sponsored a national C.N.S. conference and members of the C.N.S., administrative, and education teams frequently were speakers for programs sponsored by professional organizations, as well as for local universities' CE departments.

The approach to developing CE offerings was to conduct a human resource assessment in-house to compile areas of expertise. Many authors suggest beginning with a needs assessment that will identify consumers' interests (Cooper, 1983; Johnson, 1985; Jordan, 1985). The needs assessment should be structured to gather information to allow accurate targeting of the market.

Johnson (1985) suggests that monitoring regional and local as well as national economic changes will help the CE provider make accurate cost-effective changes in marketing plans. She also recommends a close watch on changes affecting participants (e.g., nurses' salaries, reimbursement issues, work environment problems) as essential in offering well-timed, responsive CE.

## THE HOW-TO OF PLANNING CE

Most valuable in planning, after market goals are set, are concrete ideas on how to put a CE offering together from start to finish. The Consortium received consultation from Johnson (1985) and Jordan (1985) in developing its plans. Of prime importance in planning any CE offering is the interplay and balance among key factors: program (product), participant, price, and service variables.

Jordan suggests that the purpose of any continuing education offering is solving a problem. The CE provider must know the audience and its problems, and find answers to those problems. Because the Consortium is part of an active service setting, the initial assumption was that what was working well in that location would be of interest to others. The target market for the Consortium was other settings' administrators and staff.

It is important to understand what motivates participants to attend and build these factors into the marketing plan. Jordan (1985) suggests that need for CE, desire to save or make money, networking, increasing skill, and just the need for a paid day off all may be motivators. Johnson (1985) warns that nurses are very selective in their choice of program style, topics, and faculty.

## Choosing Dates and Location

The literature is full of conflicting information on choosing dates and locations (Holtz, 1983; Johnson, 1985; Jordan, 1985). The Consortium found midweek conferences held in hotels worked best. One-day seminars, particularly for nurses, appeared to draw the largest attendance. Location choices may vary, depending on the audience. For a national offering, a hotel near the airport often is the best site; for a regional conference, a downtown one works well. In informal surveys, all nurses agree they like to get away from the institutional setting and regard a hotel as relaxing and pleasant.

## Advertising

Designing advertising for a CE offering is time-consuming and exacting. Trends in brochure design change quickly. (One "hot" trend used engraved invitations with return envelopes included.) The brochure must be checked and double-checked before printing to avoid errors in details such as date, spelling, location, or content. Direct mail has worked well in some cases for the Consortium. Buying appropriate mailing lists as well as developing one's own is important. The latter might be achieved by amassing a file of individuals who attend conferences; this should be added to as CE expands.

In pricing the conference, it is the Consortium's experience that when nurses offer CE they tend to underprice. Johnson (1985) suggests that it is important to identify a price ceiling by checking the brochures of others in the area and setting the charge under that figure.

Mailings for the Consortium were handled initially through the nursing department. This proved extremely time consuming so the task was turned over to either an outside mail service or the hospital mail department.

Time lines and budgets must be developed during the initial planning phase. Good examples of these available in the literature can be adopted to meet individual needs (Holtz, 1983; Johnson, 1985; Jordan, 1985).

## Evaluation

If a nursing entity is to continue growing as a CE provider, the success of each offering must be evaluated. Evaluation at its best includes soliciting the reactions of the participants, the presenters, and a financial analysis. The Consortium has found that evaluation forms are filled out when kept short and to the point—a mix of open-ended and forced choice or Likert Scale questions. Likert scales are a series of items worded either favorably or unfavorably; respondents indicate their degree of agreement or disagreement with each statement (Polit and Hungler, 1978, p. 374). Feedback from presenters is valuable in making future plans. Financial analysis completes the evaluation phase.

## A Word About Cancelling

There are mixed feelings about whether or not CE offerings should be cancelled when registration is low. The trend appears to be toward permitting late registration, often at the door (Johnson, 1985). It usually is best not to cancel offerings because of the potential effect on the host entity's reputation.

## CONSULTATION

The philosophy of the consultation service offered through the Consortium is one that maintains the quality of the product as a high priority. As the Consortium evolved, requests increased for sharing quality innovations on patient care. It was imperative to maintain high standards in the quality of any product offered.

The Consortium's activity focused on several areas: consulting nationally with organizations on quality assurance, consulting with administrators on specific programs (e.g., competency-based evaluations), on-site visits to clinics, provision of education on specific topics such as nursing diagnosis, the ANA *Social Policy Statement,* and provision of a percentage of clinical nurse specialist time to cover a variety of needs in a small hospital. As most of the consultation is done with small hospitals, the discussion here focuses on the process of developing services with such institutions.

To anyone interested in establishing or increasing nursing consulting services, small hospitals have become an attractive market. Changes in health care budgets have reduced their access to education and the expertise that clinical nurse specialists had provided. This has occurred in smaller hospitals to a greater degree because they began with fewer resources. Ironically, although the supply of resources is reduced, demand has risen because of increased acuity, higher patient turnover, and shortened lengths of stay.

When considering small hospitals as a target market, it is best to look outside the local area. The old adage about "never a prophet in your own land" remains accurate even though well-worn. This is especially true if the provider is located in a large metropolitan area or university town that may be resource-heavy.

A target area may be identified by market surveys, random phone calls, interest shown from advertising, or informal networking. Once an area is targeted, several approaches may be used for increasing exposure or selling services. The Consortium identified certain key conferences for presenting posters displaying specific programs being marketed (quality assurance) to increase opportunities to discuss offerings. Area or district nursing administration conferences, which often include poster sessions as part of their program, are best for direct exposure to individuals responsible for decision-making and budgets. Sponsorship of workshops with local hospitals may be a way to gain access to those interested in consultation. Short presentations at district and specialty nursing meetings proved successful.

The Consortium's resources include several clinical specialists from different areas as well as other clinicians (many master's prepared) who have developed a specialty. Once a hospital is targeted, it is given a list of resources according to specialty. The Consortium coordinator matches needs of the requesting entity with resources of the Consortium and develops a contract outlining the specifics.

The contract with one hospital has involved a variety of resources. One C.N.S. worked with a nursing department to develop monthly nursing grand rounds. In the beginning, different C.N.S.s presented topics on a monthly basis (e.g., pain, nursing stress, chronic illness, depressed elderly, etc.). Eventually, staff nurses from each unit took over presenting different topics on a monthly rotation basis.

Implementation of nursing grand rounds is a successful method for integrating the C.N.S.s into the client hospital. It allows staff members to be introduced to the C.N.S. in a nonthreatening manner; it also gives them an opportunity to test the credibility of the C.N.S. This works especially well if the rounds are informal enough to promote discussion between C.N.S. and staff.

Other offerings have included the following:

- A C.N.S. with mental health and group process expertise worked with a nursing unit on team building.
- A C.N.S. in chronic disability helped form a support group with the staff of a newly opened rehabilitation unit.
- A C.N.S. worked with the emergency department on crisis intervention and communication with difficult patients.
- A C.N.S. and a parent-child head nurse both worked with a pediatric unit on educational and organizational needs of the pediatric unit.
- Several C.N.S.s worked with groups of staff members on implementing nursing diagnoses.

In addition, individual C.N.S.s were requested to work with staff on problems in certain specialty units, specifically: ventilator-dependent patients, families of dying patients, and helping staff identify approaches to angry and demanding patients.

## CONSULTATION: THE ADMINISTRATOR'S (USER'S) VIEW

Many small and midsized hospitals are faced with the problem of expanding the professional nursing role while facing economic pressures and a lack of qualified nursing practitioners in multispecialty roles. These hospitals can use the Consortium as a strategy to fill gaps in their nursing care delivery systems.

Professionalization is described by Little (1981) as having four components:

1. autonomy, which includes decisionmaking and independent functioning using the nursing process
2. authority, representing both legal authority as in state nurse practice acts and as invested in nursing positions through the responsibilities demanded
3. advocacy, which demonstrates nursing support and protection of the patient, family, and community
4. accountability, which represents giving first priority to the patient/client/family.

Embracing these concepts and recognizing the generally accepted major role functions of the C.N.S. as those of expert clinician, teacher, consultant, and researcher (Clayton, 1984), it can be seen that the use of a Consortium can influence the growth of nursing toward professionalization.

When the Consortium, through St. Michael Hospital in Milwaukee, began marketing its services, nursing administrators at St. Mary's Medical Center in Racine, 30 miles to the south, were attracted to the possibility of developing a formal arrangement for the Consortium to provide clinical specialist coverage. Although the clinical specialist role already had been introduced successfully at St. Mary's, it was difficult for this midsized hospital to hire enough C.N.S.s to cover the broad range of diagnostic entities found on its general units.

Through the Consortium, a larger number of specialists with specific hospital-based experience in clinical practice, education, and research were expected to be available to meet the needs of the nursing staff at St. Mary's. The Consortium could attract high-quality nurses to its staff and promote an environment of peer support to its members, a problem at St. Mary's and not unlike the dilemma faced by other smaller facilities with a limited number of clinical specialist positions.

To a consumer of consultation services, the Consortium constitutes a group of professionals prepared for autonomous practice; for smaller hospitals, it offers advantages over other models for introducing advanced nursing roles. Clinical specialists at the smaller hospital may not have a substantial peer group to draw upon for support. Shared positions, often with schools of nursing, may create tension because of diverging interests and may require multiple individual contracts to meet hospital needs.

The Consortium provides an environment for integrated and coordinated professional practice, giving its members opportunities for shared governance and peer review. When the Consortium contracts its services to other health care entities, its staff members have additional opportunities to gain experience and for professional networking, adding to their knowledge and expertise.

Institutions that turn to consultation add a new depth of human resources to their staff. The Consortium can be utilized at a variety of levels in an organization, from administrative requests for assistance in program development, to the staff nurse who may desire consultation directly with a patient, to hospital education staff members, who may use the Consortium staff's expertise in presenting specialized topics. It is through these and other mechanisms that the Consortium staff can contribute directly to developing the autonomy, authority, advocacy, and accountability of a nursing staff.

Before establishing a relationship with a consortium, the client hospital should complete an assessment of its own nursing division. Areas of concern or need will surface and become negotiating points. At a minimum, this should include the nursing administrator's assessment of the strengths and weaknesses in nursing care delivery. Information that might be reviewed in the assessment includes survey data on patient and community satisfaction, physician satisfaction with nursing services, and the capabilities of the nursing staff to function autonomously. Coupled with an awareness of the nursing division's communication network and responsiveness to change, the administrator will have adequate information to begin a dialogue with the consultation staff on which services are needed and how they might best be introduced to the nursing staff.

Once the assessment has been completed, negotiations with consultants can start. General terms of the agreement include the amount and method of reimbursement, the availability of consulting staff, and scheduling. Specific goals based on assessed needs, and plans for integrating consultants into the agency, are important next steps.

At St. Mary's, the goals and priorities centered on three areas: (1) the need for its staff to gain knowledge and awareness of the importance and application of clinical research, (2) staff education in specific areas such as the diagnostic process in nursing, and (3) staff exposure to advanced clinical role models.

## STRATEGIES FOR IMPLEMENTATION

Introducing consultants into an organization is not unlike the management of any major change. Lewin (1951) suggests that a force-field analysis, or an analysis of the positive and negative forces influencing the change, will yield useful information in developing strategies to assure successful implementation of a desired change. There are general strategies to consider when introducing consultants, although each organization will need to address its own specific restraining forces, such as budget, staffing limitations, and those mentioned in the previous paragraphs.

After the contract has been signed, credentialling of consultants according to hospital protocol becomes a priority. Any privileges requested during the credentialling process must be consistent with the contractual arrangements agreed upon. General areas for consideration include the ability to consult with patients and to provide direct care in complex situations, commensurate with the education and experience of individual Consortium staff members, and documentation in the medical record. Licensure, evidence of graduation and certification, job-related experience, and other information required by the credentialling body in the client organization must be available from consultants. It is through this process that an institution is safeguarded and practitioners are held accountable for the privilege of practicing.

Politically, it can be advantageous to share specific information about consulting services with the medical staff. In many hospitals, physicians compose the majority on the credentials committee, so this may be one of the first groups to gain an understanding of advanced practice issues related to the Consortium. If advanced nursing roles in clinical practice, education, and research have not been introduced previously in an organization, it is imperative that a capable spokesperson from nursing administration be present to answer questions.

By no means should dialogue with physicians end with the credentialling body. The nursing staff should adopt a positive attitude, with the goal of building bridges with the medical staff, and seek opportunities to communicate about the clinical and staff enhancements available through affiliation with the consultants. Medical/nursing liaison groups, medical staff department heads, and executive staff members are significant groups who share an interest in nursing department activities and can offer support if kept well informed.

Ideally, key nursing leaders will have been involved throughout the needs assessment, contract negotiations, and credentialling process. It is important, in establishing relationships, to restate the purpose of the association with the consultants to middle managers, evening and night supervisors, the education staff, and others who will use the consultants' services.

During the initial phase, it can be helpful to hold a forum for resolving operational questions, seeking input from all participants. Areas to be covered include communication linkages, availability of consulting staff, special interest areas for beginning collaboration, consultants' expertise, and accountability mechanisms between agency staff and the consultants.

An informal luncheon or reception may provide a relaxed environment to pave the way for creating new relationships, particularly if ample time is allowed for small-group discussion. Next, time should be provided for consultants to meet with the general staff in the areas in which they will be involved to stimulate interest and questions. This should occur before the consultant actually begins work. Finally, an orientation program designed to acquaint consultant(s) with the client will fulfill the objective of assuring an understanding of hospital operations.

One final strategy relates to the efficient use of consultant time. This is of particular importance when travel time and distance are involved. A suggested method for reducing the chance for duplication or misdirected time is to appoint a coordinator to interface with the consultant. The coordinator maintains a calendar of scheduled visits, manages requests for services, and lists the appointments for various units. The Consortium facilitator (consultant) similarly arranges for appropriate Consortium expertise to be available when needed by the hospital. These persons are the keys to assuring that the end product is a productive and efficient use of time and talent.

The future use of the Consortium looks positive. The image of the nursing department has been enhanced because of the availability and utilization of Consortium services. Marketing opportunities exist because of the expanded specialization of nursing services. Managers consider the use of the Consortium in program development when establishing goals. The scope of expertise available gained acceptance with the nursing staff members who, with increased exposure, more readily called upon the Consortium's services. As the staff identifies with strong practitioner/role models, professional networking increases with the aim of enhancing job satisfaction.

## VALUE TO NURSING

The ability to be involved in offering continuing education and consultation increases nurses' satisfaction. Even indirect association enhances their self-image in the institution. Despite the frustrations of starting up a new program, the autonomy associated with these endeavors is rewarding.

Nurses on the other side—that is, those who attend the seminars or receive consultation—benefit directly by being able to apply what they learn to their jobs.

The nursing profession benefits as well. Networking through use of consultation services or CE is a win-win situation for all. No one person or place can know it all; only through well-established networks will the profession continue to grow.

## REFERENCES

American Nurses' Association. (1980). *Nursing: A social policy statement* (ANA Publication Code: NP-63 35M 12/80). Kansas City, Mo.: Author.

Caplan, G. (1970). *The process of mental health consultation.* New York: Basic Books.

Clayton, G.M. (1984). The clinical nurse specialist as leader. *Topics in Clinical Nursing, 6* (1), 17-27.

Cooper, D. (1983). *The practice of continuing education in nursing.* Rockville, Md.: Aspen Publishers, Inc.

Holtz, H. (1983). *How to succeed as an independent consultant.* New York: John Wiley.

Johnson, S.H. (1985). A model for marketing continuing education in a recession. *The Journal of Continuing Education, 16,* 19-24.

Jordan, B. (1985). *Developing and marketing successful seminars and workshops.* (Workshop manual). Los Angeles: Bob Jordan Associates.

Lewin, K. (1951). *Field theory in social science.* New York: Harper & Row.

Little, D.E. (1981). "A" formula for professional nursing care. *Rehabilitation Nursing, 6,* 19-22.

Polit, D.F., & Hungler, B.P. (1978). *Nursing research: Principles and methods.* Philadelphia: J.P. Lippincott.

*Professional Nursing Development and Clinical Research Consortium.* (1984). (Brochure). Milwaukee: St. Michael Hospital.

Schroeder, P.S., & Maibusch, R. (1984). *Nursing quality assurance: A unit-based approach.* Rockville, Md.: Aspen.

**Epilogue:**

# The Need for Coordination

*Lila Smick*

The issue of coordination of support services must not go unmentioned. The success and smooth operation of the Consortium depends on the operating efficiency of its office staff. The work to be accomplished must be planned, organized, and coordinated carefully. Coordinating a project is a little like getting all of the members of a team in the right positions and playing together. Hiring or appointing the right person for a support service coordinator position makes the whole operation run efficiently.

The Consortium operates out of a busy nursing division and shares these support services. The benefits of this arrangement are working with a staff whose strengths are well known. Hiring completely different people for a specific project creates a different set of potential problems. The most important factors in starting up are the costs and unpredictability of work flow.

Because of the dual role these support people have, several strategies are used to make their jobs easier. For example, a separate phone line was established and a laminated sheet with instructions on how to handle incoming calls was developed, decreasing potential confusion.

Attention to the details of mailings and the creation of appropriate (computerized) mailing lists is essential. Planning ahead reduces costly time spent in dealing with the task of getting everything together on time.

Members of the support services department are essential members of the Consortium team and must feel this way. The successes of the Consortium are their successes as well.

# Part VII

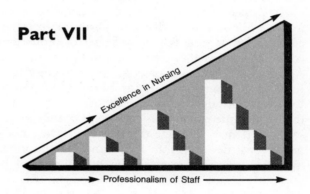

Excellence in Nursing

Professionalism of Staff

# The Commitment to Excellence: A Continuing Process

*Patricia Schroeder*
Section Editor

Parts I through VI built upon the guiding model that describes professional development in a nursing department. In many ways, such evolution of the role of nurses at St. Michael Hospital provides a microcosmic view of the development of professional nursing as a whole.

In Part VII, Chapter 30 reviews the content and direction of excellence as described throughout this book. It pulls together the importance of the activities described and their implications for nursing as a whole.

The Appendix addresses an additional issue that may have crossed readers' minds while reviewing this text. Given the constraints of the health care environment as well as the challenges of professional developments, how could 32 contributors from one institution pull this book together? The Appendix describes that process, incorporating anecdotal and empiric data. Ideas about the process as well as strategies to support it can provide direction for writing at other health care entities as well as completing other projects that require the participants' long-term commitment.

Part VII may complete this text but it does not complete the work of professional development. The arrows on the model indicate continuing movement, necessary in addressing the challenges of the profession of nursing in today's complex health care environment. The objective of professional development and excellence is not the ultimate achievement of a fixed goal but rather the continuing process and growth itself.

# Chapter 30

# Summary

*SueEllen Pinkerton*

A professional nursing staff by definition would practice autonomously, based on a unique body of knowledge and a code of ethics, organized through a professional association, recognized by the government through licensure, and compensated for its true economic worth. Nursing is a profession in process and hence does not yet practice in such a total professional environment (Bucher & Strauss, 1961). As it strives toward such practice, it needs support to test, reject, or accept components of such a model.

This book is written to describe the testing of some of the components and the resultant effects. It is intended to contribute to the body of knowledge about nursing that always will be limited to some degree to what is available in print or other materials. It also is designed to give individuals ideas for trying other models and approaches and to report those attempts so that in the end all nursing will grow and move in the process of becoming a profession.

Certainly nursing is further ahead in some components of professionalism than in others. It is recognized by the government as providing a needed service and is licensed in each state. This protects the health and safety of the public. The nurse practice acts are the governing state laws and the board of nursing is the administrative agency that implements the statute.

The basic components of the nurse practice act are a definition of professional nursing, an outline of the requirements for licensure, provisions for endorsement or sanctioning of persons licensed in another state, specifications of exemptions from licensure, list of grounds for discipline, and provisions for the board of nursing with an outline of its responsibilities (Pinkerton,

1985). This overview of nursing reflects the advances in the progress toward professionalism as shown in government recognition.

Nursing also has a Code of Ethics (American Nurses' Association, 1976) that delineates ethical practice standards. This code was established in 1926 as a response to the need to upgrade nursing education and improve nursing services (Flanagan, 1976). The code has been revised several times since and has remained an important standard for nursing, marking the growth of the profession itself.

There are many professional associations in nursing, but the American Nurses' Association usually is recognized as the organization that represents the profession. Flanagan (1976) reports that a survey of the history of the development of modern professions shows that once a profession becomes clearly defined, competent practitioners form an association in an attempt to establish standards of practice and enforce a code of conduct based on ethical principles.

The first national organization of superintendents of training schools for nurses was organized in 1894 and the first national association for nurses in 1897 (Flanagan, 1976). These were the forerunners for the ANA (organized in 1911) and the National League for Nursing (1912). The ANA, although it does not have a majority of practicing nurses as members, often is called upon to represent nursing and present testimony to legislative and regulatory bodies on its behalf—an important role for nurses beyond the organization in which they are employed (Chapter 26).

Compensation for its true economic worth is an area in which the profession is still in process. Peirin (Kleiman, 1987) of the ANA says that as of the end of 1986 there were about 1.5 million registered nurses and that their salaries for that year averaged $20,340. This is not seen as competitive by students entering college, given the long hours, shift rotations, and weekend and holiday work.

Not until a more attractive work environment is created for nursing, including equitable compensation, will young men and women be attracted to it as a career choice or will it achieve further professional status. Efforts to demonstrate nursing's ability to contribute as a revenue-producing department, such as thorough revision of a patient classification system (Chapter 25), are helping to change attitudes about its worth to health care entities.

This leaves autonomous practice and a unique body of knowledge as the areas that need the most development as nursing progresses. Obviously, a body of knowledge should be developed in a systemic, scientific manner, using the research process. Since so much of the practice of nursing takes place in acute care facilities, the data collected there should be a rich source for contributing to this knowledge. To benefit the most from these data, they should be collected and stored in a manner that enhances their utility.

Thus, nurses should understand research and its process, its value to practice, and the importance of protecting human subjects of research (Part III). Helping nurses to understand the research process is best done by utilizing something already familiar to them, so it is a matter of transferring information and the application of appropriate components from one process to an already entrenched process such as quality assurance (Part II).

Familiarity with the research process also enhances nurses' understanding of a conceptual framework for use in practice to help build theory (Chapter 17). Nursing diagnosis (Chapter 20) gives format and direction for the storage of data.

All of this knowledge, and the importance of commitment to generating it, is based on nurses' required information that enables them to make judgments on the practice of other nurses. This is the basis for the development of peer review (Chapter 22), which supports autonomous practice, competency-based evaluations (Chapter 24), and primary nursing as a delivery system for autonomous practice (Chapter 21). Structure for implementing this practice is presented through a system for staff nurse decisionmaking such as shared governance (Part IV) and a way to work out conflicts with physicians through physician-nurse committees (Chapter 19).

As nurses advance in the process of professionalization, they create new arenas for practice that offer increasingly more independence and autonomy or control over practice (Chapter 18) and can lead eventually to a mechanism for sharing professional development with other nurses either within the institution through nursing grand rounds (Chapter 23) or outside of the hospital through the Consortium (Part VI).

The professionalization process is best defined in the ANA *Social Policy Statement* (Chapter 16). It also creates enormous changes that need constant attention and monitoring, as described in Chapter 3. But the end results are worth the input. Being able to be part of creating an organizational climate that promotes professionalism helps nurses resolve issues of trust and creates a healthier organization (Chapter 2).

All the elements to help move nursing through the process of becoming a profession are available. That process takes commitment and direction, but it can build on (1) existing programs such as quality assurance that are enhanced through educating the staff about the research process, and (2) programs related to theory, autonomous practice, and development of a body of knowledge. It also takes investment in human potential, which includes the intellect, emotions, character, and personality.

Organizations and personal experiences in life help people learn maturity. A professional organizational climate supports personal growth with warmth and caring and visionary leaders. Each entity must set standards of organizational excellence that do not inhibit individual excellence and provide access and openness. Leaders at all levels need to decrease nurses' feelings of powerlessness by stimulating their motivation to achieve shared values and to believe in themselves. If nursing expects a lot, it will get a lot. If leaders and organizations lose the capacity to inspire high individual performance, the great days are over (Gardner, 1984).

Professional excellence implies competence and a striving for high standards in every aspect of life. As Gardner (1984) states, the individual spirit will not stand unattended. In that regard, everyone has a role.

---

## REFERENCES

American Nurses' Association. (1976). *Code for nurses with interpretive statements*. Kansas City, Mo.: Author.

Bucher, R., & Strauss, A. (1961). Professions in process. *American Journal of Sociology 66*, 325-334.

Flanagan, L. (1976). *One strong voice*. Kansas City, Mo.: American Nurses' Association.

Gardner, J.W. (1984). *Excellence*. New York: W.W. Norton.

Kleiman, C. (1987, June 6). Jobs: Nursing profession looks for shot in arm. *Chicago Tribune*, Section 8, p. 1.

Pinkerton, S.E. (1985). Legislative issues in licensure of registered nurses. In J.C. McCloskey and H.K. Grace (Eds.), *Current issues in nursing* (2nd ed.), (pp. 469-479). Boston: Blackwell Scientific Publications.

# Developing The *Commitment to Excellence:* Strategies for Multiple Authorship

*Patricia Schroeder*

*Writing for publication has long been considered a scholarly and professional pursuit. It is something which is supported, at least in theory, by professional nurses in many settings and areas of practice. When many members of one nursing department become the predominant contributors to a text, however, the process takes on a new meaning. Although patient care and ongoing department business does not stop, it must be considered a department's high priority commitment rather than a "nice project." It goes from an activity which is "fit in if you have spare time" to one which must be planned for, invested in, and nurtured.*

This book adds to the increasing number of texts developed by a group of professionals who work within the same organization. Although much has been written about the process of writing in general, little has been written about how such a project can be coordinated when emanating from one agency. When the ideas for this text were originally outlined, a plan for chronicling the process was implemented. It was decided that this could most effectively be done by anecdotally tracking the process as well as collecting empiric data. It is the intent of this chapter, then, to describe the experience of "putting it together."

## THE PROCESS OF PUTTING IT TOGETHER

Identifying the idea for the book was only the beginning of determining its content. The process was nurtured by the development of the model, which split the concept into well-defined stages of evolution through which this nursing department had passed. These evolutionary stages became parts, and were then subdivided into manageable chapters. The process of determining the initial table of contents flowed smoothly, and was completed in less than a week.

It was determined that overlap of material could be an issue because of the number of chapters which were related to similar content. Therefore, editors developed initial chapter outlines in an attempt to define parameters of content. This did not eliminate the overlap, but certainly decreased its degree.

Identifying initial authors was an important and political process. The major criterion for selection of authors was involvement in the activity described in the chapter. Writing skills and experience in writing for publication were considered a bonus if present, and something that could be supported by others if absent. Interest and enthusiasm about the project was assumed— usually correctly.

Selecting authors based on their involvement with the chapter's content area seemed to be the best way to glean the most pertinent "real life" information. However, because so much work at St. Michael Hospital is done based on shared governance and a participative process style, at times it was difficult to narrow down who played the major role in the activities and who should be invited to participate in the book. Some had played a major role in the development of ideas or groups, but no longer participated. Should the original developer or the current leader be included? How many coauthors could reasonably write together? Invitations to author a chapter made the department extremely sensitive to "ownership" of activities. Writing the chapter was at times equated with "owning" the content.

Once invitations to contribute (along with a prospective table of contents) were sent to authors, the tension began to mount. The invitation included the name of other potential contributors to that chapter, if coauthorship was desired. They were not informed of those who were invited to author chapters other than their own. This was done to protect the identity of anyone who would choose not to participate.

The nurses reacted in a variety of ways to the invitations to write. Many were enthusiastic and responded immediately. Some reacted with discomfort, not knowing who else was invited; there was a sense that nurses not invited might feel badly about not being involved. Some did not react at all. It was hard to determine what that meant.

A scheduled meeting of all contributors was held at the beginning of the project describing the idea in detail, reviewing the model, defining conceptual threads, and discussing many specifics regarding the writing process and strategies planned to support it. These details relieved some and stressed others. The meeting concluded with authors receiving a contract defining terms of the agreement to write (Exhibit A). Section editors, who had consented to coordinate the work of each content section, had received their own job description previously, which defined expectations for the work they would carry out (Exhibit B).

## SUPPORT STRATEGIES

A number of strategies were planned to support the work of many authors within the department. This began with the provision of chapter outlines, which were strongly encouraged to be adapted based upon the authors' knowledge base. Clear descriptions of what was expected if authors chose to contribute assisted them in deciding whether to participate and in assessing whether they were proceeding on track. The entire writing time was planned to last nine months, which although short, was intended to promote interest and decrease procrastination. This was supported with a time line and structured deadlines. Although not followed exactly, it gave authors benchmarks against which to measure progress, as well as assurance that the long and arduous process would eventually reach completion.

Prior to inviting authors, the editors arranged assistance with library staff, the typist, and a word processor. Although the library was always available, library staff had to take on a large volume of requests at once, without stopping their other ongoing work. To assist with this situation, extra workers were requested to assist with such activities as filling out article request slips and duplicating articles. A limited contract with a local university also assisted authors with literature searches.

An astute typist was an invaluable resource to the development of this manuscript. Far beyond manuscript typing, the typist provided feedback on the completeness of sections, assisted in attaining deadlines, and proofread the manuscript for basic understanding. Typists in most agencies are extremely busy; therefore, maintaining a primary commitment to a book can be difficult. However, the ongoing involvement of one typist maintained timely completion of the project.

**Exhibit A**

---

**CONTRIBUTORS AGREEMENT**

1. _____ (hereinafter called the Contributor(s)) will prepare an approximate _____ page chapter (tentatively titled: _____) manuscript in typewritten form, double-spaced on one side of an 8-1/2 x 11 inch page with one inch margin (hereinafter called the Work) and based on the attached outline, for publication in *Commitment to Excellence: Developing a Professional Nursing Staff* to be edited by SueEllen Pinkerton and Patricia Schroeder (hereinafter called the Editors) and to be published by Aspen Publishers, Inc. (hereinafter called the Publisher). The Contributor will deliver two copies of the Work to the Editors by April 4, 1986.

2. The Contributor grants the Publisher ownership of the Copyright of the Work. Work will contain no materials from other copyrighted or unpublished works without the written consent of the owner of such material. Such consent will be obtained by the Contributor and will be delivered to the Editors with the Work.

3. The Contributor agrees to revise the Work in accordance with the Editors' suggestions at the Editors' discretion. Should the Contributor be unwilling or unable to perform the necessary revision(s) within a reasonable amount of time, as determined by the Editors, the Editors will have the right to revise the work themselves and will be listed as coauthors of the Work.

4. If the Work is not delivered to the Editors by the date specified in clause 1 or if the Work is unacceptable in form or content, the Editors may choose not to include the Work in *Commitment to Excellence: Developing a Professional Nursing Staff*.

5. The Publisher may use the Contributor's name and professional affiliation in *Commitment to Excellence: Developing a Professional Nursing Staff* and promotional and advertising material for the aforementioned book.

Agreed:


Editors: _____     _____
         SueEllen Pinkerton                    Patricia Schroeder

Contributor(s):

_____

_____

_____

_____

---

**Exhibit B**

**Job Description—Section Editors**
Section editors will be cited in the book for their contributions to the manuscript. The responsibilities will be as follows:

*Act as contact person to field questions from their authors and provide support

*Notify Sue Pinkerton and Patti Schroeder of potential problems/crises

*Monitor progress on chapters to ensure completion by deadline

*Review all chapters in section (first draft) to determine:
—flow of information
—completeness of section—check for gaps or missing information
—overlap between chapters
—readability
—scholarliness
—correct citations
—correct number of pages
—condition of manuscript

*Deliver edited manuscripts (first draft) to Patti Schroeder and Sue Pinkerton by *Friday, May 2, 1986*

*Meet with individuals to review edited first draft prior to revision

*Monitor progress on chapters to ensure completion by deadline

*Receive and review all chapters for integration of suggestions and editing

*Deliver 2nd draft to Patti Schroeder and Sue Pinkerton by *Friday, June 20, 1986*

*Editors return manuscripts to Section editors and authors *Friday, May 9, 1986*

*Revise chapter based upon editing

*Manuscripts to Leann Hamann for revisions to be made on word processor by *Friday, May 23, 1986*

*Manuscripts from typist to section editors *Friday, June 6, 1986*

*Manuscripts from section editors to editors *Friday, June 20, 1986*

*Final revisions

*Manuscript due to Aspen Publishers, Inc. *Friday, July 25, 1986*

Manuscripts will be reviewed and copy edited at Aspen, and our original copies will be returned with comments written on the pages. Aspen will give us a very short deadline to review these comments and either approve or make changes. We will review the manuscript and thereafter receive galley proofs (which look like pages of a book) which will need to be reviewed for corrections. Only then are we done with our part of the book.

The use of the word processor has revolutionized the process of writing: changes in chapters were easily made; it was no longer a terrible event to modify a sentence or delete a paragraph. Using a word processor substantially decreases the time and cost of developing a book.

Strong encouragement was given to writing during work time. Although authors varied dramatically in their ability to plan time from their busy schedules to write, this allowance was often described as supportive.

Writing days were established, and a quiet room for writing was made available. Available in the writing room were coffee and donuts in the morning and soft drinks and popcorn in the afternoons, paper, pencils, and a section or book editor. Some contributors stated that although they did not use the writing room, they scheduled these days on their calendars to write in private. Many responded to the food and drink in the room, which was seen as supportive and made people feel more comfortable.

The deadline for the first draft was considered very significant. Contributors would have initial ideas on paper, editors would be able to address the whole manuscript rather than pieces, and the typist would have a draft of each chapter on the word processor. In an effort to encourage all contributors to meet this deadline, a party was planned for that evening. All were encouraged to attend, whether or not they had met the deadline; however, this proved to be a significant motivator in completing the first draft.

From the inception of the project, the editors worked to achieve deadlines without exerting excessive pressure or promoting undue competitiveness. This is always difficult to achieve. Using the premise that professionals will be accountable, contributors were supported rather than goaded.

## THE STUDY

The editors wanted empirical data as well as anecdotal reports to describe the process of developing this book. They decided that the collection of data over the course of the process would identify how authors were feeling about the process, how much time they were spending on writing, and to what degree planned support strategies were helpful. The editors developed an anonymous questionnaire and a cover letter describing the study and assuring authors of the option to choose not to participate without ramifications. The two page questionnaire and attached letter was sent to all contributors from St. Michael Hospital at four time intervals: 1) the time of initially agreeing to participate, 2) four weeks into the process, 3) the time of the first draft deadline, and 4) the time of the second draft deadline. This time frame covered five months. The survey instrument was reviewed for content and construct validity by a doctorally prepared nurse administrator and three clinical nurse specialists with experience in research methods.

Four issues were addressed: demographics, a description of current feelings about writing the manuscript, a description of the amount of time spent per week working on the manuscript, and a rating of the degree of helpfulness of support strategies.

Demographic data included the number of chapters in which the person was participating and whether the person had previously written for publication. A continuum for indicating progress toward completion of the chapter(s) was provided to identify where in the writing process the authors were.

The section on feelings listed ten positive and negative feelings about writing the manuscript and asked authors to rate the degree to which the feelings were currently felt. These feelings included frustration, being overwhelmed, being energized, and being challenged. A Likert Scale of 0 to 5 was used for rating.

Participants were asked to indicate the approximate number of hours per week which were spent on writing. A Likert Scale was again provided to rate how much of this time was spent at home versus at work.

Finally, ten system and personal supports were listed, and participants were asked to rate the degree of helpfulness on a 0 to 5 scale. These supports included items such as preparation of the initial outline, scheduled writing times, meeting with section editors, structured deadlines, and assistance from the library staff and typist.

## RESULTS/DISCUSSION

One hundred twenty-four questionnaires were sent out, 31 for each of four time periods. Eighty-three were returned (a response rate of 66 percent), evenly distributed over the four time periods.

The most dramatic overall finding was the significance of the third time period, which was the time that the first draft was due. At this time, authors reported they felt less challenged and energized, but more frustrated, pressured, and overwhelmed. Data indicated that all support strategies, with the exception of assistance from the typist, were seen as less helpful during time period three. Finally, the amount of time spent on writing almost doubled at time period three, and most of the writing was reported to have been done after work hours. All of these findings were significantly different from the other three time periods.

Because the study findings were significant and could provide important direction for planning such a project, the editors wanted to validate the analysis. Another author questionnaire was developed with a cover letter and distributed to contributors. A data summary was developed and attached. Each item was then analyzed individually in writing, followed by the question "Is the description accurate?" and "comments." Overall, the original data analysis was supported. One respondent stated that at the time of the first draft, there were other personal and professional activities which contributed to the stress level. It is unknown whether this was true for others as well.

The results of this study can provide a strong base for planning in a department in which many are contributing to a text. The time frames should be carefully developed, with the date for the first draft planned for a time of least possible stress. Placement at least one month following other major changes or deadlines will support authors in the writing process. Although this will still not entirely remove the "pain" of getting initial ideas on paper, it is important to be aware that stress levels of contributors may be higher at deadline time, and therefore personal support may be helpful.

The process of putting together a text such as this can be labelled a mixed blessing. The professional growth, enthusiasm, commitment, and pride are matched by frustration, confusion, anxiety, and questioning. The reward—the final product—always seems to take a long time. It is not until the work is published that one's contribution to the profession can be felt. It is therefore critical that leaders of the project not only plan the work to be completed, but also plan to celebrate the accomplishment. The ultimate goal to be achieved goes beyond mere publication and should be considered to include the facilitation and provision of the professional experience of the contributors.

# Index